Workouts and Maidens

Vincent Reo

Bonus Books, Inc., Chicago

98 97 96 95 94   5 4 3 2 1

Library of Congress Catalog Card Number: 93- 74134

International Standard Book Number: 1-56625-000-5

Bonus Books, Inc.
160 East Illinois Street
Chicago, Illinois 60611

Charts and statistics courtesy of the *Daily Racing Form* and Equine Line

Cover photo courtesy of Breeder's Cup Ltd.

Typesetting by Point West, Inc., Carol Stream, IL

Printed in the United States of America

*To my wife, Carolyn, the late Vincent Reo,
Gordon, and my parents Sam and Theresa,
without their support none of
this could be possible.*

Contents

Workouts

1

If a thoroughbred runs every week, he or she should be in shape, right? Wrong! Just because a horse has been running does not mean he is fit. Actually, a horse might not run too badly and still be out of shape. Those horses you want to spot. They show a handicapper future potential. A horse can easily fall out of shape if he is not jogged daily and worked out before a start. All it takes is a few days. For this reason, workouts are critical. Handicappers must pay attention to them.

Not everyone does, according to a survey of various handicappers on three different days at New Jersey's Monmouth Park racetrack. An astonishing 63 percent of the handicappers didn't know where the "Latest Workout" page was located in the *Daily Racing Form*. But they all knew where the actual workouts for a horse were located, underneath its entries.

In forthcoming chapters, we will show how to incorporate workouts into your handicapping strategies. Among the factors we cover are:

- Additional Workouts
- Working Farther Than Running
- Workouts That Appear Better Than They Are
- Great Workouts/Bad Trainer
- Reading into Workouts

- Working at One Track, Running at Another
- Leaving Your Race in Your Workout
- Comparing Workouts

There are two different types of workouts, **breezing** and **handily**. These workouts are performed at two different speeds. Breezing means the horse is working under no pressure, but is in stride and is not galloping. Handily means the horse is under urging by the jockey, but is not under the pressure and stress of racing conditions.

In the example below, *Sham's Groom* shows four breezing workouts in a time period of one month. He is training to make his three year old debut.

Sham's Groom — **Ch. c. 3(May), by Icy Groom—Sham Passion, by Sham**
Br.—Seeger RObert J (Pa)
Own.—Plumstead Stables — **Tr.—Seeger Robert J (37 2 4 3 .05)** — **120**

Lifetime 10 2 2 1 $36,866 — **1993 3 1 1 0 $16,470** — **1992 7 1 1 1 $20,396**

16May93-10Pha	fst	1^{70}	$:48^{1}$	$1:13^{1}$	$1:42^{3}$	3↑ [S]Alw 20925	**78**	3	2	$2^{\frac{1}{2}}$	$1^{\frac{1}{2}}$	1^{2}	$1^{2\frac{1}{4}}$	Vigliotti M J	Lb	112	2.70	83-19	Shm'sGrm$112^{2\frac{1}{4}}$HvyMdlMn$116^{1\frac{3}{4}}$ChmnySwpJ106	Driving	7
26Apr93- 7Pha	fst	$6\frac{1}{2}$f	:22	$:44^{4}$	$1:18^{3}$	3↑ [S]Alw 19575	**62**	3	4	2^{hd}	2^{3}	3^{2}	$2^{2\frac{3}{4}}$	Vigliotti M J	L	114	12.80	82-18	LmmnPppr$116^{2\frac{3}{4}}$ShmsGr114^{hd}ChnSpJ107	Regained 2nd	9
2Jan93- 5Pha	fst	6f	$:22^{2}$	$:46^{2}$	$1:12^{2}$	Alw 14980	**26**	7	5	$6^{5\frac{1}{4}}$	$8^{8\frac{3}{4}}$	8^{16}	$8^{17\frac{3}{4}}$	Madrigal R Jr	L	116	12.60	61-19	Cool Blu Hue111^{nk} Lean Marine$122^{\frac{3}{4}}$Quija122	No threat	8
5Dec92- 9Pha	fst	7f	$:22^{4}$	$:46^{4}$	$1:28^{1}$	[S]Pa Futy	**40**	6	2	4^{4}	$5^{2\frac{3}{4}}$	5^{11}	5^{17}	Madrigal R Jr	L	122	4.00e	49-33	TrifortheGold122^{no}ProxyContest$122^{4\frac{1}{2}}$Temo122	Outrun	7
21Nov92- 5Pha	fst	6f	:22	:45	$1:11^{3}$	Alw 17545	**47**	2	3	$1^{1\frac{1}{2}}$	2^{hd}	$3^{2\frac{1}{2}}$	$4^{11\frac{1}{4}}$	Cruz C	L	118	2.10e	72-21	TrifortheGold$115^{2\frac{1}{2}}$TomTylor$115^{8\frac{1}{2}}$PcfulVill121	Stopped	7
11Nov92- 8Pha	fst	7f	:22	$:44^{4}$	$1:24^{4}$	Alw 16627	**58**	2	4	$5^{5\frac{3}{4}}$	4^{2}	2^{2}	3^{7}	Cruz C	L	115	8.10	76-23	SilverKy$110^{3\frac{1}{2}}$Tmo$115^{3\frac{1}{2}}$Shm'sGroom115	Bumped, hung	6
29Oct92- 7Pha	fst	6f	$:22^{1}$	$:45^{2}$	$1:11^{1}$	Alw 14980	**64**	6	2	$1^{\frac{1}{2}}$	$1^{\frac{1}{2}}$	1^{2}	$2^{1\frac{1}{2}}$	Cruz C	L	120	35.80	83-18	NoNmDncr$114^{1\frac{1}{2}}$Shm'sGrm120^{1}PckhsRd117	Drftd, gmly	9
17Oct92- 2Lrl	fst	$6\frac{1}{2}$f	$:22^{3}$	$:46^{4}$	1:20	Alw 16800	**13**	1	1	1^{1}	2^{hd}	6^{10}	$7^{19\frac{3}{4}}$	Guerra W A		117	7.90	57-18	JorgofMxco$114^{\frac{1}{2}}$WldAbotHrry116^{3}PontTkr115	Fell back	7
8Oct92- 6Lrl	fst	6f	$:22^{3}$	$:46^{2}$	$1:12^{2}$	Alw 16800	**52**	2	2	2^{hd}	2^{hd}	$3^{1\frac{1}{2}}$	$5^{4\frac{1}{2}}$	Guerra W A		117	27.80	74-20	GoldnMony112^{nk}PointTkr$115^{1\frac{3}{4}}$Pddy'sFlir120	Gave way	7
7Sep92- 2Pha	fst	6f	$:22^{2}$	:46	$1:13^{1}$	[S]Md Sp Wt	**49**	4	1	1^{2}	1^{1}	1^{2}	1^{hd}	Madrigal R Jr		120	4.10	75-20	Shm'sGroom120^{hd}Temo$120^{8\frac{3}{4}}$MyBrothrGorg120	Driving	9

LATEST WORKOUTS — **May 11 Pha 4f fst $:48^{4}$ B** — **●Apr 21 Pha 5f fst $1:01^{1}$ B** — **Apr 16 Pha 4f fst $:48^{4}$ B** — **Apr 9 Pha 4f fst $:48^{1}$ B**

The guidelines for horses that work out are as follows: If a horse works 48 breezing, he should be able to work 46 handily and 44 or 45 in actual race conditions and under stress. This will only prove true with a horse that is working on a regular basis or a horse that has been working for his debut.

On April 9, *Sham's Groom* worked $48\frac{1}{5}$. He worked $48\frac{4}{5}$ breezing on the 16th and $101\frac{1}{5}$ breezing for five furlongs on the 21st. On April 26th, *Sham's Groom* made his 1993 debut. The leader hit the half mile pole in $44\frac{4}{5}$. With *Sham's Groom* three lengths off the lead, he was running $45\frac{2}{5}$. If we look back to his works, the average of the three were $48\frac{3}{5}$. If we deduct three to four seconds (two for handily and 1 to 2 for race conditions), this means he should have been running between $44\frac{3}{5}$ and $45\frac{3}{5}$. The only reason to perform this is to make sure the horse we are betting on will be able to compete. We cannot trust last year's performances, because horses can change dramatically during that layoff period.

If a particular horse is working 50, 50, 50 breezing and the competition is running 44 or 45 in actual races, this horse most likely will not be able to keep up and can be eliminated. Thus, if the track condition is the same as those races that may have been run.

In this example, *Sham's Groom* did run between those parameters. But, in his next race, he ran a 48 to the half. Why was that? This test can only be used to see if a horse is in condition. It depends on how fast he can go in a sprint. Obviously, if he was running between 45–47, that would have been too fast for that distance and he would have tired.

Also, many times when a horse has run distance races the year before and is making his debut in a sprint, he might use that race as a workout and then score when put in a longer race.

Denizen — Dk. b. or br. g. 5, by State Dinner—Giostra, by Imperial Prince
Br.—Johnson Donald T (Ky)
$6,250
Own.—Lawson Russell — Tr.—Goodridge Ronald O (12 2 1 2 .17) — **117**

Lifetime							
48 7 4 7	1993	8	1	2	1	$7,250
	1992	17	1	1	4	$8,487
$46,714	Turf	6	1	0	2	$7,058
	Wet	5	0	0	0	$1,590

10May93- 2AP	fst	7f	:22^4	:46^2	1:25	3↑Clm 8000	60	1	3	3^{nk}	2^{hd}	3^4	$4^{5\frac{1}{2}}$	Sibille R	Lb	117	6.60	72-25	LmpkinCche117$^{4\frac{3}{4}}$VrsityTem117$\frac{1}{2}$ElgiB 117	Faded inside	8
16Apr93-10RP	fst	1$\frac{1}{16}$	:47^1	1:13	1:47^4	Clm 8000	48	9	1	2^1	$6^{4\frac{1}{2}}$	9^{10}	9^{18}	Sides K L	Lb	116	*1.90	59-23	Yodddy116^{2}AndyOrphn112^{hd}Scndlizd116	Speed stopped	9
1Apr93- 4RP	fst	170	:46^4	1:12^4	1:43^1	Clm 8000	73	5	1	$1^{1\frac{1}{2}}$	1^2	$1^{2\frac{1}{2}}$	3^2	Sides K L	Lb	116	*1.90	83-24	ShttertheStrs115$^{1\frac{1}{4}}$Scndlized112$\frac{3}{4}$Denizn116	Broke in air	9
21Mar93- 3RP	gd	170	:47^4	1:14	1:46	Clm 8000	80	4	2	2^1	1^{hd}	1^{hd}	2^{nk}	Sides K L	Lb	116	*1.00	71-32	KngrooDwn116^{nk}Denizen116$^{7\frac{1}{4}}$TobieRy114	Game inside	7
7Mar93- 7RP	fst	170	:47^3	1:13^1	1:42^2	Clm 8000	85	4	1	1^1	$1^{1\frac{1}{2}}$	2^{hd}	$2^{\frac{1}{2}}$	Sides K L	Lb	120	5.20	88-16	Roaron116$\frac{1}{2}$ Denizen120$^{4\frac{3}{4}}$ Andy Orphan113	Game inside	10
21Feb93- 3RP	fst	170	:48^1	1:14^2	1:44^4	Clm 11500	68	4	2	1^{hd}	$3^{\frac{1}{2}}$	$5^{2\frac{1}{2}}$	$5^{7\frac{3}{4}}$	Sides K L	Lb	114	5.40	69-24	Alyrun116^3 Yodaddy116^{no} EditorialPolicy116	Weakened	8
12Feb93- 1RP	fst	1$\frac{1}{16}$	:48	1:13^2	1:45^4	Clm 8000	82	1	1	$1^{\frac{1}{2}}$	$1^{1\frac{1}{2}}$	$1^{4\frac{1}{2}}$	$1^{6\frac{3}{4}}$	Sides K L	Lb	116	*2.00	87-22	Dnizn116$^{6\frac{3}{4}}$NorthrnCptiv116^{2}PrvtChnc116	Off step slow	8
30Jan93- 6RP	fst	7f	:22	:44^4	1:24^2	Alw 8000s	68	8	1	2^{hd}	$2^{\frac{1}{2}}$	2^1	4^4	Sides K L	Lb	116	14.90	82-16	DremLight116^{nk}MstrJck116$^{3\frac{3}{4}}$EightPointr116	Weakened	9
5Dec92- 6RP	gd	1	:47^3	1:11^4	1:36^3	3↑Alw 14400	72	3	1	1^{hd}	3^3	$4^{6\frac{1}{2}}$	$6^{9\frac{1}{2}}$	Sides K L	Lb	116	23.00	100 —	HrrynJerry114^{1}Jute'sReject114$^{6\frac{1}{4}}$Mmbolo116	Weakened	10
5Dec92-Originally scheduled on the turf																					
28Nov92- 4RP	fst	6$\frac{1}{2}$f	:22^1	:45^1	1:17^4	3↑Clm 8000	77	3	4	$1^{\frac{1}{2}}$	$1^{1\frac{1}{2}}$	$1^{\frac{1}{2}}$	$1^{\frac{3}{4}}$	Sides K L	Lb	116	15.30	95-17	Denizen116$\frac{3}{4}$ScondNotion112^{1}Mrkbl114	Drifted entering	10

LATEST WORKOUTS May 20 AP 4f fst :54 B

Denizen, a five year old gelding, was making his '93 debut on January 30 at Remington Park. On this date, *Denizen* tried to get to the front, but chased the eventual winner while posting some very good fractions. In his next start, he was put back in a distance race at one mile and one sixteenth. Also, he was dropping from an allowance 8,000 race to the claiming level of 8,000. This level is where *Denizen* performed well last year. The "tightener" that Denizen had received in the seven-furlong sprint put him in top condition for his next start, a winning one. He covered the distance in 145$\frac{4}{5}$, winning by 6$\frac{3}{4}$ lengths and paying $6.00. This angle is just a sample of the different ways first starts and workouts will bring profits. This past example will be more profitable when one spots this pattern with a horse that is not dropping, as was *Denizen*, who only paid $6.00 because of his drop in company.

If a particular horse is making his first start of the year and has workouts at a comparable distance to what is being run, this horse's chances increase tremendously. Rest upon it: this is one horse that will not tire in the stretch.

Additional Workouts

2

Additional workouts are either workouts that the *Daily Racing Form* clockers missed or workouts that are called in by a trainer.

It is obvious that it could be possible for a horse to be missed, but why would a trainer call in a workout? The next six examples answer this question. They'll help you understand how additional workouts can take your tickets to the cashier.

The first four examples show the difference between legitimate and non-legitimate workouts. Legitimate workouts are workouts that were performed in which the horse (usually a maiden) was not named, was working under a different name, or was just missed by the clockers. If the horse's name is not spelled exactly correctly, the computer will not pick up the workout. When a horse is going to workout, he will pass a guard as the horse walks toward the entrance to the track. The guard will ask the name of the horse and how far he will be working. The guard will take the information (Ex: "*Twinkle In My Eye* - ⅝ of a mile") and use his walkie talkie to transfer the information to the clockers. As one can imagine, some names are rather difficult and can be misspelled or misunderstood in the process. That is why maidens, especially, often will not be recognized and can have their names misspelled. A horse who is making his first start must have at least one official workout. This is one reason why trainers will call these workouts in. If the horse is entered and the computer says the horse has no workouts, the trainer will be called by the racing office to see why this is. Thus, additional workouts have been created. Usually, for maidens, these are legitimate workouts.

Non-legitimate workouts arise because a horse has not run in the last thirty days. If this occurs, the horse that is entered must have at least one official workout to show the horse is sound and able to run without physical injury. In these cases, it is very obvious, usually the day before the horse is running, that an additional workout will appear. Most of the time, it will be only one workout and this is the reason it is non-legitimate. If the horse had two or three additional workouts and was posted the day before he was running, then it would seem that these were actually performed, but, when only one workout appears, the trainer clearly just wants his horse to be eligible to run.

In the first example, *Clean Wager* was making his first start on June 11 at Monmouth Park in the 1st race. *Clean Wager* had two additional workouts on June 9's list at Monmouth Park. Either *Clean Wager* was not named at the time and was not able to work officially, or he was working under a different name. *Clean Wager* posted two workouts and that would make them legitimate. In addition, he worked on that same day officially. If they just wanted the horse to start they would have posted just one workout and would not have worked him officially two days before his race.

MONMOUTH PARK – Track Muddy

Three Furlongs		Texas Melody	:38 B	Mr. Frizz	:49² Bg	Keratoid	1:02 B
Al's Prospect	:36 B	Very Sentimentl	:36² B	Ms.SilverWillow	:51² B	Late Night	1:04 Bg
CpturethCrown	:38⁴ B	Windy Dunes	:36³ B	Perfect Star	:49 B	Mickeray	1:04² B
Clean Wager	:37¹ B	**Four Furlongs**		Semester Miss	:49² Bg	Neon's Delite	1:02³ B
Gate Line	:36 B	CapabilityGreen	:49 Bg	Super Nip	:48 H	Phi Beta	1:02³ B
Majestic Hero	:38 B	Concorde Finale	:49⁴ Bg	Sweet Baby V.	:52¹ Bg	Slip Mahoney	1:02² Bg
Miss Toni	:37 B	Danazatiz	:51⁴ B	**Three Timer**	:48 Hg	Tru Mac	1:04³ B
Mistcapade	:37⁴ B	Fight Ain't Over	:49² B	Tojours Jolie	:49² B	**Six Furlongs—1:07⁴**	
Modern Melody	:38⁴ B	Froze	:50² B	True by Two	:50³ B	Concord'sFutur	1:14 B
My SweetTalker	:38 Bg	Kind One	:51⁴ B	Turpial	:51² B	Fleethoof	1:17 Bg
Nantucket Sky	:38 B	LightOnYourFet	:50² B	**Five Furlongs— :56¹**		Proud Pete	1:17² B
No Stalling	:36² B	Like Them All	:49¹ B	Breath Tester	1:04⁴ B	WoodsofWindsor	1:13 H
NorthernStrtgy	:36⁴ B	Miss Con Court	:49 Bg	Gallant Warfare	1:04² B	**1 Mile—1:33⁴**	
Sea Connection	:36⁴ B	MomntofSpring	:48³ Bg	HereFromHeven	1:02² B	**Friendly Lover**	1:41 B
Snazzy LilBroad	:36⁴ B	MoneyofthMind	:49 Hg	Holy Bull	1:01 Hg	Mighty Avanti	1:41² B

Notes: WOODS OF WINDSOR (6f) went nicely. Fractions: 36, 48.3, 100.3 and galloped out in 1:27; MIGHTY AVANTI (1m) finished strong. 26.4, 40, 52.4, 104.4, 1:16.2, 1:28.4 with jockey C. Lopez up. Additional works: CLEAN WAGER 5/17 (3f) 27.1b CLEAN WAGER 5/26 (4f) 49.2bg. TEXAS MELODY 5/28 (3f) 38b. MY SWEET TALKER 6-2 (4f) 50bg.

```
EQUINE LINE * PRODUCT 18B  *  7/03/93 * Clean Wager              * PG.   1


Clean Wager 1991 DK B/ filly, by Bet Big 80 --- Above Suspicion 85
                                                 by  Great Above 72

Breeder:  Pelican Stable


(SPR=69)

1993 in USA and Canada:

      trk     dist  trk  race    value of                         wnrs   claim  #
date  race#   turf  con  type      race    wt  pp fp lngths earned time   price  rn
----  -----   ----  ---  ----    --------  --  -- -- ------ ------ -----  -----  --
0623  MTH01   5.00  FST  FO2MCL    10,000 117 03 04  5 3/4     500 1:00.1 30,000 09
      1st  Spunky Prospect                    2nd   Northern Focus
      3rd  Always Rome
      Owner:   Pelican Stable
      Trainer: Croll Warren a Jr
      Jockey:  Wilson R
0611  MTH01   5.00  FST  FO2MCL    10,000 112 01 03  9 3/4   1,200 1:00.0 32,000 07
      1st  Innocent Bystander               2nd   Doc n Trope
      3rd  Clean Wager
```

I do not like additional workouts, but if I can find a legitimate excuse it will help. Maidens have an excuse because it is possible that they were not named at the time, but horses that have been running have no excuse and these workouts must be frowned upon and not trusted. Also, we must refer back to the trainer to see if we can trust these workouts with maidens. Many times you will see two or three workouts that are posted as additional workouts and appear to be legitimate. When this set of workouts is very fast, one must find when these workouts were performed to see how the track was. Perhaps everyone was putting up these numbers, making them less impressive. Also, check the trainer and see if he is trustworthy! Trainers on occasion will post false workouts to make the public think the horse is better than it is.

In our second example, *My Brother Gary* posted two additional workouts on June 15, the day before he was scheduled to run. *My Brother Gary* was also trained by a trustworthy conditioner, James Crupi. Unlike *Clean Wager*, *My Brother Gary* did not work out on that same day.

Although these are legitimate workouts it must be stressed that one has to be very careful how much trust to put into them. Always check to see how many additional workouts there are and who the trainer is.

MONMOUTH PARK — Track Fast

Three Furlongs							
AmericanLouisa	:37¹ B	Sommerset Hill	:40 Bg	Miss Con Court	:50² Bg	I'm Harriet	1:03³ B
Beaujus Boy	:38¹ Bg	SoverignMgicin	:38 B	Olympic Park	:48⁴ B	Jeb	1:04³ B
BurningChstnut	:37³ B	StrikeCommndr	:39 B	OnTimeDelivery	:50 Bg	Jill's Brother	1:02¹ B
Charsal	:37 B	Sunny Cookie	:36² B	Outlaw Proof	:51 B	Late Night	1:03⁴ B
Easy Buck	:36 B	True Slew	:37 B	Pacific Express	:50¹ B	Light Them All	1:02⁸ B
FmilyEnterprize	:35² B	Via Search	:38 B	PremirCommndr	:48¹ H	Ms. Goldilocks	1:03³ B
HagglesNHssels	:40 B	Who's Paying	:38 Bg	Prospect Girl	:52³ B	Northern Windy	1:01⁴ H
HereFromHeven	:36³ Bg	**Four Furlongs**		Raise A Crafty	:52 B	OneMityMomnt	1:03 B
Jesse Jet	39 B	BloominBusiness	:50 B	RsoundingProof	:51 B	Shiela'sRevenge	1:01⁴ B
Jet Forth	:39³ B	Blue Colony	49² B	Sacred Honor	:51¹ B	Slip Mahoney	1:03² B
Joe Casey	:40 Bg	Call Me Guy B.	:49³ B	Savvy Sammy	:49 B	Tinbar	1:02 Bg
Lulu's Lullabye	:35³ B	CallMeMr.Tibbs	:48⁴ B	Screen Trial	:51 B	Toujours Jolie	1:01² Hg
Mask Marvel	:37 B	Celtic Choice	:48⁴ B	SouthernPrdise	:51² B	WhimsiclMlody	1.05 B
Miss Tarbeck	:37³ B	Danazatiz	:50 B	Stress Buster	:51 B	World Island	1:01⁴ H
Nantucket Sky	:37¹ B	DefenseofLibrty	:50 B	Total Kaos	:51² B	**Six Furlongs—1:07⁴**	
National Kid	:36⁴ B	Feel ThatBreeze	:50 B	Turbo Woman	:52³ B	Desperado Josh 1:16² B	
National Spirit	:36 B	Gallant Step	:51 B	**Five Furlongs— :56¹**		**Seven Furlongs**	
PeruvinPrincess	:37² B	Golden Pro	:51⁴ B	Big Ann Taylor	1:04 B	Keratoid	1:28 B
Quick Courage	:37¹ B	Kosablanca	:49⁴ B	Bloomn'goodTrl	1:02 B	**1 Mile—1:33⁴**	
Randomizer	:36 Bg	Leve Springs	:50 Bg	Distinct Effort	1:05 B	Future Pretense 1:38³ B	
Sea Reef	38² Bg	LuckyShe'sMine	:50 B	Froze	1:02⁴ B		
		Madam Jinsky	:54 Bg	Good for Poppy	1:02 B		

FAMILY ENTERPRIZE (3f) went nicely; **OLYMPIC PARK (4f)** and **CALL ME MR. TIBBS (4f)** worked nicely in company; **KERATOID (7f)** finished strong. **ADDITIONAL WORKOUTS: 6/6 MY BROTHER GARY** 5f gd 1:03B G. 6/11 **MY BROTHER GARY** 5f fst 1:03B G.

EQUINE LINE * PRODUCT 18B * 7/03/93 * My Brother Gary   * PG.   1

My Brother Gary 1991 DK B/ colt, by Imperial Falcon 83 —- Maritza 79
                                                  by High Roll 73

Breeder: Summerplace Farm

(SPR÷59)

1993 in USA and Canada:

date	trk race#	dist furl	trk con	race type	value of race	wt	pp	fp	lngths	earned	wnrs time	claim price	# rn
0616	MTH01	5.00	FST	02MCL	10.000	118	06	04	14 1/2	500	1:00.1	35,000	07

1st Duelling Knight   2nd Carry a Rose
3rd River Clare
Owner: Martucci William C
Trainer: Crupi James J
Jockey: Squartino R A

In our third and fourth examples, you will learn about non-legitimate workouts and how to spot them.

Harrington received an additional workout on June 18. The additional workout read that on June 14 *Harrington* went three furlongs in 39²/5 breezing. *Harrington* was entered on June 22, then scratched and entered again on June 28.

DELAWARE PARK – Track Fast

Three Furlongs		Sweet Entrophy :37¹ B		Iron Groom	:49³ B	Gray's Ferry	1:03¹ B
Bushie Blue	:36³ B	**Four Furlongs**		Mss. Highness	:49² B	ScoreforUsBaby	1:02⁴ B
HtchAnothrDott	:37¹ B	A Quickie	:48¹ B	Top Grade	:49¹ B	**Toss A Trick**	1:02² B
Persia	:39² B	Ancient Lust	:49³ B	**Five Furlongs—**	:56¹	**Six Furlongs—**	1:08¹
PrecisionLeader	:38⁴ B	**Irish Trim**	:48 B	Good Wishes	1:03¹ B	Tis Awd	1:16² B

Additional workout: 6–14 HARRINGTON (3f) fast :39 2/5 B.

Another tip-off to these additional workouts when they are non-legitimate is the time between workouts and the actual starting date.

Harrington 1986 DK B/ colt, by Recusant 78 –– Harani 75, by *Hawaii 64

Breeder: Mr. & Mrs. Don Ball

(SPR=80)

1993 in USA and Canada:

date	trk race#	dist furl	trk con	race type	value of race	wt	pp	fp	lngths	earned	wnrs time	claim price	# rn
0628	DEL07	6.00	FST	3UCL	3,500	112	08	04	1/2	210	1:12.1	3,500	13

1st   Pretty Product   2nd   Cloudy's Castle
3rd   Loughborough Lane
Owner: R M L Stable
Trainer: Somerville Henry F
Jockey: Rodriguez a F

1992 in USA and Canada:

date	trk race#	dist furl	trk con	race type	value of race	wt	pp	fp	lngths	earned	wnrs time	claim price	# rn
0913	PHA07	6.00	FST	3UCL	4,500	116	12	11	18 3/4	0	1:11.2	4,000	12

```
     1st   Hot Song                    2nd   Portland Park
     3rd   Talented Pirate
0831 PHA09  8.50   FST   3UCL      5,000 116 08 08 19 3/4        0 1:46.3  4,000 12
     1st   Frigid Dancer               2nd   Jack Boot
     3rd   Bardi's Challenge
0821 PHA04  9.00T  SFT   3UCL      6,750 116 03 07 18            0 1:55.1  6,500 09
     1st   Top Floor                   2nd   Bina's Patrick
     3rd   Duca d'Aosta
0813 PHA01  9.00   FST   3UCL     10,890 112 04 05  9 3/4      270 1:54.1  8,000 06
     1st   Seasjohnspower              2nd   Singh's Raja
     3rd   Phantom Knight
0726 PHA03  7.00   FST   3UCL      4,500 116 02 03  2          495 1:25.0  4,000 09
     1st   Cajun Fox                   2nd   Talk Nice
     3rd   Harrington
0719 PHA09  5.00T  FRM   3USAL     7,759 116 10 08  9 3/4        0  :59.0        10
     1st   Beyond all Odds             2nd   Rebelde
     3rd   Northforest Dancer
0706 PHA08  7.00   FST   3UCL      6,000 116 03 05 18 1/2      180 1:23.4  6,500 07
     1st   Johns I. D.                 2nd   Chocolate Too
     3rd   Halo Judge
0615 PHA07  6.00   FST   3UCL      6,000 116 01 09 15 3/4        0 1:11.3  7,500 10
     1st   Chancellor Forbes           2nd   Talented Pirate
     3rd   Bob Balfe
0518 PHA09  6.00   FST   3UCL      9,000 116 09 09 14            0 1:10.3 11,000 09
     1st   Ima Smarten                 2nd   Attacka Sack
     3rd   Easy Appeal
```

Harrington was making his first start of the year and he needed a workout, since he did not start in the last thirty days. As we have noted, all horses must have an official workout if they have not started in thirty days.

Harrington finished fourth, beaten by half a length, suggesting that if he had trained a little longer and better, he might have won. The result is not important in all of these examples, but the fact that we can identify which ones we can trust and which ones we cannot will definitely be to our advantage.

Chelly M., on the surface, may look like the same example as *Harrington*, but *Chelly M.* had a disturbing twist. *Chelly M.* had an additional workout posted on June 11, saying that on June 7 she worked 118²/₅ breezing. As mentioned in Chapter 1, if we adjust this workout of 118²/₅, Chelly M. should be able to perform around 114²/₅.

MONMOUTH PARK — Track Fast

Three Furlongs						
Artic Conquest	:36¹ Bg	Toroweep	:38 B	Mircleofmircles	:52³ B	Advance Word	1:04³ B

Three Furlongs
Artic Conquest :36¹ Bg
Charlie Angel :37 B
Cold Filter :37² B
ConfederateFlg :35³ H
Cosmic Candy :35¹ H
Dazzling Smile :36 Bg
Desert Drive :37² B
Devilish Boy :37² B
Duke's Joy :39 B
Gorgeous Phil :35² H
Incredible Me :36 B
Jersey Dimon :37³ B
Joe Casey :38 B
Kinklets :37⁴ B
Kitchen N Yon :37² B
Magic ofVictory :37² B
Mr. Impatience :37² B
Ms. Ultimate :36¹ B
Nashua One :37³ Bg
Paper Weight :37² B
Pixie's Greatest :35³ H
Quaker Bonnet :37⁴ B
Sand Kicker :39² B
Sincere Endever :35² Bg
Six Peak :35³ B
Slim Pas Suel :37² B
Snippet :38³ Bg
Sommerset Hill :38 B

Sterling Royalty :35³ H
Sylvester V. :37³ B
Taroz :35 H
Tears N Time :35³ H

Toroweep :38 B
Traffect Feast :39 B
Turkey Tom :37⁴ B
Very Careless :37 B
VictoriTyndrum :37³ B
Wild Peace :38⁴ B

Four Furlongs
Afar :49³ B
AlyshebaDancer :50 B
Be Back :49² B
Book of Power :52³ B
Buckey'sDstroy :51 B
Caranna C. :51 B
Casino Magic :50 B
Celtic Choice :50² B
Colorful Patch :51 B
DarnedAlarming :48 H
Disaster Master :48 H
Facts of Love :53² B
Future Answer :49 B
Glamour Gal :47 H
HotTimesAreHr :50 B
Inga's Bo :49 Bg
Jericho Blase :48 B
Jersey Go*ld :48 B
Justinthefastme :48³ Bg
KeytotheNursry :48⁴ H
Keys Idle :51 B
Learn Quick :48 H
MhogoneyLight :49 B
Medical Record :49³ Bg
MichelleDanielle :51 B
Mineral Ice :49⁴ B

Mircleofmircles :52³ B
Mr. Vincent :48⁴ Bg
My Protege :47¹ H
Myerdon :50⁴ B
Not A Scratch :49⁴ B
PleasantDilemm :50⁴ H
Polorctte :51² B
PopcornNHoney :50⁴ B
Private Enough :48 Hg
Private Terry :53² B
Seven Cadet :54 B
Seven Layer :48³ H
Shansnie's Lane :49 Bg
Shesahe :54 B
Sir Angel :49¹ B
Slew City Melba :48³ H
Smartan's Hero :48³ Bg
Soar Ciello :49² H
Solly Honor :48¹ Hg
Sporty Card :50¹ B
Stand of Blue :49 B
Sunny's Magic :49 B
Thank's forcandy :47 B
U.S. Loyalty :48³ H
Uwillbeking :49¹ B
Wake Up Alarm :48 H
White Coners :49 B
Worlds to Go :50¹ B
Yeckley :48² H
Youmkmyhrtsng :51² B

Five Furlongs :56¹
A Shakey Queen 1:04 B
AdelphiAccount 1:03³ B

Advance Word 1:04³ B
Azorica 1:04 B
Basques Ad 1:03² B
Belle's Rider 1:02⁴ B
Bound Above 1:02⁴ Bg
CasanovaChrlie 1:02⁴ B
Crafty Afrel 1:01² B
End of Time 1:05² B
Fifty CentDollar 1:05⁴ B
Hi Berger 1:04² B
Make Us Laugh 1:04¹ Bg
Marshall Blake 1:03 B
McStew 1:02 B
Melanie Mark 1:03⁴ B
Motel Amiss 1:05 B
OnTimeDelivery 1:05 B
Oncetherwaswy 1:05 B
Onherwayhome 1:05 B
Ox 1:04 B
Perfect Vodka 1:03² B
Sabin Major 1:04 B
Salajak 1:03¹ B
Snomite 1:05 B
Special Illusion 1:03 B
Timely Warning 1:04 B
Wild Zone 1:03 B

Six Furlongs —1:07⁴
Cravinsky 1:17 B
Oreo Man 1:16¹ B
ProgrssivMotion 1:15⁴ B
Show d'Or 1:17² Bg
Turn Away 1:19 B

Additional Works: **CHELLY M.** 6/7/93 Mth Mt, Fast (6f) 1:18 2/5 b.

On June 22, *Chelly M.* was making her 1993 debut, dropping to the lowest level in her short career, a maiden claiming $20,000 event.

Chelly M. 1989 B filly, by Valid Appeal 72 — Penny's Chelly 78, by *Rixdal 63

Breeder: Harriet Heubeck & Elmer Heubeck Jr.

(SPR=51)

1993 in USA and Canada:

date	trk race#	dist furl	trk con	race type	value of race	wt	pp	fp	lngths	earned	wnrs time	claim price	# rn
0622	MTH01	6.00	FST	F3UMCL	9,000	118	03	06	23 3/4	90	1:14.2	20,000	08

```
      1st  Arc Melody                        2nd  Krislynns Dream
      3rd  Afternoon Star
      Owner:   Heubeck Harriet C
      Trainer: Kelly Edward I
      Jockey:  Santagata N

1992 in USA and Canada:
```

date	trk race#	dist furl	trk con	race type	value of race	wt	pp	fp	lngths	earned	wnrs time	claim price	# rn
0903	BEL09	6.00	MUD	F3UMCL	12,000	118	06	07	8 1/4	0	1:12.2	30,000	12
	1st Miraflores							2nd	Out of Line				
	3rd Gunner Lil												
0802	MTH11	6.00	FST	F3UM	15,500	117	08	09	21 3/4	155	1:12.3		10
	1st Dial a Babe							2nd	Georgia Anna				
	3rd Cometti Slew												
0724	BEL01	6.00	SY	F3UM	24,000	116	04	04	8	1,440	1:12.4		05
	1st Her Greeting							2nd	Open Marriage				
	3rd Imposing Light												

On this day, *Chelly M.* finished sixth, beaten by 23¾ lengths. The winner, *Arc Melody*, finished the race in 114²⁄₅. If we adjust *Chelly M.'s* actual race time, she finished the six furlongs in 119¹⁄₅. *Chelly M.* was not overmatched, because she was dropping in class, just out of condition. *Chelly M.* could not even run her workout time of 118²⁄₅, a workout that was performed under no pressure. We know this by the breezing mark on the side of the workout. That is why we cannot trust these non-legitimate workouts. *Chelly M.* could not even run her supposed workout time.

The fifth example of additional workouts will be covered more thoroughly in Chapter 15. As one can see below, *Pagofire* has legitimate workouts, and, in Chapter 15, we will show how we definitely know this horse has worked out.

MONMOUTH PARK — Track Sloppy

Three Furlongs								
Cndlelight Dinnr	:37 B	National Kid	:37 B	Wave Form	:39 B	Get Long Gold	1:04² Bg
Dinner Affair	:37² B	Pappa Way	:36³ B	**Four Furlongs**		Thrilla InManilla	1:02³ Bg
Easy Buck	:37² B	Quick Courage	:36³ B	Call Me Guy B.	:51² B	Viola D.	1:04 B
Esmerldo's Gem	:37² B	Slady Roberto	:35⁴ B	Kirby Slew	:54 B		
		Timber Ghost	:35 B	Lost Another	:51 B	**Six Furlongs—1:07⁴**	

Front Line	:35^4 B	TowerofWisdom	:39 B	Lucky She'sMine	:49^1 Bg		
Lynn'sNotebook	:37 B	Via Search	:38^4 B	Five Furlongs—	:56^1	All the Honor	1:16 B

Additional workouts: May 14, track fast, PAGOFIRE (4f) :49 4/5 b. May 22, track fast, EXPERT PLAY (4f) :47 4/5 hg and PAGOFIRE (4f) :48 3/5 b. May 28, track fast, PAGOFIRE (5f) 1:02 b. May 29, track fast, EXPERT PLAY (5f) 1:02 4/5 b. May 31, track fast, DEFENIE POLICY–IR (3f) :36 b. May 31, track fast, SHAKE AND SHIVER (3f) :38 1/5 b, SLIM PAS SUEL (3f) :37 b, TSNAMI SPANGLER (3f) :35 hg and BARBADES (6f) 1:30 b.

FIFTH RACE
Monmouth
JUNE 2, 1993

5 FURLONGS. (.56^1) MAIDEN SPECIAL WEIGHT. Purse $17,000. Fillies 2–year–olds, weights, 117 lbs.

Value of race $17,000; value to winner $10,200; second $3,230; third $1,700; fourth $680; balance of starters $170 each. Mutuel pool $42,604. Exacta Pool $36,485 Trifecta Pool $37,559

Last Raced	Horse	M/Eqt.A.Wt	PP	St	$\frac{3}{16}$	$\frac{3}{8}$	Str	Fin	Jockey	Odds $1
	Pagofire	2 117	10	3	1^1	$1^{5\frac{1}{2}}$	$1^{7\frac{1}{2}}$	$1^{11\frac{1}{2}}$	Wilson R	1.40
21Apr93 ^{3}Hia^2	True By Two	b 2 112	9	4	$6^{2\frac{1}{2}}$	$5^{2\frac{1}{2}}$	2^{hd}	$2^{3\frac{3}{4}}$	Homeister R BJr^5	8.90
	Dixie Brat	2 117	3	6	5^{hd}	$4^{\frac{1}{2}}$	3^2	$3^{3\frac{1}{4}}$	Bravo J	5.30
	Evening Tease	2 117	1	8	$7^{\frac{1}{2}}$	6^{hd}	$4^{\frac{1}{2}}$	$4^{1\frac{1}{4}}$	Rivera L Jr	34.80
	Preciseness	2 117	5	10	9^{hd}	$9^{\frac{1}{2}}$	7^1	$5^{2\frac{1}{2}}$	Castillo H Jr	7.20
	Sterling Royalty	2 117	11	1	3^2	3^{hd}	$5^{1\frac{1}{2}}$	6^{nk}	Santagata N	31.30
	Premier Mombo	2 117	4	11	8^3	7^{hd}	6^1	7^{nk}	Bruin J E	19.60
	Always Rome	2 112	6	7	10^{hd}	$10^{2\frac{1}{2}}$	$8^{\frac{1}{2}}$	$8^{5\frac{3}{4}}$	Duross A C^5	77.10
24May93 ^{3}Bel^3	Lori's Passion	2 117	8	2	4^{hd}	8^3	10^6	9^5	Marquez C H Jr	2.90
	Ray's Trial	2 117	7	5	2^1	$2^{\frac{1}{2}}$	9^2	10^7	Lopez C C	36.30
	Sea the Connection	2 117	2	9	11	11	11	11	Ferrer J C	35.50

OFF AT 3:00 Start good, Won easily. Time, :22^1, :46^1, :58^4 Track fast.

$2 Mutuel Prices:			
10–PAGOFIRE	4.80	3.20	3.40
9–TRUE BY TWO		6.20	4.60
4–DIXIE BRAT			5.80

$2 EXACTA 10–9 PAID $61.20 $2 TRIFECTA 10–9–4 PAID $273.60

Ch. f, (Jan), by Island Whirl—Horsafire, by Hold Your Peace. Trainer Perkins Ben W Jr. Bred by Harder Lois C (Fla).

PAGOFIRE disposed of RAY'S TRIAL on the turn and drew off in an easy effort. TRUE BY TWO, five wide into the lane, bested the rest. DIXIE BRAT lodged a bid on the turn and weakened in the drive. EVENING TEASE saved ground and lacked the needed stretch bid. PRECISENESS dropped back soon after the start, moved outside and offered a mild stretch bid. STERLING ROYALTY raced forwardly placed to the drive and tired. PREMIER MOMBO broke a bit slowly and bothered some leaving the gate, advanced outside into the turn and offered little in the drive. LORI'S PASSION, a bit fractious in the gate, raced between foes on the turn and gave way. RAY'S TRIAL prompted the early issue and gave way in upper stretch.

Owners— 1, New Farm; 2, Homeister Rosemary; 3, Summit Stable; 4, Winbound Farm & Old Brookside Farm; 5, Hooper Fred W; 6, Sears Michael; 7, Snowden Guy B; 8, Windy Acres; 9, Spina Nicholas; 10, Mamone Raymond; 11, Polo Hill Farm.

Trainers— 1, Perkins Ben W Jr; 2, Jennings Lawrence Jr; 3, Serpe Philip M; 4, Contessa Gary C; 5, Pierce Joseph H Jr; 6, Sears Leon B; 7, Salzman John E; 8, Hamer William E; 9, Spina Chuck; 10, Vincitore Michael J; 11, Boniface Kim.

Scratched—My Protege; B. J.'s Kat; Normandy Belle (5May93 ^{4}Bel^5); Shouldnt Say Never.

The next example focuses on *Feel That Breeze* and *Patti's Gift.* These two horses, most likely, were missed by the clockers. How do we know this?

MONMOUTH PARK — Track Muddy

Three Furlongs							
Cheneli's Titanic	:34 H	Southern Sign	:38² B	Martini for All	:49³ B	Cometti's Slew	1:02⁴ B
Dare toRemeber	:36⁴ B	Timeforathrill	:36² B	Ocean Drive	:52 B	DecidedPlesure	1:04 B
Fire Bullet	:36² B	Wahool	:36 B	Oh So Wise	:50¹ B	Future Pretense	1:04 B
Madame Jinsky	:37³ B	Woodster	:36³ B	Preciseness	:48 H	Spanish Kiss	1:03¹ B
Momento	:37³ B	**Four Furlongs**		SecretAssembly	:50 B	TomsRiverIndin	1:04⁴ B
PleseDon'tRing	:37 B	Front Line	:49¹ B	Sky Box	:48 H		
Prospect Girl	:37 B	Glady Roberto	:49¹ B	SouthernPrdise	:53 B	**Six Furlongs—1:07⁴**	
Ready Alara	:38 B	Good for Poppy	:50 B	Tank'sRajectrte	:53¹ B		
		Jill's Brother	:49³ B	**Five Furlongs— :56¹**		I'mABig	1:16 B
						Necklace Place	1:20 B

Additional workouts: Feel That Breeze 6/9 Mth (4F) Muddy 49 2/5 B. PATTI'S GIFT 6/9 Mth (4F) Muddy 49 2/5 BG.

The immediate attempt to get these workouts in the paper tells us that they are legitimate. These workouts were performed on June 9th, and they were printed the next day. In our examples of non-legitimate workouts, there are usually weeks in between the work and the display on the workout sheet. Also, these two are maidens who were probably missed by the clockers, and the trainer noticed this error and called them in.

Working Farther Than Running

CHAPTER 3 This angle is my favorite. One of the hardest things to figure out with first time starters is if they can last. Many good two year olds can work 35 for three furlongs from the gate, but it is extending the speed and endurance to last five, five and one half, and six furlongs that separates the men from the boys.

---

7 **5 ½ FURLONGS.** (1.02⁴) MAIDEN SPECIAL WEIGHT. Purse $15,500. 2-year-olds. Weight: 118 lbs.

Coupled—Shu Fellow and Super Nip.
LASIX—Inagroove.

Inagroove	Ch. c. 2(May), by Groovy—Rose Of Darby, by Roberto		Lifetime	1992 0 M 0 0
	Br.—Prestonwood Farm (Ky)		0 0 0 0	
Own.—Spina Nicholas	Tr.—Spina Chuck (12 0 1 2 .00)	**118**		
LATEST WORKOUTS	Jly 19 Mth 6f fst 1:14² Bg	Jly 15 Mth 5f fst 1:01³ Hg		

Wading Castelli	B. c. 2(Apr), by Leo Castelli—Wading Power, by Balance of Power		Lifetime	1992 0 M 0 0
	Br.—Edwards Robert L (NJ)		0 0 0 0	
Own.—Castelli Stables	Tr.—Anderson William D (31 3 5 1 .10)	**118**		
LATEST WORKOUTS	●Jly 15 Mth 3f fst :35 H	Jly 10 Mth 5f fst 1:02² Bg	Jly 1 Mth 5f fst 1:03 B	Jun 30 Mth 5f fst 1:06 B

Stately Fighter	Dk. b. or br. c. 2(Apr), by Fit To Fight—Statuesque, by Gay Mecene		Lifetime	1992 0 M 0 0
	Br.—Wakefield Farm (Ky)		0 0 0 0	
Own.—Polin Mrs Charlotte C	Tr.—Forbes John H (101 15 6 18 .15)	**118**		
LATEST WORKOUTS	Jun 29 Mth 4f fst :51 B			

Armagh County	Dk. b. or br. g. 2(Mar), by Distinctive Pro—Black Bess, by Riverman				Lifetime	1992 0 M 0 0	
	Br.—Lusararian Inc (Fla)				0 0 0 0		
Own.—Equity Horse Farm	Tr.—Thrasher Clint D (18 2 3 1 .11)			**118**			
LATEST WORKOUTS	Jly 17 Mth 4f fst :48³ Bg	Jly 10 Mth 5f fst 1:01¹ H	Jly 2 Mth 4f fst :49 B		Jun 16 Mth 3f fst :36³ B	

Strand of Blue	Gr. c. 2(Mar), by Blue Ensign—Strand of Gems, by Accipiter				Lifetime	1992 1 M 1 0	$2,945
	Br.—Francis W. Lucas (Fla)				1 0 1 0		
Own.—Char-Mari Stable	Tr.—Perkins Ben W Jr (34 6 8 7 .18)			**118**	$2,945		
1Jly2-10Mth fst 5f :22 :45² :57³ Md Sp Wt	70 4 7 3¾ 3⁵ 2⁸ Wilson R	118 3.50	85-17 GrtNgtr118⁸StrndfBl118½NrthrnWtnss118	Earned place 1
LATEST WORKOUTS	Jly 21 Mth 4f fst :50 B	●Jun 27 Mth 4f fst :47¹ Hg	Jly 14 Mth 4f fst :50⁴ B		Jun 22 Mth 4f fst :50 B	

Shu Fellow	B. c. 2(Feb), by Saratoga Six—Video Babe, by T V Commercial				Lifetime	1992 0 M 0 0	
	Br.—Red Bull Stable Inc & Eaton Farms (Ky)				0 0 0 0		
Own.—Due Process Stables	Tr.—Nobles Reynaldo H (24 2 4 4 .08)			**118**			
LATEST WORKOUTS	Jly 15 Mth 4f fst :49 Bg	Jly 8 Mth 4f fst :49 Bg	Jly 3 Mth 5f fst 1:02¹ Bg		Jun 28 Mth 4f fst :48³ Bg	

Carnival Knight	Dk. b. or br. c. 2(Apr), by Carnivalay—Codette, by Codex				Lifetime	1992 2 M 1 0	$1,485
	Br.—Ivy Dell Stud (Pa)				2 0 1 0		
Own.—Armbrister Carl D	Tr.—Armbrister Carl D (1 0 0 0 .00)			**118**	$1,485		
1Jly2-1Atl fst 5½f :22³ :47³ 1:07¹ Md Sp Wt	30 1 4 2² 3¹ 1¼ 2¾ Rodriguez E	b 118 19.50	80-14 KickthTr118²CrnvlKnght118³QuckScoot118	Bid tired 10
1Jly2-10Mth fst 5f :22 :45² :57³ Md Sp Wt	12 11 8 8¹¹ 9¹⁹10²³10²⁶¼ Rodriguez E	b 118 39.30	66-17 GrtNvgtor118⁸StrndofBlu118½NorthrnWtnss118	Outrun 11
LATEST WORKOUTS	●Jly 21 Atl 3f fst :35² H	Jun 27 Atl 3f fst :35³ H	●Jun 19 Atl 5f fst 1:01 Hg		Jun 13 Atl 5f fst 1:01³ Bg	

In my first book, *Finding HOT Horses,* I used this example in chapter 5, but for different reasons. *Inagroove* will be the only example from 1992 in this book. Too many handicapping books show examples from ten years ago. If they have to go ten years in the past to prove their theories, they don't work. All the examples in this book are in a two-month time span, showing the currentness and consistency of all my theories and systems.

As one will learn in the next dozen chapters, "stupidity" is what I do. One can learn to live off it at the racetrack. If it wasn't for "stupidity" I could not and would not make any money at the track. *Inagroove* is a perfect example of this "stupidity".

The 7th race at Monmouth Park at five and one-half furlongs offered exacta and trifecta betting. As one glances down at the past performances, the race consisted of three horses who had already started and seven first-time starters. Two horses, *Inagroove* and *Major Manila,* had worked over five and one-half furlongs. *Inagroove* worked 114²/₅ breezing from the gate and *Major Manila,* 116 breezing. First of all, *Inagroove* came from out of the gate. If the works were identical, *Inagroove* would get the nod, but *Inagroove's* time was 1 and ³/₅ better, clearly showing superior ability.

Whenever one handicaps a maiden race, one has to look for those "stupidity" horses that he or she will learn to bet against instead of betting with the losers at the track. In this race, *Strand of Blue* finished second behind *Great Navigator,* but he was eight lengths behind. As will be shown throughout this book, it is good to finish 1-3 lengths behind a good or great horse but when he gets dominated, as was the case of *Strand Of Blue*, such horses have to be examined for what they are. His two workouts after that race were poor. He is a prime example of a "stupidity" horse. *Tricky Catman* was the other; he ran second at Atlantic City. If the horse finished second at a lower class track with below average horses, how in the world is he going to win at Monmouth Park? *Strand Of Blue* went off the 9-5 favorite with *Tricky Catman* at 7-1.

Inagroove, because of his 114⅖ breezing from the gate workout, was superior to anything this field could possibly do. If we adjusted Inagroove's workout, he should perform between 110⅖ and 111⅖. With horses that work farther than running, condition will never be a problem.

SEVENTH RACE **5 ½ FURLONGS. (1.02^{4}) MAIDEN SPECIAL WEIGHT. Purse $15,500. 2–year–olds. Weight: 118 lbs.**

Monmouth

JULY 24, 1992

Value of race $15,500; value to winner $9,300; second $2,945; third $1,705; fourth $620; balance of starters $155 each. Mutuel pool $78,688. Exacta Pool $85,266 Trifecta Pool $97,746

Last Raced	Horse	M/Eqt.	A.	Wt	PP	St	¼	⅜	Str	Fin	Jockey	Odds $1
	Inagroove	Lb	2	118	1	8	3^{2}	3^{3}	2½	1¾	Marquez C H Jr	7.80
	Armagh County		2	118	4	4	1^{hd}	1½	1½	$2^{1½}$	Vega A	2.20
1Jly92 ^{10}Mth^{2}	Strand of Blue		2	118	5	7	$4^{1½}$	4^{5}	3^{hd}	$3^{1¾}$	Wilson R	1.80
	Major Manila	Lb	2	118	9	1	8^{2}	7½	5½	4^{nk}	Purdom M D	22.10
28Jun92 ^{1}Atl^{2}	Tricky Catman		2	118	8	2	2^{2}	2^{2}	$4^{5½}$	5¾	Gryder A T	7.40
	Super Nip		2	118	10	5	6^{3}	6½	6^{1}	$6^{2¼}$	Santagata N	6.20
10Jly92 ^{1}Atl^{2}	Carnival Knight	b	2	118	6	3	5½	5^{2}	7^{3}	7^{2}	McCormick M L	43.60
	Wading Castelli		2	118	2	9	9½	10	8^{2}	$8^{2½}$	Romero J A	12.20
	Stately Fighter		2	118	3	10	10	9^{hd}	9^{hd}	$9^{3½}$	Lidberg D W	35.50
	Strike Commander	b	2	118	7	6	7½	8^{3}	10	10	Picon J	67.50

OFF AT 3:51 Start good, Won driving. Time, :22^{1}, :46^{1}, 1:06^{1} Track fast.

$2 Mutuel Prices:

1–INAGROOVE	17.60	8.60	4.40
4–ARMAGH COUNTY		4.00	3.20
5–STRAND OF BLUE			2.80

$2 EXACTA 1–4 PAID $73.40 $2 TRIFECTA 1–4–5 PAID $273.00

Ch. c, (May), by Groovy—Rose Of Darby, by Roberto. Trainer Spina Chuck. Bred by Prestonwood Farm (Ky).

INAGROOVE, angled out nearing the turn, advanced into the lane and challenged in upper stretch, came over approaching the sixteenth pole then bested ARMAGH COUNTY. The latter held a narrow edge into the lane while removed from the rail and gave way grudgingly. STRAND OF BLUE advanced along the rail through upper stretch and tired late. MAJOR MANILA offered a late gain from the outside. TRICKY CATMAN showed the early way, raced outside of ARMAGH COUNTY into the lane, steadied nearing the sixteenth pole and tired. SUPER NIP lacked the needed rally. WADING CASTELLI was outrun. STATELY FIGHTER failed to menace.

Owners— 1, Spina Nicholas; 2, Equity Horse Farm; 3, Char-Mari Stable; 4, Marla Farm; 5, Canonie Tony Jr; 6, Due Process Stables; 7, Armbrister Carl D; 8, Castelli Stables; 9, Polin Mrs Charlotte C; 10, Carabelli Robert.

Trainers— 1, Spina Chuck; 2, Thrasher Clint D; 3, Perkins Ben W Jr; 4, Crupi James J; 5, Velez Roberto; 6, Nobles Reynaldo H; 7, Armbrister Carl D; 8, Anderson William D, 9, Forbes John H; 10, Tronco William L.
Scratched—Shu Fellow.

Northern Witness — Dk. b. or br. g. 3(Feb), by Ankara—Silent Times, by Silent Screen
MIGLIORE R (76 12 12 11 .16) — Br.—Starsfell Farms Inc (Fla)
Own.—Sabarese Theodore M — Tr.—Parisella John (—)
110

Lifetime								
9 2 1 3	1993	3	2	0	1	$28,900
$39,256	1992	6	M	1	2	$10,356

3May93- 6Aqu	fst	6½f	:23	:46^2	1:18^4	Alw 26500	78	5	3	5^4	5^3	$3^{1\frac{1}{2}}$	1^{nk}	Migliore R		117	6.80	87-17 NorthrnWtnss117^{nk}Brd'sFly117$^{\frac{3}{4}}$IrnGvl117 Wide,driving	8
1Apr93- 7Hia	fst	6f	:21^4	:45^2	1:11^3	Alw 15000	72	5	8	$9^{7\frac{3}{4}}$	$7^{6\frac{3}{4}}$	$6^{1\frac{3}{4}}$	$3^{2\frac{1}{4}}$	Vasquez J	L	116	7.80	85-14 Ecdd116$^{2\frac{1}{4}}$DstnctG116^{hd}NrthrnWtss116 Late rally 7 wd	9
1Jan93- 6Crc	gd	7f	:22^4	:46^3	1:25^3	Md Sp Wt	69	4	7	$7^{3\frac{3}{4}}$	4^3	1^{hd}	1^{hd}	Lee M A	L	120	2.40	87-13 NorthrnWitnss120^{hd}L'sGoldnKnight115^{9}SpnishPrnc120	12
1Jan93-Fully extended drifted out then drifted in																			
17Oct92- 3Crc	fst	170	:48^1	1:14^1	1:45^4	Md Sp Wt	57	2	1	$1^{\frac{1}{2}}$	2^{hd}	2^3	$5^{10\frac{1}{4}}$	Bailey J D	Lb	117	*1.40	74-11 BayMinister117^{8}Nuseatle117$^{1\frac{1}{2}}$WolfRidgeRod117 Faded	8
3Oct92- 6Crc	fst	7f	:22	:45^2	1:27	Md Sp Wt	57	1	7	$6^{5\frac{1}{4}}$	$5^{6\frac{1}{2}}$	$5^{1\frac{3}{4}}$	3^3	Rodriguez P A	L	118	*1.30	77-15 BdFrGld118$^{1\frac{1}{2}}$LsGldKht118$^{1\frac{1}{2}}$NrtrWtss118 Late rlly 6 wd	10
19Sep92- 6Crc	fst	1	:48^4	1:13^4	1:40^2	Md Sp Wt	56	5	5	2^{hd}	2^{hd}	$3^{6\frac{1}{2}}$	$8^{13\frac{1}{2}}$	Rodriguez P A	Lb	116	*1.00	79-04 SanImagination116^{8}TonyBlue116$^{1\frac{1}{2}}$SirTim116 No threat	12
1Aug92- 9WO	fst	6½f	:22^2	:45	1:18^3	Swynford	60	6	3	$6^{6\frac{1}{2}}$	$6^{5\frac{1}{2}}$	$6^{6\frac{1}{2}}$	$4^{3\frac{3}{4}}$	McKnight J		115	9.80	78-15 RchthGld117$^{1\frac{1}{2}}$OStpHfStp117^{1}TrIThS119 Closed mildly	7
11Jly92- 2Mth	fst	5½f	:22^4	:46^4	1:06	Md Sp Wt	60	4	5	$3^{\frac{1}{2}}$	$2^{\frac{1}{2}}$	$3^{1\frac{1}{2}}$	$2^{2\frac{1}{4}}$	McKnight R E		118	3.70	82-14 Gerson118$^{2\frac{1}{4}}$NorthernWitness118^{1}Btct118 Earned place	7
1Jly92-10Mth	fst	5f	:22	:45^2	:57^3	Md Sp Wt	69	7	2	5^6	5^8	4^9	$3^{8\frac{3}{4}}$	McKnight R E		118	2.40	84-17 GrtNvgtor118^{8}StrndofBl118$^{\frac{3}{4}}$NrthrnWtnss118 Late gain	11

LATEST WORKOUTS May 24 Aqu 7f fst 1:28^1 H Apr 26 Crc 5f fst 1:04 B Apr 20 Crc 7f fst 1:30 B Apr 10 Crc 5f sly 1:02 B (d)

Northern Witness was coming off a good try at Hialeah when he entered on May 3, 1993. In *Northern Witness*'s last start, he made a big move and tired slightly through the lane. After that start, *Northern Witness*'s connections worked him an impressive five furlongs around the dogs on a sloppy track in 102 breezing. His next workout was a condition workout to build up stamina, not too fast, but effective. On May 3, 1993, *Northern Witness* showed his come-from-behind kick to nip 4-5 *Birdie's Fly*. *Northern Witness* paid $13.60 and also keyed a $46.00 exacta.

The next two examples show an obvious condition angle of "step-up" workouts. The "step-up" angle is only effective when a horse is returning from a long layoff. *This Is My Mystery* and *Fightin Force* are just two of the many examples of "step-up" conditioning. *This Is My Mystery* had four workouts before making her '93 debut, On April 15, 1993, at Finger Lakes, *This Is My Mystery* worked three furlongs in 38 breezing; then on April 21 she worked 50 breezing at four furlongs. On May 2, she worked five furlongs in 104⅗ breezing, and on May 9, she performed a slow conditioning workout at six furlongs in 121 breezing. All of these workouts were breezing, and each one stepped up to a longer distance. Conditioning is not a factor when one works longer then he is running or one is using the "step-up" theory.

This Is My Mystery made her awaited debut on May 16, winning by ½ length in 1:15, paying $12.80—a beautiful price for an obvious angle.

All angles that involve workouts must be accompanied by conditions that suit the particular horse. If a horse is placed too high in competition, no matter how good his workouts are, he will not win. *This Is My Mystery* has always run in claiming 3,000 at Finger Lakes and has been consistently close.

This Is My Mystery — B. m. 5, by Who's For Dinner—Heavenly Mystery, by Great Above — $3,000 — Br.—Novaton J I (Fla) — Tr.—Milian Michael (6 1 1 1 .17) — 122
Own.—Sanchez Adrian

Lifetime						
40 7 5 4	1993	1	1	0	0	$1,800
$24,883	1992	20	3	3	4	$9,876
	Wet	7	1	0	1	$3,935

16May93- 1FL	fst	6f	:22^4	:47^1	1:15	3↑ⒻClm 3000	43	9	1	1^1	$1^{\frac{1}{2}}$	$1^{\frac{1}{2}}$	$1^{\frac{1}{2}}$	Messina R	b	120	6.40	71-24 ThsIsMyMystry$120^{\frac{1}{2}}$ChSDcc120^{hd}HrsHgCnd120	Driving 9
8Dec92- 6FL	gd	6f	:22^3	:46^2	1:13^1	3↑ⒻClm 3000	37	1	7	$3^{2\frac{1}{2}}$	3^2	2^3	$3^{5\frac{1}{2}}$	Messina R	b	119	2.10	74-16 LdsGrl119^1AsIsObsss$116^{4\frac{1}{2}}$TsIsMMstr119	Flattened out 9
28Nov92- 6FL	my	5½f	:23^2	:48	1:07^2	3↑ⒻClm 3000	28	9	7	$8^{4\frac{3}{4}}$	$8^{8\frac{1}{4}}$	$5^{6\frac{1}{2}}$	5^7	Messina R	b	119	7.00	70-24 La Carr116^2 Sweet Kity$122^{2\frac{1}{2}}$ Lydian's Girl122	Even try 11
22Nov92- 6FL	gd	5½f	:23^2	:48^1	1:08^1	3↑ⒻClm 3000	28	4	5	2^{hd}	$2^{1\frac{1}{2}}$	3^4	$3^{6\frac{3}{4}}$	Messina R	b	116	4.50	66-23 SssySmnth$116^{1\frac{1}{4}}$Amysn$119^{5\frac{1}{2}}$ThsIsMMstr116	Weakened 8
10Nov92- 4FL	gd	6f	:22^3	:46^2	1:13^2	3↑ⒻClm 3000	46	8	5	$2^{\frac{1}{2}}$	2^1	2^2	$5^{5\frac{1}{2}}$	Messina R	b	119	4.80	73-22 Shawnee119^3 Amyson119^2 Retalc116	Gave way 10
30Oct92- 4FL	gd	5½f	:23	:47^2	1:07^1	3↑ⒻClm 3000	51	3	4	1^1	$1^{1\frac{1}{2}}$	$1^{\frac{1}{2}}$	$2^{\frac{1}{2}}$	Messina R	b	119	3.00	77-22 Amyson$116^{\frac{1}{2}}$ThsIsMyMystry119^3OrBoldRs119	Good try 7
18Oct92- 2FL	fst	6f	:22^4	:46^1	1:13^2	3↑ⒻClm 3000	62	1	5	$1^{2\frac{1}{2}}$	$1^{5\frac{1}{2}}$	1^{10}	$1^{7\frac{1}{2}}$	Messina R	b	116	3.50	79-22 ThsIsMMstr$116^{7\frac{1}{2}}$AbArs$116^{2\frac{1}{2}}$VntgWn116	Much the best 9
9Oct92- 4FL	sly	5½f	:22^3	:47^2	1:08^4	3↑ⒻClm 3000	36	1	7	$3^{4\frac{1}{2}}$	$3^{7\frac{1}{2}}$	3^7	$3^{6\frac{1}{2}}$	Messina R	b	116	21.00	63-33 Bdrck$116^{4\frac{1}{2}}$Stv'sLckLd116^2ThsIsMMstr116	No solid bid 7
2Oct92- 6FL	fst	5½f	:22^1	:45^2	1:05^1	3↑ⒻClm 3000	39	3	8	8^4	8^{11}	6^{13}	$5^{8\frac{1}{2}}$	Messina R	b	115	16.70	79-20 MetllicGlss$115^{3\frac{1}{2}}$Amyson119^2YellowPrincess114	Outrun 8
12Sep92- 5FL	fst	6f	:22^4	:46	1:12	3↑ⒻClm 3000	43	4	8	6^6	$6^{8\frac{3}{4}}$	6^8	6^{11}	Messina R	b	115	7.70	75-16 MarksOutrage$115^{4\frac{1}{2}}$ConnieD.119^2ArcadiMiss119	Outrun 8

LATEST WORKOUTS May 9 FL 6f fst 1:21 B — May 2 FL 5f fst 1:04^3 B — Apr 21 FL 4f fst :50^2 B — Apr 15 FL 3f fst :38 B

Fightin Force — Dk. b. or br. g. 8, by Fifth Marine—Foolish Image, by Dancer's Image — $4,000 — Br.—Audley Farm Inc (Ky) — Tr.—Hall Aimee D (49 6 6 2 .12) — 122
Own.—Hall Aimee D & John A

Lifetime						
58 10 9 11	1992	16	1	5	4	$13,163
$52,617	1991	9	4	1	2	$15,290
	Turf	2	0	0	0	
	Wet	6	1	0	2	$7,150

26Dec92- 4Suf	fst	6f	:22^3	:46^4	1:14^1	3↑Clm 4000	55	9	5	4^3	2^2	2^4	$7^{4\frac{3}{4}}$	Caraballo J C	LBb	122	*1.90	71-24 SingulrSm$122^{2\frac{1}{2}}$MjesticAct122^{nk}SocilProspect122	Tired 12
2Dec92- 5Suf	fst	6f	:22^3	:47	1:13^2	3↑Clm 4000	68	8	4	3^3	2^1	2^{hd}	$3^{\frac{1}{2}}$	Caraballo J C	LBb	122	7.00	79-19 HlloRngoon122^{hd}MHst$122^{\frac{1}{2}}$FghtnFrc122	Bid, weakened 12
13Nov92- 4Suf	fst	6f	:22^3	:46^1	1:12^1	3↑Clm 4000	51	10	6	$6^{3\frac{1}{2}}$	$4^{3\frac{1}{2}}$	$7^{7\frac{1}{4}}$	$6^{10\frac{1}{2}}$	Baez R	LBb	122	*1.50	75-17 GinndBittrs122^4RdThMilkmn$122^{1\frac{3}{4}}$FirwyPhl122	Wd, dull 12
25Oct92- 7Suf	my	6f	:22^3	:46^2	1:12^1	3↑Clm 5000	69	4	4	$5^{3\frac{3}{4}}$	6^4	4^2	$3^{3\frac{1}{4}}$	Caraballo J C	LBb	117	6.20	83-18 Decoy'sRelity$116^{\frac{1}{2}}$IrishAlrm$116^{2\frac{3}{4}}$FightinForce117	Hung 11
5Oct92- 4Suf	fst	6f	:22^4	:46^4	1:12^3	3↑Clm 5000	68	9	2	$4^{4\frac{1}{2}}$	$2^{2\frac{1}{2}}$	2^2	$5^{4\frac{1}{2}}$	Caraballo J C	LBb	117	*2.80	79-16 LstLnk$116^{3\frac{3}{4}}$KnghtfMlt116^{hd}HlfWAsk119	Flattened out 11
7Sep92-10Rkm	fst	6f	:22^3	:46^3	1:12^3	3↑Clm 5000	70	4	3	3^1	$2^{\frac{1}{2}}$	2^{hd}	2^1	Caraballo J C	LBb	118	*2.00	81-24 HlfWAsk116^1FghtnFrc$118^{\frac{3}{4}}$Mtt'sSchtck116	Outfinished 12
12Aug92- 7Rkm	fst	6f	:22^3	:46^2	1:12^2	3↑Clm 5000	73	10	3	$5^{2\frac{1}{2}}$	3^2	3^1	2^3	Caraballo J C	LBb	117	3.70	80-23 BscUnt119^3FghtnForc117^{hd}FoolshMcDuff116	No match 12

LATEST WORKOUTS May 17 Suf 6f fst 1:19 Hg — May 11 Suf 5f fst 1:02^4 B — May 4 Suf 4f fst :49^4 B

Fightin Force is another who is working toward a '93 debut. *Fightin Force* worked four furlongs in $102\frac{4}{5}$ on May 11. The final condition work occurred on May 17 when he worked 119 for six furlongs handily from the gate. *Fightin Force* has consistently ran well in this company and proved it again as he drew off in deep stretch to win easily. *Fightin Force* is another example of "stupidity". In *Fightin Force*'s last seven races, he has been the favorite four of those seven times. Actually, *Fightin Force* was in higher company in four of the seven starts, boasting a 7-0-2-2 record. Despite all of that, the public sent him off 9-1. *Fightin Force* covered the six furlongs in 112 flat, while returning $20.00 to win.

FIRST RACE   Probable Post 1:00

6 FURLONGS. 3-Year-Olds and Up. Maidens Claiming ($8,000 to $7,000). Purse $4,500.

PP	HORSE	PR. RIDER	WT.	COMMENT.	PR.ODDS
2	Going to Pieces	Lloyd J S	114	Can better last	3-1
5	Crystal Grail	BrennanMJ	5109	Good money shot	4-1
3	R. D. Golden Land	MadriglRJr	122	Mustn't tire	9-2
6	Speakin Out	Cruz C	122	Might get part	5-1
4	Wishful Groom	Jocson G J	114	Eased last; drops	6-1
7	Let Him Rip	Pena R D	5115	An outsider	10-1
9	Ninety Plus	Arroyo E R	114	Drops a notch	10-1
8 ·	Bench	MadriglRJr	120	Dull winner form	15-1
1	Dandy Son	BaddeleyLJ	7113	Outrun debut	20-1

Coupled—Crystal Grail and Ninety Plus.

Blinkers On: Going to Pieces.

The first race at Philadelphia Park was filled with many bad maidens that probably could not win if they were running by themselves. Anyway, there was an outstanding favorite in the race, *R.D. Golden Land*. This four-year-old gelding was deserving of the favorite's role. In *R.D. Golden Land*'s second start, he came up lame while in the lead, and was in the process of cutting some awfully quick fractions at 3-5. In his next start, he led and then tired at 6-5. The favorite role was not a surprise, as *R.D. Golden Land* dropped further down the maiden ladder to claiming 8,000. Before I conceded that *R.D. Golden Land* was going to win, I wanted to make one last check or look for an exacta horse. *Bench* had made nine career starts, and had never finished on the board. This gelding, also four years old, had shown absolutely nothing, but with those workouts for his debut, his connections obviously have found out what was wrong. On May 22 at Rockingham, *Bench* worked five furlongs from the gate in 102 handily, and then came back with an effective 100⅘ breezing at Philadelphia Park and a six furlong conditioning workout of 117⅕ breezing.

Bench rallied to finish second, losing by three lengths. He went off at odds of 15-1 and was a healthy play by himself, but also completed a nice exacta. All indications would point to play Bench alone but *R.D. Golden Land*, though a beaten favorite before, was clearly the best with a clean trip. The fact is that Bench never had finished on the board, and, even if he was 100 percent, this might not have been enough. As it turned out, it was not. Nevertheless, the condition factor helped *Bench* make his turn around and return a nice price despite finishing second.

Bench — B. g. 4, by Roberto—Glimmer Glass, by The Axe II
$7,000 Br.—Mill Ridge Farm Ltd (Ky)
Own.—Hasbany Elias L — Tr.—Hasbany Daniel L (9 1 3 1 .11) — **120**

Lifetime						
9 0 0 0	1993	2	M	0	0	$80
$480	1992	7	M	0	0	$400
	Turf	4	0	0	0	
	Wet	1	0	0	0	

22Jan93-10GS	gd	6f	:223	:462	1:124	Md 7500	21	7	3	86½	89¾	911	914¾	Madrigal R Jr	Lb	122	8.50	63-16	SenyhExpress1175¼CddyDon117nkIt'sforLife122	Outrun 11
15Jan93- 2GS	gd	170	:473	1:16	1:491	Md 7500	22	7	5	43½	51½	77¼	811½	Madrigal R Jr	Lb	122	3.70	47-30	WeNeed'm122nkKhlMArnold122¾ChiquitoRojo122	Tired 9
3Dec92- 1Med	fst	170	:48	1:141	1:444	3↑Md 12500	40	3	8	64	53	35½	412¼	Sousonis S	Lb	119	3.50	62-19	TcitCrtel1153¾RullhJudge1156VluedEvnt115	No late bid 11
17Nov92- 7Med	fst	6f	:222	:452	1:102	3↑Md Sp Wt	34	5	8	89½	911	813	712¾	Sousonis S	Lb	120	66.80	78-11	SfeDepositBox120½BrvoGinni1202SrtogRidg120	Outrun 10
4Sep92- 5Bel	yl	1 1/16	Ⓣ:481	1:123	1:433	3↑Md Sp Wt	9	8	3	74	810	827	849¼	BrocklebankGV	b	118	36.50	31-20	Nlsn'sNv1187¾Thrhrvrdvn1185IfWrRdgmn118	Wide trip 8
27Jly92- 9Bel	yl	1⅜	Ⓣ:481	1:392	2:173	3↑Md Sp Wt	59	4	7	75¼	98	79½	715¾	Brocklebank G V		116	64.10	47-29	MarkedDown116¾OpeningDnce1161¼L'Bby122	No factor 10
4Jly92- 9Bel	my	1 1/16	:464	1:101	1:424	3↑Md Sp Wt	49	4	5	59½	49	49½	519½	Brocklebank G V		116	18.50	68-21	Dnzig'sDnc1168CollinsCrt1161½MrkdDown116	No factor 7
4Jly92-Originally scheduled on turf																				
15Jun92- 5Bel	fm	1 1/16	ⓣ:472	1:111	1:413	3↑Md Sp Wt	66	10	6	63	64	86¼	910¼	Santos J A		114	8.80	78-10	SpctclrTd114nkCrnshsCrnr122hdAdncWrd114	Wide tired 12
25May92- 2Bel	fm	1	ⓣ:453	1:093	1:34	3↑Md Sp Wt	68	6	8	95¾	95¾	79½	510¾	Santos J A		115	8.90	81-14	RylMntnInn1154¼Nlsn'sNvy115nkStpRylly115	No factor 12

LATEST WORKOUTS Jun 20 Pha 6f fst 1:171 B ●Jun 9 Pha 5f fst 1:004 B ●May 22 Rkm 5f fst 1:02 Hg

Conditioning is a very big factor, as shown in the past examples. Many times, one sees a horse on the lead, doing moderate fractions and emptying out. This is solely due to a horse not having the stamina to finish out. Trainers know this and avoid tiring their horses by working them farther than they are running. This is an angle that cannot be afforded to be left out of our handicapping repertoire.

Workouts That Appear Better Than They Are

CHAPTER 4

If a horse works out in 100⅕ breezing for five furlongs, would it seem to be a good workout? On the surface, it may appear to be. As one will find out in this chapter, looking up workouts is very important and profitable. The procedure in this chapter shows another reason to look up workouts. A time of 100⅕ breezing may be a good workout on the surface, but may turn out to be just an okay or bad workout.

PHILADELPHIA PARK — Track Fast

Three Furlongs		Four Furlongs— :45		Wizzy	:47² B	Pewter Cowboy	1:00¹ Bg
Irish Incite	:39⁴ B	Feriado	:50¹ B	Five Furlongs— :56²		Royal Cinch	1:00³ B
Pasta n'Peas	:38¹ B	LnchAChowChw	:51³ B	Amberfax	1:03⁴ B	Valiant Emzee	1:04 B
Perfect Witness	:38² B	LemmonPepper	:50³ B	Aye Blue	1:06¹ B		
Rare Silence	:34³ H	Persuasive	:50 B	Diagnostic	1:00³ B		
Rob Gelb	:36² B	Round My Door	:48³ B	Don'tfightoverme	1:00¹ B	Seven Furlongs—1:21¹	
Sir Robert Jr.	:36 Bg	Sitting On Top	:48 Bg	I'm Maxine	1:06¹ B		
Water Skipper	:37⁴ B	St. Haven	:47⁴ H	Mr. Excellerator	1:00³ B	Direct Approach	1:29 B

RARE SILENCE (3F) sharp blowout. PEWTER COWBOY (6F) broke very well from the gate.

On April 19, there were nine workouts at five furlongs, but we are only interested in five.

- *Diagnostic* 100³/₅ B
- *Don't Fight Over Me* 100¹/₅ B
- *Mr. Excellerator* 100³/₅ B
- *Pewter Cowboy* 100¹/₅ BG
- *Royal Cinch* 100³/₅ B

On an individual basis, one might think these were all very good workouts, and, in turn, wind up betting a bad horse. If any of these horses worked that same time, and no one was within a second or two of his workout, this would be more impressive than if five or ten horses did the same time on that particular day.

Royal Cinch 1986 DK B/ filly, by Royal and Regal 70 —— Shirley's Vol 73
                                                          by *Voluntario III 61

Breeder: E. C. Wetherington

(SPR=88)

1993 in USA and Canada:

date	trk race#	dist furl	trk con	race type	value of race	wt	pp	fp	lngths	earned	wnrs time	claim price	# rn
0504	PHA04	7.00	FST	F3UCL	9,095	119	05	06	9 1/4	0	1:25.0	11,000	06
	1st Splendid You							2nd	Opinion				
	3rd Basque Song												
	Owner: Konrad Diana U												
	Trainer: Velazquez Alfredo												
	Jockey: Matz N												
0424	PHA06	5.50	FST	F3USAL	9,346	122	02	02	2 3/4	1,800	1:04.3		06
	1st Country Chelsie							2nd	Royal Cinch				
	3rd Be'un a Rex												
0405	PHA08	6.00	FST	F4UCL	10,000	116	04	03	2	1,100	1:12.1	16,000	05
	1st Ri's Rondezvous							2nd	Lucky Cassie				
	3rd Royal Cinch												
0322	PHA05	6.00	FST	F4UCL	8,500	119	03	01	3 1/2	5,100	1:12.2	11,000	06
	1st Royal Cinch							2nd	Splendid You				
	3rd Cheeseball Ann												
0228	PHA05	6.00	FST	F4UCL	8,500	114	07	01	2 3/4	5,100	1:13.0	9,000	08
	1st Royal Cinch							2nd	Inciting				
	3rd Emperor's Darling												

Royal Cinch is the first to run of the bunch, and competed in the sixth race at Philadelphia Park on April 24. *Royal Cinch* finished second in a six horse field at five and one-half furlongs. The seven year old mare went on to run sixth in her next start, while dropping from Allowance $9,500 to Claiming $11,000.

```
Don't Fightover Me 1988 B filly, by Fight Over 81 -- Lady of the Court 83
                                                     by  Lord Avie 78

Breeder:  Richard Landeis


(SPR=79)

1993 in USA and Canada:

       trk      dist  trk  race     value of                          wnrs   claim  #
date  race#     furl  con  type       race      wt  pp fp lngths earned time   price  rn
----  -----    ------ --- ------  ---------- --- -- -- ------- ------- ------ ------- --
0501 PHA11      6.00  FST F3USTK    26,900  116 07 ff               0 1:11.3          07
        MINT JULEP S.-O (25,000A)
     1st  Proven Pullet                     2nd   Fast Fingers
     3rd  Ms. Copelan
     Owner:   Asbell Joseph
     Trainer: Garcia Efrain T
     Jockey:  Madrigal R Jr
0410 GS 08      5.00  SY  F3UAL     20,000  115 01 05  8          600   :58.1          05
     1st  Princess Sybil                    2nd   Jazzy One
     3rd  Practical Susan
0402 PIM08      6.00  MUD F4UAL     22,300  114 02 05 11 3/4      660 1:11.4          07
     1st  Bless Our Home                    2nd   Musical Bride
     3rd  Mighty Rose
0305 PHA08      5.50  SY  F4UAL     21,500  116 07 06 11 1/2        0 1:04.2          07
     1st  Jazzy One                         2nd   Laura Who
(dh) 3rd  Tasteful T. V.
(dh)      Meetmenow

1992 in USA and Canada:

       trk      dist  trk  race     value of                          wnrs   claim  #
date  race#     furl  con  type       race      wt  pp fp lngths earned time   price  rn
----  -----    ------ --- ------  ---------- --- -- -- ------- ------- ------ ------- --
0112 PHA09      6.00  FST F4USTK    26,800  122 06 08  8 1/4        0 1:11.4          08
        CAMELIA S.-OR (25,000A)
     1st  Idle Isle                         2nd   Country Chelsie
     3rd  Asadorable
```

Don't Fight Over Me, who shared a bullet workout on April 19, was next to attempt a victory. On May 1, *Don't Fight Over Me* did not even finish, as she was outrun early on.

```
Diagnostic 1988 B colt, by Brogan 80 -- Analysis 76, by  Reviewer 66

Breeder:  Mr. & Mrs. James Moseley


(SPR=96)

1993 in USA and Canada:

       trk     dist  trk  race   value of                          wnrs   claim
date race#    furl  con  type    race     wt  pp fp lngths earned  time   price
---- -----  ------  ---  ----- ---------- --- -- -- ------ ------- ------ ------
0611 BEL07 10.00T FRM  3UAL      32,500 117 04 04    3/4   1,950 2:01.0
     1st  Wild Acclaim                           2nd  Wesaam
     3rd  Square Cut
     Owner:   Ardboe Stable
     Trainer: McCarthy William E
     Jockey:  Krone J A
0528 PHA08  8.50T FRM  3UAL      25,000 116 01 02  1 1/2   5,000 1:42.3
     1st  Ogle                                   2nd  Diagnostic
     3rd  Frozen Reef
0513 BEL06  8.50T FRM  3UAL      32,500 117 06 02    NK    7,150 1:41.4
     1st  Marabella Star                         2nd  Diagnostic
     3rd  Mucho Precious

1992 in USA and Canada:

       trk     dist  trk  race   value of                          wnrs   claim  #
date race#    furl  con  type    race     wt  pp fp lngths earned  time   price  rn
---- -----  ------  ---  ----- ---------- --- -- -- ------ ------- ------ ------ --
1002 MED09 11.00T FRM  3USTK     50,000 126 07 03  5 3/4   5,500 2:14.4         08
     NEW JERSEY TURF CLASSIC H.-G3 (50,000A)
     1st  Royal Ninja                            2nd  Forlibend
     3rd  Diagnostic
0909 BEL04 10.00T FRM  3UAL      31,000 117 08 01  4 1/2  18,600 2:00.2         09
     1st  Diagnostic                             2nd  Timber Cat
     3rd  Captive Tune
```

Diagnostic started on May 13 in an Allowance $32,500 event and
was beaten by thirteen lengths, while finishing fifth. He was making his
first start of the year. This five year old colt was not over matched, as he
finished first in an Allowance $31,000 event at Belmont and third in a
$50,000 stake race at the Meadowlands in his last two starts of '92.

Mr Excellerator 1990 B colt, by Red Attack 82 -- Fedora 82, by Exceller 73

Breeder: Michael Hunter Farm

(SPR=64)

1993 in USA and Canada:

date	trk race#	dist furl	trk con	race type	value of race	wt	pp	fp	lngths	earned	wnrs time	claim price	# rn
0620	PHA06	8.50T	FRM	3UCL	12,000	115	05	02	1	2,400	1:47.3	16,000	07
	1st Colonel's Sonata								2nd Mr Excellerator				
	3rd Krispy Peach												
	Owner: Nagel Dietmar												
	Trainer: Velazquez Alfredo												
	Jockey: Aguila G E												
0612	PHA09	8.32	FST	03MCL	6,500	122	08	01	NO	3,900	1:46.2	15,000	11
	1st Mr Excellerator								2nd W O Officer				
	3rd Caro's Swan Song												
0606	PHA11	7.00	FST	03MCL	7,000	122	06	03	8 3/4	770	1:27.3	17,500	09
	1st Blue Summer								2nd Puorro				
	3rd Mr Excellerator												
0525	PHA01	6.00	FST	03MCL	6,000	122	04	05	8 1/4	180	1:13.3	15,000	07
	1st Papa Danny								2nd Wishful Groom				
	3rd Bear Grass												
0517	PHA04	6.00	FST	3UM	13,500	113	05	04	12 1/4	810	1:11.0		07
	1st Slew's Sensation								2nd Storm Reef				
	3rd Earsie												

Mr. Excellerator was the fourth of the bunch and made his career debut on May 17. In a Maiden Special Weight contest, Mr. Excellerator finished fourth, beaten by twelve and three-quarters of a length. He was then dropped into maiden claiming $15,000 event and finished fourth. This colt did not win until his fourth start on June 12 at odds of $3.40 - 1.

Pewter Cowboy 1989 RO colt, by Leematt 68 -- Powder Face 80, by Mister Pitt 59

Breeder: Peter Giangiulio

(SPR=74)

1993 in USA and Canada:

date	trk race#	dist furl	trk con	race type	value of race	wt	pp	fp	lngths	earned	wnrs time	claim price	# rn
0409	PHA07	6.00	FST	4UAL	14,500	116	04	06	10 3/4	0	1:13.4		09

```
        1st   Lawyers Delight                2nd   Saratoga Fever
        3rd   Prince Cozzene
        Owner:    Geraghty Barbara
        Trainer: Boulmetis James P
        Jockey:   Black a S

   1992 in USA and Canada:

        trk     dist   trk   race   value of                            wnrs     claim   #
   date race#   furl   con   type     race      wt  pp fp lngths earned  time     price  rn
   ----  -----  -----  ---   -----  --------    --  -- -- ------ ------  ------   ------  --
   1108 PHA07   6.50   FST   03CL     9,000   116  07 08 12 3/4       0 1:19.3   15,000  09
        1st   Clark Cable                      2nd   Birthday Bash
        3rd   Gilded Tea
   1020 PHA09   6.00   FST   03AL    14,000   122  07 07  8 1/2       0 1:12.0           10
        1st   Speedy Lover                     2nd   Peace Royale
        3rd   Gold Pro
   0905 PHA06   6.50   FST   03AL    14,000   122  06 05  5 1/4     420 1:18.0           09
        1st   Birthday Bash                    2nd   Speedy Lover
        3rd   Gold Pro
   0824 PHA03   7.00   FST   3UM     18,225   116  02 01  5 1/4  10,935 1:23.3           08
        1st   Pewter Cowboy                    2nd   Smarten's Best
        3rd   Davids Affair
```

Pewter Cowboy, the other half of the bullet workout, has not run and was probably injured.

In the four starts of the five horses, these horses compiled a record of 4-0-1-0.

BELMONT PARK — Track Fast

Three Furlongs		Dante's Brew	:491 B	Max Fax	:502 B	Boots andChaps	1:013 B
CorprtInvstmnt	:39 B	Daring Fly	:481 H	Naval Guardian	:483 H	Border Cat	:594 H
DavidsJustClssi	:374 Bg	Deputy Snoop	:481 H	Our Emblem	:51 B	Clever Knave	:59 H
Dovey	:364 H	Dispute	:502 B	Pay Phone	:53 B	Cougalore	1:011 H
Grand It Is	:36 H	Dolly's Back	:483 H	Pick 'n Roll	:512 B	High Regent	1:014 H
Kerfoot Corner	:373 Bg	Eden Isle	:493 Bg	Pot Pong	:52 B	Isn'tThatSpecial	:59 H
Klondike Clem	:394 Bg	ExcellentTipper	:493 B	Precious Bird	:501 B	Jolly Jack	1:031 H
Lucky Eight	:39 B	Eyesight	:482 H	RoscommonLssi	:482 H	Majestic Hawk	1:023 B
McDee	:353 Hg	Flying Phoenix	:494 Bg	Salina	:522 Bg	Malmo	1:02 B
Mrs. Marcos	:36 H	Freeze the Gold	:49 H	Silky Feather	:481 H	Mio Robertino	1:04 B
Potentilla	:372 Bg	Frozen Ammo	:493 Bg	Smartweed	:50 Bg	Mobile	:594 H
Scoop the Gold	:373 Bg	Garendare	:52 B	Sovereign Kitty	:49 Hg	Russian Bride	1:04 B
Strikany	:35 H	Gingerland	:493 Bg	Tanako	:50 B	SeductiveSavge	1:022 Hg
Swap Dancer	:353 Hg	He's the Usher	:493 B	Tarq	:484 B	Share the Glory	1:033 B
Teasing Charms	:363 H	HeavenlyHoofer	:482 H	Trvelin'Edmond	:503 B	Silver of Silver	:583 H
ThirtyGoodOnes	:353 Hg	Irish Harbour	:48 H	WcoConnection	:512 B	Sylva Honda	1:00 H
Twilight Classic	:363 H	Javavoom	:503 Bg	Wajir	:53 B	Wildest Dreams	1:013 H
Four Furlongs		La Toque Blanc	:494 Hg	West by West	:48 B		
Bold Spector	:484 Hg	Look Ahead	:52 B	Who's to Pay	:502 B	Six Furlongs—1:074	
CaptinBinbridge	:512 B	Lord Cardinal	:48 H	World Truth	:52 B	All Ability	1:151 H
Classy Hat	:474 H	Lusu	:51 Bg	Five Furlongs— :561		Crnshw'sCorner	1:163 B
Cox's Sword	:483 H	Master Kong	:512 B	AlybobConnctn	1:02 H	Track Topper	1:163 Hg

MCDEE, SWAP DANCER and **THIRTY GOOD ONES** (3f) went together in a sharp effort. **WEST BY WEST** (4f) had an easy spin. **DISPUTE** (4f) looks good. **ISN'T THAT SPECIAL** and **CLEVER KNAVE** (5f) went in company.

On June 16 at Belmont Park, six horses worked roughly the same.

- *Border Cat* 59⅘ H
- *Clever Knave* 59 H
- *Isn't That Special* 59 H
- *Mobile* 59⅘ H
- *Silver of Silver* 58⅗ H
- *Sylva Honda* 100 H

I cannot stress enough the fact that looking up workouts will increase one's profits. It is obvious that if six horses work the same very fast time, then the track had something to do with it, and they are not as impressive. If all of the horses were stakes and grade one horses, than there would be an explanation, but, when $17,000 claimers are working roughly the same time as Silver Of Silver, the track definitely had an effect on the workouts.

Border Cat 1989 B colt, by Storm Cat 83 — Muriesk 79, by Nashua 52

Breeder: Overbrook Farm

(SPR=98)

1992 in USA and Canada:

date	trk race#	dist furl	trk con	race type	value of race	wt	pp	fp	lngths	earned	wnrs time	claim price	# rn
1217	AQU08	6.00	SY	03STK	52,400	119	03	04	13 3/4	3,144	1:09.3		05
	PHILOSOPHY S.-L (50,000A)												
	1st Preporant							2nd	Permit				
	3rd Nowhere Man												
	Owner: Young William T												
	Trainer: Lukas D Wayne												
	Jockey: Romero R P												
1204	MED05	6.00	FST	03STK	35,000	119	04	02	4	7,000	1:09.3		05
	MENDHAM S.-O (35,000A)												
	1st Concorde's Tune							2nd	Border Cat				
	3rd Nowhere Man												
1116	AQU08	6.00	FST	3UAL	41,000	117	02	02	2 1/4	9,020	1:09.1		07
	1st Nowhere Man							2nd	Border Cat				

```
         3rd   Jessie Jet
1024 AQU05  6.00  FST  3UAL      41,000 117 08 02    NK    9,020 1:10.1            08
     1st   Good Scout                          2nd   Border Cat
     3rd   Heart of a Hero
1010 BEL01  6.00  MUD  03STK     54,600 119 01 03   9 1/4   6,552 1:08.2           06
         GULCH S.-L (50,000A)
     1st   Detox                              2nd   Belong to Me
     3rd   Border Cat
0918 MED06  6.00  FST  03STK     35,000 115 03 01    NK   21,000 1:09.0            05
         BERGEN COUNTY S.-O (35,000A)
     1st   Border Cat                         2nd   Wardrobe Test
     3rd   Sticks and Bricks
0830 SAR04  6.00  FST  3UAL      28,000 112 06 01   9      16,800 1:09.0           07
     1st   Border Cat                         2nd   Case Study
     3rd   The Great M. B.
0819 SAR09  7.00  MUD  3UAL      28,000 112 04 02    NK    6,160 1:23.3            10
     1st   Keratoid                           2nd   Border Cat
     3rd   Prioritizer
0810 SAR01  8.00  FST  03CL      29,000 117 02 01    NK   17,400 1:36.2 75,000 06
     1st   Border Cat                         2nd   Roman Chorus
     3rd   Wooden Wagon
0729 SAR01  8.50T FRM  03CL      32,000 112 04 04   6 1/4   1,920 1:40.0 75,000 10
     1st   Kiri's Clown                       2nd   Freight Bill
     3rd   Sennacherib
```

Border Cat must have gotten hurt and did not run off that workout.

```
Clever Knave 1989 DK B/ gelding, by Clever Trick 76 -- Face Nord 83
                                      by  Northjet (IRE) 77

Breeder:  George Strawbridge


(SPR=94)

1993 in USA and Canada:
```

date	trk race#	dist furl	trk con	race type	value of race	wt	pp	fp	lngths	earned	wnrs time	claim price	# rn
0625	BEL05	6.00	FST	4UCL	19,500	117	08	06	8	0	1:11.1	35,000	08

```
     1st   I'll Take a Stand              2nd   Red Hot Red
     3rd   Quickest Blade
     Owner:   C'Est Tout Stable
     Trainer: Daggett Michael H
     Jockey:  McCauley W H
```

```
0416 AQU02  6.00  FST  4UCL    21,500 117 07 06  6 3/4       0 1:10.1 50,000 07
     1st  Explosive One                   2nd  Meaghan's Toy
     3rd  Nymphist
0401 AQU07  7.00  SY   3UAL    29,500 112 01 03  7 1/4   3,540 1:24.0        04
     1st  Walking Street                  2nd  Will to Reign
     3rd  Clever Knave
0310 AQU06  6.00  FST  4UAL    30,000 114 03 02  2       6,600 1:10.0        05
     1st  Peerless Performer              2nd  Clever Knave
     3rd  Walking Street
0225 AQU07  6.00  FST  4UAL    28,000 117 03 01  1 1/2  16,800 1:11.0        09
     1st  Clever Knave                    2nd  Winloc's Rabbett
     3rd  Ben Ali's Rullah
0211 AQU07  6.00  FST  4UAL    28,000 117 06 03  HD      3,360 1:11.2        12
     1st  Like Itor Leave It              2nd  Roscommon Proud
     3rd  Clever Knave
0121 AQU08  6.00  FST  4UAL    28,000 117 07 08  5 1/4       0 1:11.2        10
     1st  Explosive One                   2nd  Ocean Splash
     3rd  Storm Boot
0101 AQU06  6.00  FST  4UAL    28,000 114 01 07  7           0 1:11.0        08
     1st  Appealing Tracy                 2nd  Chanels Titanic
     3rd  Ocean Splash

1992 in USA and Canada:

     trk      dist  trk  race   value of                      wnrs  claim  #
date race#    furl  con  type   race    wt  pp fp lngths earned time  price  rn
---------------------------------------------------------------------------------
1210 AQU06  6.00  FST  3UAL    27,000 110 07 01  NO     16,200 1:11.4        08
     1st  Clever Knave                    2nd  Patience of Jove
     3rd  Freezing Fun
1118 AQU07  6.00  FST  3UAL    27,000 110 03 03  2 3/4   3,240 1:10.3        09
     1st  Ocean Splash                    2nd  Snappy Landing
     3rd  Clever Knave
```

Clever Knave is a four year old gelding who is currently running in the claiming $35,000 ranks. On June 25, *Clever Knave* made his first appearance at Belmont following a two month absence. *Clever Knave* finish sixth, beaten by eight lengths.

```
Isn't That Special 1986 GR colt, by Private Account 76 —— Lucy Belle 75
                                      by  Raise a Native 61

Breeder:  Robert B. Raphaelson
```

(SPR=94)

1993 in USA and Canada:

date	trk race#	dist furl	trk con	race type	value of race	wt	pp	fp	lngths	earned	time	claim price	# rn
0621	BEL04	8.00	MUD	4UCL	24,500	113	04	06	11 1/4	0	1:37.3	45,000	07

1st Will to Reign   2nd Dibbs n' Dubbs
3rd Carrdiographer
Owner: C'Est Tout Stable
Trainer: Daggett Michael H
Jockey: Velazquez J R

| 0524 | BEL06 | 7.00 | FST | 4UCL | 28,500 | 116 | 08 | 07 | 13 | 0 | 1:22.3 | 85,000 | 08 |

1st Look Ahead   2nd Drummond Lane
3rd Maraud

| 0513 | BEL08 | 8.50 | FST | 3UAL | 46,000 | 117 | 02 | 06 | 28 | 0 | 1:40.4 | | 07 |

1st West by West   2nd Berkley Fitz
3rd Fabersham

| 0502 | AQU06 | 7.00 | FST | 4UCL | 28,500 | 118 | 01 | 02 | 2 1/4 | 6,270 | 1:23.3 | 90,000 | 07 |

1st Sunnybutcold   2nd Isn't That Special
3rd Friendly Lover

| 0327 | AQU06 | 6.00 | FST | 4UH | 41,000 | 117 | 05 | 05 | 7 1/4 | 0 | 1:10.0 | | 06 |

1st Fabersham   2nd Preporant
3rd Wild Dante

1992 in USA and Canada:

date	trk race#	dist furl	trk con	race type	value of race	wt	pp	fp	lngths	earned	time	claim price	# rn
1018	BEL07	8.00	FST	3UH	47,000	114	01	04	12 1/2	2,820	1:37.3		06

1st Jacksonport   2nd All Smarts
3rd Look Ahead

| 0927 | BEL07 | 8.50 | SY | 3UH | 47,000 | 116 | 04 | 04 | 11 1/4 | 2,820 | 1:41.3 | | 06 |

1st Richman   2nd Crackedbell
3rd Killer Diller

| 0903 | BEL08 | 8.50 | MUD | 3UH | 47,000 | 115 | 05 | 01 | HD | 28,200 | 1:41.2 | | 06 |

1st Isn't That Special   2nd Majesterian
3rd Crackedbell

| 0810 | SAR08 | 9.00 | FST | 3USTK | 52,700 | 115 | 05 | 02 | HD | 11,594 | 1:48.2 | | 05 |

UPSET S.-L (50,000A)
1st Tank's Number   2nd Isn't That Special
3rd Alyten

| 0729 | SAR05 | 8.00 | FST | 3UH | 47,000 | 116 | 01 | 03 | 6 3/4 | 5,640 | 1:35.3 | | 05 |

1st Richman   2nd Killer Diller
3rd Isn't That Special

   Isn't That Special is owned and trained by the same connection as
Clever Knave. He made his next start a week before, on June 21. *Isn't
That Special*, a seven year old colt, took a tremendous drop in class,
from claiming $85,000 to claiming $45,000. He ran a dismal sixth, and
has finished on the board only once in five starts, a second on May 2.
   There is no such horse as Mobile. It must be someone working
under a different name.

Sylva Honda (GB) 1988 CH colt, by =Adonijah 80 — =Wolverhants 78
                                                  by =Wolver Hollow 64

Breeder: Someries Stud

(SPR=88)

1993 in USA and Canada:

date	trk race#	dist furl	trk con	race type	value of race	wt	pp	fp	lngths	earned	wnrs time	claim price	# rn
0628	BEL08	8.50	FST	3UAL	46,000	117	04	03	6 1/4	5,520	1:44.2		06
1st Farewell Wave								2nd Alyten					
3rd Sylva Honda (GB)													
Owner: Grimstead Edwin													
Trainer: Moubarak Mohammed													
Jockey: Velasquez J													
0607	BEL08	8.50	FST	3UH	46,000	113	03	03	16 1/2	5,520	1:43.2		04
1st Pure Rumor								2nd Key Contender					
3rd Sylva Honda (GB)													
0522	BEL06	8.00	FST	3UAL	46,000	117	01	02	NK	10,120	1:35.4		06
1st Sand Lizard								2nd Sylva Honda (GB)					
3rd Farewell Wave													
0501	AQU09	8.50T	FRM	3USTK	92,100	109	04	08	8 3/4	0	1:42.1		11
FORT MARCY H.-G3 (75,000A)													
1st Adam Smith (GB)								2nd Kiri's Clown					
3rd Casino Magistrate													
0331	GP 08	8.50T	FRM	4UH	55,000	113	06	02	1	10,450	1:41.4		07
1st Paradise Creek								2nd Sylva Honda (GB)					
3rd Flying American													
0319	GP 08	9.00	GD	4UAL	29,000	113	03	01	5 1/2	17,400	1:50.0		06
1st Sylva Honda (GB)								2nd Silver Conquest					
3rd Elk River													
0203	GP 08	7.00	FST	4UAL	22,000	112	10	08	4 3/4	220	1:23.3		10
1st Hidden Prize								2nd Contarito					
3rd Lordly Ruckus													

```
0112 GP 09  7.00  FST  4UAL      23,900 112 12 08 12 3/4      200 1:20.4          12
     1st  Tough and Rugged                   2nd   Brookshire
     3rd  Skinman
```

1992 in England:

date	trk	dist furl	trk con	race type	frgn race value	frgn wt	fp	lengths behind	earnings in Pounds	# rn
1002	NEW	8.00	FRM	3U W	14,750	136	08	NO	0	08

```
        MAIN REEF S.-L  (12,500)
     1st =Inner City                      2nd =Soiree (IRE)
     3rd $John Rose (GB)
```

| 0910 | DON | 7.00 | GD | 3U W | 40,305 | 130 | 10 | 1/2 | 0 | 10 |

```
        KIVETON PARK S.-G3 (30,000)
     1st =Pursuit of Love                 2nd  Prince Ferdinand (GB)
     3rd  Storm Dove
```

Sylva Honda on June 28 finished third in an Allowance $46,000 race.

Silver of Silver 1990 GR colt, by Silver Buck 78 —— Genuinely Gold 82

                              by Gold Stage 77

Breeder: Charles Patton & Herman Heinlein

(SPR=99)

1993 in USA and Canada:

date	trk race#	dist furl	trk con	race type	value of race	wt	pp	fp	lngths	earned	wnrs time	claim price	# rn
0703	BEL08	9.00	MUD	03STK	200,000	123	02	03	7 1/4	24,000	1:47.3		06

```
        DWYER S.-G2 (200,000A)
     1st  Cherokee Run                    2nd  Miner's Mark
     3rd  Silver of Silver
     Owner:   Chevalier Stable
     Trainer: Shapoff Stanley R
     Jockey:  Vasquez J
```

| 0605 | BEL09 | 12.00 | GD | 03STK | 1,740,900 | 126 | 11 | 04 | 5 | 44,454 | 2:29.4 | | 13 |

```
        BELMONT S.-G1 (500,000A)
     1st  Colonial Affair                 2nd  Kissin Kris
     3rd  Wild Gale
```

| 0501 | CD 08 | 10.00 | FST | 03STK | 985,900 | 126 | 09 | 08 | 8 3/4 | 0 | 2:02.2 | | 19 |

```
        KENTUCKY DERBY-G1 (500,000A)
     1st  Sea Hero                        2nd  Prairie Bayou
```

```
         3rd  Wild Gale
0418 KEE08  8.50  FST  03STK    140,675 121 08 07  4          0 1:43.3        09
         LEXINGTON S.-G2 (125,000A)
         1st  Grand Jewel                      2nd  El Bakan
         3rd  Truth of It All
0320 GP 10  9.00  SY   03STK    500,000 122 09 05  4 3/4  15,000 1:51.1        13
         FLORIDA DERBY-G1 (500,000A)
         1st  Bull Inthe Heather               2nd  Storm Tower
         3rd  Wallenda
0227 GP 08  8.50  FST  03STK    188,490 122 08 03  2 3/4  20,734 1:45.0        09
         FOUNTAIN OF YOUTH S.-G2 (150,000A)
         1st  Duc d'Sligovil                   2nd  Bull Inthe Heather
         3rd  Silver of Silver
0109 CRC10  9.00  SY   03STK    100,000 122 09 03  2 1/4  11,000 1:53.4        10
         TROPICAL PARK DERBY-G3 (100,000A)
         1st  Summer Set                       2nd  Duc d'Sligovil
         3rd  Silver of Silver
```

1992 in USA and Canada:

date	trk race#	dist furl	trk con	race type	value of race	wt	pp	fp	lngths	earned	wnrs time	claim price	# rn
1114	AQU08	9.00	FST	02STK	200,000	122	08	01	1/2	120,000	1:50.1		11

```
         REMSEN S.-G2 (200,000A)
         1st  Silver of Silver                 2nd  Dalhart
         3rd  Wild Gale
1017 CRC11  8.50  FST  02STK    410,000 120 12 01  4       246,000 1:47.3      15
         FLORIDA STALLION/IN REALITY S.-LR (400,000A)
         1st  Silver of Silver                 2nd  Crafty
         3rd  Fiery Special
0930 BEL07  8.00  FST  02AL      29,000 117 12 03  8         3,480 1:36.3      12
         1st  Dalhart                          2nd  Living Vicariously
         3rd  Silver of Silver
```

Silver Of Silver probably was the only one to deserve the workout. He finished third in the Dwyer, losing to Cherokee Run.

As discussed in the previous chapter, one must handicap these races and use these workouts as an advantage. As one can see, with the emphasis above we had all kinds of horses from claimers to grade 1 caliber, and one has to judge workouts for how they are performed and what company they are performed with.

If a lot of horses work out on the same day at about the same speed, don't get too excited even if the time is fast. There are some exceptions to this generalization, which we will cover in chapter 8.

Good Workouts/ Bad Trainer

5

For most handicappers, maiden races are something most people shy away from because of lack of information. Every trainer wants to have a good horse and some believe that if they work their horses fast, they will be good. In the examples below, one will see both sides of the coin. Is there a difference between Anthony Tropia and Ron McAnally? Of course, we know whom we would select. Is there a difference between working four furlongs in 47 breezing and 47 handily? Of course! This difference is the edge and angle the handicapper is looking for. Let us explain with a quick example:

Horse X Trainer John Doe 17-0-3-1
5 furlongs 59 H 4 furlongs 47³/₅ HG 4 furlongs 47²/₅ HG

Horse Y Trainer Fred Smith 17-7-4-2
Same As Above

With both horses having the same workouts, the better trainer seems automatic, but not just because of his record, but the trust that Fred Smith knows what he is doing, based on his results in the past. There is more trust placed by the handicapper in the trainer than even the handicapper realizes.

SIXTH RACE 5 FURLONGS. (.561) MAIDEN SPECIAL WEIGHT. Purse $17,000. 2-year-olds. Weight, 118 lbs.

Monmouth
JUNE 4, 1993

Value of race $17,000; value to winner $10,200; second $3,230; third $1,870; fourth $850; balance of starters $170 each. Mutuel pool $65,109. Exacta Pool $75,882.

Last Raced	Horse	M/Eqt. A. Wt	PP	St	¼	⅜	Str	Fin	Jockey	Odds $1
	Sacred Honour	2 118	2	4	1²	1¹	15½	11¹	Wilson R	3.00
13May93 4Pim³	British Raj	b 2 118	3	7	6ʰᵈ	52½	3ʰᵈ	2¹³	Bruin J E	b-2.70
	Parella Fella	2 118	9	2	5¹	3ʰᵈ	4¹	3ʰᵈ	Marquez C H Jr	1.20
21May93 1GS³	Outlaw Proof	2 118	6	3	2¹½	2³½	2²½	4³	Castillo H Jr	20.40
	Distinct Effort	b 2 113	5	6	3ʰᵈ	4½	5³	52½	Homeister R BJr⁵	b-2.70
12May93 3Hia⁵	Candlelight Dinner	2 118	7	1	4ʰᵈ	6ʰᵈ	6²	62½	Santagata N	a-19.00
	Bound for Dixie	2 118	8	5	7¹½	72½	72½	72½	Bravo J	8.20
21May93 1GS⁴	Lure's Champion	2 116	4	9	8⁷	8⁶	8⁹	8¹¹	Rivera L Jr	21.90
6May93 3Hia⁸	Esmeralda's Gem	2 118	1	8	9	9	9	9	Bracho J A	a-19.00

a-Coupled: Candlelight Dinner and Esmeralda's Gem; b-British Raj and Distinct Effort.

OFF AT 3:28 Start good. Won ridden out. Time, :22³, :46³, :59¹ Track fast.

$2 Mutuel Prices:

4-SACRED HONOUR	8.00	4.20	2.80
2-BRITISH RAJ (b-entry)		3.20	2.40
8-PARELLA FELLA			2.40

$2 EXACTA 4-2 PAID $23.20

B. c, (Mar), by Stalwart—Found a Jewel, by Diamond Prospect. Trainer Perkins Benjamin W. Bred by Mary Anne DeWitt (Fla).

SACRED HONOUR responded when challenged on the turn, widened under intermittent urging then drew off while being ridden out. BRITISH RAJ steadied and raced wide while trying to get out entering the turn, advanced outside turning for home and finished well. PARELLA FELLA lacked the needed stretch bid. OUTLAW PROOF challenged the winner on the turn and tired in the drive. DISTINCT EFFORT saved around and faded in the drive. CANDLELIGHT DINNER, between foes into the turn, tired. BOUND FOR DIXIE had no response. LURE'S CHAMPION was outrun as was ESMERALDA'S GEM.

Owners— 1, New Farm; 2, Whip Stables; 3, Roseland Farm; 4, Outlaw Biker Stable; 5, Snowden Guy B; 6, Aljure David A; 7, Polo Hill Farm; 8, Vizzoni Pat; 9, Aljure David A.

Trainers— 1, Perkins Benjamin W; 2, Salzman J Edwin Jr; 3, Tropia Anthony; 4, Martin Gregory F; 5, Salzman John E; 6, Romero Jorge E; 7, Boniface Kim; 8, Costa Frank; 9, Romero Jorge E.

Scratched—Wake Up Alarm (3Jun93 3Bel5); Ambraco.

In our first example, this trend becomes apparent right away. The 6th race at Monmouth Park featured nine two year olds going five furlongs.

Esmeralda's Gem was making his second start of his career coming off a last place finish at Hialeah. Off of this poor performance in the claiming ranks, Jose Romero had now decided to move this colt to a Maiden Special Weight—a strange move, considering his first race. Also, the absence of Carlos Marquez Jr., Romero's top jockey, makes *Esmeralda's Gem* unplayable.

Sacred Honour was the hot horse. By the time the entries were published for this race, the word had been out about New Farm. On June 2, New Farm sent out their first two year old, *Pagofire*. This filly responded with a twelve length victory, returning $3.00 to its backers. After this victory, there was a rather long article published on New Farm, stating how they spent $2 million on 24 babies. For these reasons, I figured I would be setting for a 1-2 again. *Sacred Honour*'s works might not look impressive to the naked eye, but when one looks them up, they tell a different story. On May 14, *Sacred Honour* worked 3 furlongs in 40 breezing. This is not a particularly good workout, but when we look it up, we see that he was in company with another promising baby, *Code Home*. It was apparent that it was the first work for both. His next workout was on May 22, when this colt came out of the gate with *Pagofire*, working a good ½ mile in 48²/₅. *Pagofire* worked in 48³/₅. If *Sacred Honour* has ¹/₁₀ of what *Pagofire* has, he will be tough to beat.

British Raj was one of the second time starters who finished third in his debut. *British Raj* has not worked on this new surface and if he cannot win at Pimlico, I do not know how he is going to win here. The competition at Monmouth is always better than at Pimlico.

Lure's Champion might have had an excuse in his first start, as he ran off before the race, but he finished fourth, beaten by almost nine lengths in a slow 100. His adjusted time was 101¹/₅ for five furlongs, and I could guarantee these will not go that slow.

Distinct Effort has four workouts to his credit, three at Laurel and the other at Monmouth Park. The workouts are not impressive, and I would have given this one more consideration, as his work at Monmouth was tremendously better. Maybe he dislikes the Laurel surface, but the work on May 25 was actually worse. Also, the fourteen days in between works means, most likely, there was an injury involved.

Outlaw Proof, like *Lure's Champion*, is coming out of the same maiden special weight at Garden State—slow times, and if he cannot win there, he is not going to win here.

Candlelight Dinner is the other half of the Romero entry. If there is one thing I can't figure out in horse racing, it is why any trainer would enter two maidens in the same race. I do not care if the owners are different, but I cannot figure this out. Anyway, in *Candlelight Dinner*'s only start, he finished fifth, beaten by 9¹/₄ lengths. The horse that finished third in that race, *Rita's Whirl*, has been unsuccessful in his two local tries, and I would not expect much from this one, either.

Bound for Dixie has nice breeding and I love the one workout theory, as will be shown in the coming chapters, but Kim Boniface is unknown to me and will have to be very tough to compete here. A couple of more workouts might have been wise.

Parella Fella is the reason and the meaning to what we mean by great workouts and a bad trainer. Anthony Tropia is unknown to me, and it seems to me that this trainer likes to see his horses have bullet workouts. These workouts cannot be trusted because of the particular trainer. In the next example, this will be made clearer. Usually, these horses are bet down and they come up empty.

5 FURLONGS. (.56¹) MAIDEN SPECIAL WEIGHT. Purse $17,000. 2-year-olds. Weight, 118 lbs.

Coupled—Esmeralda's Gem and Candlelight Dinner; British Raj and Distinct Effort; Wake Up Alarm and Ambraco.

Esmeralda's Gem
Ch. c. 2(Apr), by Sezyou—La Esmeralda, by Baldski
Br.—Aljure David (Fla)
Own.—Aljure David A
Tr.—Romero Jorge E (2 1 0 0 .50)   **118**
Lifetime   1993   1 M 0 0 $80
1 0 0 0
$80
6May93- 3Hia fst 3f   :22   :33³   Md 25000   — 2 8   8¹⁰ 89¼   MacKinze H A   118   8.40   — — Bo'sFager114ⁿᵒPalaceFire118¹¼VodikaNtive114   Outrun 8
LATEST WORKOUTS   May 25 Mth   3f fst :38² B   May 4 Hia   3f fst :37   Bg   Apr 27 Hia   3f fst :36⁴ B

Sacred Honour
B. c. 2(Mar), by Stalwart—Found a Jewel, by Diamond Prospect
Br.—Mary Anne DeWitt (Fla)
Own.—New Farm
Tr.—Perkins Benjamin W (3 0 3 0 .00)   **118**
Lifetime   1993   0 M 0 0
0 0 0 0
LATEST WORKOUTS   May 22 Mth   4f fst :48² Hg   May 14 Mth   3f fst :40   B

British Raj
B. c. 2, by Rajab—Be Victorious, by Stevward
Br.—Schwetert F C (FL)
Own.—Whip Stables
Tr.—Salzman J Edwin Jr (—)   **118**
Lifetime   1993   1 M 0 1 $1,705
1 0 0 1
$1,705
13May93- 4Pim fst 4½f   :22³   :46³   :53²   Md Sp Wt   66 7 8   69½ 5⁵ 31½   Prado E S   b 120   *2.00e   — — RnAldn120¹¼ThrllfVctry120ⁿᵒBrtshRj120   Steadied wire 10
LATEST WORKOUTS   May 4 Lrl   3f fst :37   B   Apr 27 Lrl   4f fst :50   B   Apr 13 Lrl   4f fst :50   Bg

Lure's Champion
Dk. b. or br. c. 2(Mar), by Mountain Lure—Kitty's Misfit, by Salem
Br.—Pasquale Vizzoni (NJ)
Own.—Vizzoni Pat
Tr.—Costa Frank (2 1 0 0 .50)   **116**
Lifetime   1993   1 M 0 0 $550
1 0 0 0
$550
21May93- 1GS fst 5f   :22⁴   :46³ 1:00   Md Sp Wt   21 8 4   41½ 31½ 46½ 48²   King E L Jr   118   5.60   79-18 ⑨BlodBth118¼JdyDdy118⁵¼OtlwPrf118   Ran off pre race 8
LATEST WORKOUTS   Jun 2 Mth   3f fst :37   B

Distinct Effort
B. c. 2(May), by Distinctive Pro—Angel Dance, by Classical Ballet
Br.—Century Thoroughbreds (Fla)
Own.—Snowden Guy B
Tr.—Salzman John E (—)   **113⁵**
Lifetime   1993   0 M 0 0
0 0 0 0
LATEST WORKOUTS   May 25 Mth   4f fst :49² B   May 11 Lrl   4f fst :49³ Bg   May 4 Lrl   4f fst :50² Bg   Apr 27 Lrl   4f fst :51   B

Outlaw Proof
Dk. b. or br. c. 2(May), by Proof—Move Over Bud, by Great Above
Br.—Ljoka Daniel (NJ)
Own.—Outlaw Biker Stable
Tr.—Martin Gregory F (—)   **118**
Lifetime   1993   1 M 0 1 $1,210
1 0 0 1
$1,210
21May93- 1GS fst 5f   :22⁴   :46³ 1:00   Md Sp Wt   26 2 7   51½ 41½ 3⁵ 37   Torres C A   118   4.30   81-18 ⑨BloodBth118¼JodyDody118⁵¼OtlwProof118   Mild rally 8
LATEST WORKOUTS   May 15 GS   4f fst :51   B   May 8 GS   3f fst :36¹ Bg

Candlelight Dinner
B. c. 2(Apr), by Who's For Dinner—Miss Edgecomb, by Cherokee Fellow
Br.—Aljure David (Fla)
Own.—Aljure David A
Tr.—Romero Jorge E (2 1 0 0 .50)   **118**
Lifetime   1993   1 M 0 0 $137
1 0 0 0
$137
12May93- 3Hia fst 5f   :22⁴   :46⁴   :59²   Md Sp Wt   38 4 7   6⁶ 67¾ 57½ 59½   Velez J A Jr   116   5.80e   — — FrnkKnw116⁵¼Lynn'sNtbk116¹Rdn'sWhrl116   No threat 7
LATEST WORKOUTS   Jun 1 Mth   3f sly :37   B   May 25 Mth   3f fst :36   B   May 4 Hia   3f fst :37⁴ B

Bound for Dixie
Dk. b. or br. c. 2(May), by Dixieland Brass—Xenia, by Majestic Prince
Br.—Winn Mrs James (Ky)
Own.—Polo Hill Farm
Tr.—Boniface Kim (—)   **118**
Lifetime   1993   0 M 0 0
0 0 0 0
LATEST WORKOUTS   May 28 Mth   4f fst :49¹ Bg

Parella Fella
Ch. c. 2(Feb), by Explodent—Play Fretty, by Needles
Br.—Eagle Stone Farm In' (Ky)
Own.—Roseland Farm
Tr.—Tropia Anthony (—)   **118**
Lifetime   1993   0 M 0 0
0 0 0 0
LATEST WORKOUTS   May 29 Mth   5f fst 1:02⁴ B   ●May 22 Mth   4f fst :47⁴ Hg   ●May 8 Hia   4f fst :48³ Hg   ●Apr 24 Hia   3f fst :36   Hg

Wake Up Alarm
Dk. b. or br. c. 2(Apr), by Kris S—Morning Mirage, by Avatar
Br.—Whisper Hill Farm (Fla)
Own.—Two Sisters Stable
Tr.—Pierce Joseph H Jr (5 3 1 0 .60)   **118**
Lifetime   1993   0 M 0 0
0 0 0 0
Entered 3Jun93- 3 BEL
LATEST WORKOUTS   May 26 Mth   5f fst 1:02¹ B   May 18 Mth   5f fst 1:01² Hg   Apr 19 GP   5f fst 1:02   H   Apr 7 GP   3f fst :36   Hg

Ambraco
B. c. 2(Apr), by Copelan—Ambra Ridge, by Cox's Ridge
Br.—Hooper Fred W (Fla)
Own.—Hooper Fred W
Tr.—Pierce Joseph H Jr (5 3 1 0 .60)   **118**
Lifetime   1993   0 M 0 0
0 0 0 0
LATEST WORKOUTS   May 29 Mth   4f fst :48² H

As the board flashed for the first time after the fifth race, *Sacred Honour* and *Parella Fella* were co-favorites at 2-1. To my surprise and delight, *Sacred Honour* was going up and Parella Fella down as time wore on. When the smoke cleared *Sacred Honour* won by 11 lengths, dominating this field from the outset. As mentioned in the first few chapters, "stupidity" is what I live for at the track, and it does not get more obvious than this example. *Parella Fella* went off at odds of 6-5 and finished a dismal third, beaten by 12¾ lengths. The entry of *British Raj* and *Distinct Effort* were second choice at $2.70, with a second and fifth place finish. *Sacred Honour* paid $8.00 and I laughed all the way to the window. As I said—"stupidity," I could not live without it. I know a lot of readers might say that one example might have been a coincidence. I will prove them wrong in the next example.

HIALEAH PARK April 28, 1993

race #	dist fur.	trk con	race type	value of race	wnrs time	runners
3	3.00	FST	FO2M	$14,000	0:32.02	9

horse name	fp	lngths	wt	pp	earned	odds	claim	most recent trk/race #
Delta Lady	1	2	117	1	$8,400	2.70		061693CRC03

Fighting Fit -- Delta Key by Sauce Boat
        Owner : ROBINSON J MACK
        Trainer: GOMEZ FRANK
        Jockey : BRACHO J A

| Curvacious Cutie | 2 | 2 | 117 | 2 | $2,520 | 6.60 | | 063093CRC09 |

        Owner : LEWIS JAMES JR
        Trainer: TORTORA EMANUEL
        Jockey : RUSS M L

| Betweenthisandthat | 3 | 2 | 117 | 9 | $1,680 | 1.30 | | 062593CRC06 |

        Owner : VITTESE DOMINIC
        Trainer: VIVIAN DAVID A
        Jockey : FERRER J C

| Combat Affair | 4 | 4 | 110 | 8 | $700 | 29.10 | | 070193CRC05 |

        Owner : TRIGGS D
        Trainer: ARMSTRONG SHERMAN O
        Jockey : RUSSELL W B

| Doc n Trope | 5 | 5 1/2 | 117 | 5 | $140 | 2.80 | | 062393MTH03 |

        Owner : ROSELAND FARMS
        Trainer: TROPIA ANTHONY
        Jockey : CASTILLO H JR

Blue Puff   6 8 3/4 117 7 $140   9.90   061193CT 03
          Owner : ABDOOL A & M
          Trainer: KANHAI JOSEPH
          Jockey : SINGH R R
Tom's Sister Joann   7 9   117 3 $140 20.30   060593ATL01
          Owner : MONARCH STABLE INC
          Trainer: DANIELS EDWARD J JR
          Jockey : VELEZ J A JR
War Michie   8 10 1/4 117 6 $140 51.50   042893HIA03
          Owner : DAVIS DUKE & DECESPEDES J L
          Trainer: DAVIS DUKE
          Jockey : DOUGLAS R R
Slew of Rubies   9 14 1/4 117 4 $140 30.20   062393ATL01
          Owner : TOLIN STEFAN A
          Trainer: KNOLL PETER D
          Jockey : MARTIN C W

HIALEAH PARK May 11, 1993

race #	dist fur.	trk con	race type	value of race	wnrs time	runners
3	5.00	FST	FO2M	$15,600	1:00.03	6

horse name	fp	lngths	wt	pp	earned	odds	claim	most recent trk/race #
Time for Courage	1	1 3/4	116	6	$10,400	1.90		051193HIA03

Real Courage -- Same Thyme by Delaware Chief
          Owner : LA PIETRA WALTER
          Trainer: ALEXANDRE EDSON
          Jockey : TORIBIO A R

| Doc n Trope | 2 | 1 3/4 | 118 | 3 | $2,600 | 1.20 | | 062393MTH03 |

          Owner : ROSELAND STABLE
          Trainer: TROPIA ANTHONY
          Jockey : REDWOOD M A

| Kissmylips | 3 | 8 1/4 | 116 | 4 | $1,690 | 4.90 | | 051193HIA03 |

          Owner : MONARCH STABLE INC
          Trainer: DANIELS EDWARD J JR
          Jockey : LEE M A

| Northern Evening | 4 | 13 1/4 | 116 | 2 | $650 | 12.70 | | 051193HIA03 |

          Owner : FOUSHEE JOSEPH & JULIE
          Trainer: FOUSHEE JOSEPH
          Jockey : RODRIGUEZ P A

| Combat Affair | 5 | 14 3/4 | 116 | 5 | $130 | 3.70 | | 070193CRC05 |

          Owner : TRIGGS D
          Trainer: ARMSTRONG SHERMAN O
          Jockey : RIVERA J A II

```
Jnf'sdream              6 31 1/4 106  1        $130   19.40              051193HIA03
              Owner  : FERNANDEZ JOSE N
              Trainer: FERNANDEZ JOSE N
              Jockey : GRANA P B
```

On April 28, *Doc N Trope* made his two year old debut in a three furlong maiden special weight contest. He finished fifth, beaten by 5½ lengths. *Doc N Trope* went off at 2.80-1. On May 11, in a five furlong race, *Doc N Trope* finished second, beaten by 1¾ lengths, while going off as the 6-5 favorite. Both of these races were at Hialeah Park in Florida.

When *Doc N Trope* ventured to Monmouth Park, he was sporting two defeats and a pair of fast workouts, 47⅕ handily from the gate and 47⅖ handily.

On June 11, *Doc N Trope* was dropped into a maiden claiming $32,000 contest going five furlongs. With the drop in class, this had favorite and suckers' bet written all over *Doc N Trope*. He finished second again, this time at odds of 9-5.

```
MONMOUTH PARK June 11, 1993

         dist  trk   race      value of  wnrs
race #   fur.  con   type        race    time    runners
------   ----  ---   ----      --------  ----    -------
  1      5.00  FST   FO2MCL    $10,000   1:00.00    7
                                                           most recent
horse name              fp lngths wt  pp      earned   odds   claim    trk/race #
----------              -- ------ --  --      ------   ----   -------  ------------
Innocent Bystander       1  3 1/4 115  6      $6,000   10.20  $30,000  061193MTHO1
Skip Trial -- Sharp Maid by Sharpen Up (GB)
              Owner  : OLD BELLEVUE FARM
              Trainer: FORBES JOHN H
              Jockey : MARQUEZ C H JR
Doc n Trope              2  3 1/4 117  3      $2,000    1.90  $32,000  062393MTHO3
              Owner  : ROSELAND FARM
              Trainer: TROPIA ANTHONY
              Jockey : KING E L JR
Clean Wager              3  9 3/4 112  1      $1,200    4.20  $32,000  062393MTHO1
              Owner  : PELICAN STABLE
              Trainer: CROLL WARREN A JR
              Jockey : HOMEISTER R B JR
```

My Sweet Talker	4 11 1/2 117	7	$500	1.20	$32,000	061193MTHO1
Owner : BEACON STABLE						
Trainer: PERKINS BEN W JR						
Jockey : WILSON R						
Texas Melody	5 14 1/4 117	4	$100	20.00	$32,000	062393MTHO3
Owner : ALIBI STABLE						
Trainer: DOWD JOHN F						
Jockey : TORRES C A						
Sea the Connection	6 18 3/4 113	2	$100	16.10	$28,000	061193MTHO1
Owner : POLO HILL FARM						
Trainer: BONIFACE KIM						
Jockey : FERRER J C						
B. J.'s Kat	7 23 1/2 117	5	$100	37.70	$32,000	062393MTHO3
Owner : MAMONE RAYMOND						
Trainer: VINCITORE MICHAEL J						
Jockey : LOPEZ C C						

Doc n Trope 1991 DK B/ filly, by Sitzmark 80 —— Cornish Dame 82, by Damascus 64

Breeder: Harvey Liebeskind & Donald Dreyfuss

(SPR=79)

1993 in USA and Canada:

date	trk race#	dist furl	trk con	race type	value of race	wt	pp	fp	lngths	earned	wnrs time	claim price	# rn
0623	MTHO3	5.00	FST	FO2MCL	10,000	117	04	02	4	2,000	1:00.4	30,000	08

1st Rivkah   2nd Doc n Trope
3rd Outlaw Belle
Owner: Roseland Farms
Trainer: Tropia Anthony
Jockey: King E L Jr

0611	MTHO1	5.00	FST	FO2MCL	10,000	117	03	02	3 1/4	2,000	1:00.0	32,000	07

1st Innocent Bystander   2nd Doc n Trope
3rd Clean Wager

0511	HIAO3	5.00	FST	FO2M	15,600	118	03	02	1 3/4	2,600	1:00.3		06

1st Time for Courage   2nd Doc n Trope
3rd Kissmylips

0428	HIAO3	3.00	FST	FO2M	14,000	117	05	05	5 1/2	140	:32.2		09

1st Delta Lady   2nd Curvacious Cutie
3rd Betweenthisandthat

On June 23, it was the same story again, this time at 8-5, and more money down the drain. Right before this start, *Doc N Trope* blew out again and received a bullet work. *Doc N Trope* continued to post great workouts while draining the public dry. Great workouts + bad training = losses. By the way, I almost forgot, Anthony Tropia is the trainer of *Doc N Trope*.

THIRD RACE	5 FURLONGS. (.56¹) MAIDEN CLAIMING. Purse $10,000. Fillies, 2–year–olds. Weights, 117 lbs. Claiming Price $30,000; for each $2,500 to $25,000 2 lbs.

Monmouth
JUNE 23, 1993

Value of race $10,000; value to winner $6,000; second $2,000; third $1,100; fourth $500; balance of starters $100 each. Mutuel pool $51,536. Exacta Pool $73,164.

Last Raced	Horse	M/Eqt.A.Wt	PP	St	3/16	3/8	Str	Fin	Jockey	Cl'g Pr	Odds $1
	Rivkah	2 117	1	5	1²	1³	1³	1⁴	Rivera L Jr	30000	2.60
11Jun93 ¹Mth²	Doc n Trope	2 117	4	7	4ʰᵈ	32½	2ʰᵈ	23¾	King E L Jr	30000	1.60
	Outlaw Belle	2 113	7	2	22½	2³	35½	3⁴	Ferrer J C	25000	27.10
15Jun93 ⁵Mth⁸	Budd Lake	2 113	2	1	3²	41½	41½	43½	Ortiz F L	25000	34.40
24May93 3Bel⁶	Prejudice Eyes	2 113	3	3	5ʰᵈ	5½	5½	5ʰᵈ	Sheridan E M	25000	3.90
11Jun93 ¹Mth⁵	Texas Melody	b 2 117	8	6	7⁵	6ʰᵈ	6ʰᵈ	6¹	Bravo J	30000	4.80
	Prosperous Girl	2 112	6	4	6ʰᵈ	73½	71½	7ⁿᵏ	HomstrRBJr⁵	30000	8.90
11Jun93 ¹Mth⁷	B. J.'s Kat⁻	2 110	5	8	8	8	8	8	Garcia D⁵	27500	60.40

OFF AT 1:59 Start good Won ridden out Time, :22⁴, :47², 1:00⁴ Track fast.

$2 Mutuel Prices:	1–RIVKAH	7.20	3.40	3.60
	4–DOC N TROPE		2.60	2.80
	7–OUTLAW BELLE			5.80

$2 EXACTA 1–4 PAID $18.20

B. f, (Apr), by Valid Appeal—Golden Fingers, by Precious Boy. Trainer Goldberg Alan E. Bred by Zellen Larry (Fl).
RIVKAH rushed up along the inside to gain a clear advantage soon after the start, raced removed from the rail through the lane and was ridden out. DOC N TROPE finished well along the inside. OUTLAW BELLE chased the winner into the lane and tired in the drive. BUDD LAKE dropped back on the turn. PREJUDICE EYES, between rivals into the turn, lacked a bid. TEXAS MELODY stayed outside and lacked a rally. PROSPEROUS GIRL, between foes into the turn lacked a bid. B. J.'S KAT was no factor.
Owners— 1, Zellen Larry; 2, Roseland Farm; 3, Outlaw Biker Stable; 4, A C Stable; 5, Marine Robert J; 6, Alibi Stable; 7, Pelican Stable; 8, Mamone Raymond.
Trainers— 1, Goldberg Alan E; 2, Tropia Anthony; 3, Martin Gregory F; 4, Cash Russell J; 5, Boniface J William; 6, Dowd John F; 7, Croll Warren A Jr; 8, Vincitore Michael J.
Scratched—Sunnie Angel.

The problem with maidens like *Doc N Trope* is that until they are dropped to a level where they can win, they will continue to come close and continue to be bet down. *Doc N Trope's* winning level might be maiden claiming $15,000. Until he reaches his winning level, he will not win.

Trust is very important with maidens, and trusting great workouts with a bad trainer is a poor investment.

Working at
One Track
and Running
at Another

6

For many horses, it's not a problem working at one track, then shipping to another to run. *Lure*, *Sky Beauty*, and *Star of Cozzene* are just a few of the stakes horses that travel from course to course. Their class and talent override any inconvenience or dislike. These horses are still able to compete on a high level. How do lower class claimers compete? They don't! A cheap horse that impressed at one track, then moves to another track for whatever reason, often comes up flat. Here's why. Horses get accustomed to one track; when they are brought to a different surface and atmosphere, they have trouble adjusting if they are cheap or have an ailment or both.

Track comments of workouts are only effective when the horse runs on the track he is working out on. Some examples.

Visual Signal received a comment for working impressively on May 4.

PHILADELPHIA PARK – Track Fast

Three Furlongs			
Amarita's Gems :36¹ B	ConclusiveSecrt :50³ B	LittleToyFctory :49³ Bg	Totally Exposed :49³ B
Iways AGroom :36² Bg	Crowberry :48³ B	Lucky Cassie :49⁴ B	**Visual Signal** :48 Bg
	FinalEnggement :48² B	Mountain Ghost :50² B	

Kodari	:39³ B	FortyTwoSpecil	:49 B	Okinori	:50³ B	**Five Furlongs— :56²**	
Nicky's Ryan	:36³ B	Gallant Tower	:48¹ B	P. Willy	:49 Bg		
Pressman	:37 B	Gone High	:49⁴ B	PerfctIntntions	:49³ Bg	CarolinaChessie	1:06¹ B
Prince Batty	:37³ B	HarvrdCnGroup	:48¹ B	Potomac View	:51² B	**Hopester**	1:01³ B
Rascal Rabbit	:37 B	Iknanatoon	:50¹ B	Quja	:48² B	Kiskisa	1:02⁴ B
Regal Wish	:36⁴ B	Imallkeyedup	:51³ B	Review Readers	:51 B	RealisticChance	1:07 B
Sunshine Chez	:37³ Bg	Interco's Lady	:53 Bg	Serefe	:50 B		
Thelastcrusade	:38³ B	Italian Star	:50¹ B	Shwaka	:53¹ B	**Six Furlongs—1:08¹**	
Wrong Song	:36³ B	J. O. Lively	:49³ B	Sivler Drums	:50¹ B		
Four Furlongs— :45		JustMeanttoBee	:49⁴ B	Six for theRoad	:49⁴ B	**Dance forChance**	1:15³ B
Art's Alley Cat	:48² Bg	La Bet	:50¹ B	Tee Bruder	:51 B	Diagnostic	1:17² Bg
Awfully Busy	:50 B	Ladysecretary	:52¹ B	Tia Conchita	:48⁴ B	Lenny's Olando	1:16⁴ B
						Passel	1:17¹ B

THELASTCRUSADE (3f) went easy. VISUAL SIGNAL (4f) sharp gate effort. Additional workout: May 1, track fast, OREGONIZING (4f) :52 1/5 b.

Visual Signal then shipped to Rockingham on June 4 and ran third, beaten by three and three-quarter lengths in the bottom claiming company of 4,000. Obviously, Visual Signal was good enough to receive a comment, but, when shipped, he couldn't compete at a lower class track.

Visual Signal 1987 B colt, by Magesterial 77 --- Sign Language 81
                                        by Silent Screen 67

Breeder: Pamela H. Firman

(SPR=79)

1993 in USA and Canada:

date	trk race#	dist furl	trk con	race type	value of race	wt	pp	fp	lngths	earned	wnrs time	claim price	# rn
0623	RKM05	6.00	FST	3UCL	4,000	122	09	03	6	300	1:12.3	4,000	09
	1st Northern Secretary								2nd	Five Star Express (IRE)			
(dh)	3rd Visual Signal												
(dh)	Kid Blue Diamond												
	Owner: Bernardini Gregory P & N												
	Trainer: Figueroa Carlos R												
	Jockey: Bermudez J E												
0609	RKM04	6.00	FST	3UCL	4,000	122	04	02	1/2	800	1:12.3	4,000	07
	1st Dorado								2nd	Visual Signal			
	3rd Ocala Appeal												
0604	RKM04	6.00	FST	3UCL	3,960	122	06	03	3 3/4	480	1:13.1	4,000	06
	1st Assertified								2nd	Kee Cut			
	3rd Visual Signal												
0120	GS 02	6.00	FST	4UCL	4,000	119	06	07	17 1/2	40	1:12.0	4,000	09
	1st Loyken								2nd	New Hampshire (IRE)			
	3rd Silent Perfection												

1992 in USA and Canada:

	trk	dist	trk	race	value of						wnrs	claim	#

```
date race#  furl  con  type     race     wt  pp fp lngths earned  time    price   rn
```

```
1130 PHA07  6.50  FST  3UCL     6,000  116  08 08 14 1/4      0 1:19.1  7,500  11
     1st   Mountain Ghost                     2nd   Qui Star
     3rd   Pasta n' Peas
```

The reason we have to be careful with these shippers is because the clockers at Philadelphia are looking for performance that they know will be effective at Philadelphia Park and cannot be held responsible for what happens elsewhere.

PHILADELPHIA PARK — Track Fast

Three Furlongs		Boosin	:47³ B	Motel Madness	:49³ B	Five Furlongs— :56²	
Alice's Princess	:39 B	DremofChmpgn	:49¹ B	Naturally Eval	:49 B		
Etoile de Feu	:36 B	Edward G.	:49³ B	Never My Love	:49⁴ B		
Hafefe	:36³ B	I'm Yourking	:48¹ B	Soils of Ivory	:52 B	Gillingham	1:02³ B
Mr. Do All	:37 B	Jack the Wack	:48¹ B	Summon Thee	:50 B	Irish Incite	1:03³ B
Music in Time	:39 B	Lotto's Baby	:51¹ B	Waheal	:48¹ B	R. M's Girl	1:02³ B
Four Furlongs— :45		Moone Light	:48² B	Yogart Man	:50² B	Tish Above	1:04³ B

HEAVY FOG UNTIL 7:45 A.M. I'M YOUR KING & WAHEAL (4f) very sharp in company. Additional Workouts: 5/4 CIEL D'HIVER (3f) :36.1b QUIJA (4f) :48.2b

Waheal was next to leave Philadelphia Park on June 13 and made his career debut at Monmouth Park. *Waheal* was overmatched when placed in a maiden special weight event. No matter how good his workout was, he was going to have to come up with a big race to win with these. Now, if *Waheal* had been entered in a maiden special weight or a maiden claiming race at Philadelphia Park, the results might have been different. The competition and the benefit of a track that *Waheal* had been using would have improved his efforts.

```
Waheal 1990 B colt, by Professor Blue 83 — My Nadia 83, by  Little Current 71

Breeder:  Adnan Elussad
```

```
(SPR=36)

1993 in USA and Canada:
```

```
        trk     dist   trk   race    value of                      wnrs   claim  #
 date  race#   furl   con   type     race     wt  pp fp lngths earned time  price  rn
```

```
0613 MTH04  6.00  FST  3UM      17.000 115 07 08 28       170 1:11.0       09
     1st   Mr Miner                         2nd   Private Plan
     3rd   Woodster
     Owner.   Elassad Adnan
     Trainer:  Seeger Robert J
     Jockey:  Ferrer J C
```

PHILADELPHIA PARK — Track Muddy

Three Furlongs		Four Furlongs— :45		Nine Grand	:49 B	Halo de Naskra	1:06³ B
Bejilla Rose	:36³ B	Accession	:51³ B	Ostia	:50⁴ B	Heza Regal Win	1:05⁴ B
Don Don's Pal	:38⁴ B	Alpine Choice	:49² B	Petit Parisien	:48² B	Highinaridge	1:05 Bg
Fuzzy Slippers	:36¹ B	Bar Tat	:52³ B	**Princess Lili**	:48 Bg	Lady Czarsanna	1:05 B
Hold the Party	:38² B	Deliciosa	:49 B	Rare Valentine	:51³ B	**Lakeside Park**	1:01² Bg
I'm A Jezebell	:35 B	Erv's Duck	:50² B	So Close	:52⁴ B	Maud's Double	1:05 Bg
Joey's FirstJove	:36³ B	Flor de Fuego	:52³ B	Tres Flores	:51 B	Perfect Silver	1:02² B
Joyfull Michelle	:35 B	FortunteMinistr	:51¹ B	True Justice	:50³ B	Private Morning	1:06² B
Juke Box Jackie	:36³ B	Fully Charged	:48³ B	**Five Furlongs— :56²**		RuleroftheNight	1:04⁴ B
Saratoga Wind	:37 B	Gold Shaker	:51¹ B	Absolut Sterling	1:07 B		
StormDorJhnny	:36³ B	Lightning Show	:48³ B	Ali Gat	1:03¹ B		
Vacation Bound	:35² B	Magic Pepper	:48³ B	Charming Wolf	1:03 B		

Additional Workouts May 1, Track Fast: BIG FACE (3f) : 35 2/5 B. JOYFULL MICHELLE (3f) went very well, out (4f) in :48. JOEY'S FIRST JOVE (3f) took it easy. LAKESIDE PARK (5f) showed good early speed.

Lakeside Park received a comment on May 6 at Philadelphia Park. This eight year old colt was a hard hitting veteran, who was going to ship to Delaware to make his next start. *Lakeside* missed the Philadelphia Park racing surface as he finished last, beaten by twelve and one-half lengths.

```
Lakeside Park 1985 B colt. by Silver Buck 78 -- Sparkalot 72. by  Duel 61

Breeder:  Happy Valley Farm


(SPR=63)

1993 in USA and Canada:

       trk       dist   trk   race    value of                    wnrs     claim  #
date   race#  furl  con   type    race      wt  pp fp lngths earned  time     price  rn
----   -----  ----- ---   ----    -------   --  -- -- ------ ------ -------  -----  --
0614 DEL02  6.00  FST  3UCL    3,800 122 03 08 12 1/2      0 1:13.0  4,000 08
     1st   Sure                          2nd   Crimson Cry
     3rd   Naked Prospect
     Owner:   Friedman Ellie
     Trainer: Dare Richard S
     Jockey:  Lafler B M
0108 PHA01  6.00  MUD  4UCL    4,500 116 08 07 16 3/4      0 1:11.0  4,000 12
     1st   Bluestrum                     2nd   Gee Jamie
     3rd   Grin
```

```
1992 in USA and Canada:

      trk     dist  trk   race    value of                             wnrs    claim   #
date  race#   furl  con   type      race    wt  pp  fp  lngths earned  time    price   rn
----  -----  ------ ----  ------  --------- --- --- --- ------ ------- ------   ------ ----
1116  PHA04   6.00  FST   3UCL      4,500   116  10  11  20          0  1:13.3   4,000  11
      1st    Big Big Boy                            2nd   Ken's Hero
      3rd    Man of the Year
1011  PHA02   6.00  GD    3UCL      4,500   119  01  11  11 1/4      0  1:11.4   4,000  12
      1st    Monetary Tricks                        2nd   Wells Landing
      3rd    Ruckus
0719  PHA01   6.00  FST   3UCL      5,000   116  02  ff             0  1:11.4   4,000  07
      1st    Grey Flamingo                          2nd   Sheltered Moon
      3rd    Get the Net
```

Seattle Native continued with the Philadelphia defectors as the five year old went to Delaware. Like the others, Seattle Native lagged behind, finishing fourth of the six entrants.

All of these horses received favorable comments after their workouts and then shipped and were unsuccessful. This trend is a successful way of throwing out those low odds losers. The clockers at Philadelphia are looking at these horses and judging and rating them for what they are and how they would compete at Philadelphia Park. It would appear that, since Philadelphia Park is slightly better than Delaware, Rockingham, and Atlantic City, that these horses would do very well at these lower class tracks. It just goes to show how much the surface has to do with performance.

Leaving Your Race in Your Workout

7

One frequently asked question when I am doing a seminar goes like this: Sometimes, when handicapping, I will see a horse that works out great, gets a comment, and still runs out. Why is that?

The answer is fairly simple: a workout does and will take a lot out of any animal, and, unless given proper rest, the particular horse will not have time to recuperate.

The *Daily Racing Form* clockers do not know when a horse is planning to run, unless it is pointing toward a grade 1 stakes race. All the clocker knows is that the horse looked great running at that particular moment.

Thursday, June 3, 1993
BELMONT PARK – Track Fast

Three Furlongs							
rmuda Gai	:36 H	Aztec Hill	:49⁴ B	Mio Robertino	:50 Bg	High Regent	1:04 B
me On Joy	.35² H	Ballet Bulletin	:51² B	Miss the Alarm	:49 Hg	I of the Vortex	1:02 B
mmissionrBrt	:39 B	**Berkley Fitz**	:45⁴ H	No Holme Key	:47³ H	Intriguing	1:02¹ H
omsdagen	:36⁴ H	Border Cat	:49³ B	Noble Sheba	:49⁴ B	Jacsonzac	1:02² H
alandExpects	:37¹ B	Buffalo Trail	:50² B	Saltee Island	:52¹ Bg	Kate'sValentine	1:01³ H
ny Dare	:36 B	Dana's Wedding	.52 B	Seattle Ore	:47⁴ H	Little Tobin	1:01⁴ H
ostrada	:35⁴ B	Darn That Fool	.52 B	Six Thirty Two	:49¹ B	Memory Green	1:00⁴ H
		Eagles FlyAlone	:51 Bg	Stormy Java	:49⁴ B	Personal Bid	1:02³ B

Java Dance	.37^{2} B	Eastern Charm	:49^{1} H	Testy Trestle	:49 B	Pure Rumor	1:01 B
Key Contender	**:35 H**	El Bakan	:47^{3} B	Three Nickles	:52^{1} B	Q'S Kids	1:03^{1} H
Lord Salisbury	:36^{3} H	Fat Copper	:51^{2} Bg	Track Topper	.50^{2} Bg	Rose Indien	1:03 B
Loyal Todd	:38^{4} Bg	Fleet Talker	:49^{2} Hg	**Five Furlongs— :56^{1}**		**Satellite Signal**	**1:00^{3} H**
MemorableDate	:38 B	Green Reader	:47^{4} H	Andover Square	1:01^{2} H	Scoop the Gold	1:02^{4} B
Roger Racket	:36 H	Half A Crown	:49 B	Bellewood	1:02 H	Sharia	1:02^{4} B
Star Guest	:35^{3} H	Hawkeye Bay	:50^{3} H	Bland	1:01^{2} Hg	Tight Fit	1:02^{2} H
StelSomThundr	:36^{3} H	Huckster Rose	:47^{2} H	Chancalu	1:02 H	Toe Loop	1:04 B
Trvelin'Edmond	:36^{4} B	I'mSoAgreeable	:47^{4} H	Country Store	1:00^{4} B	Via Dei Portici	1:01^{2} B
Wilton Place	:37^{2} B	Launch's Pride	:50 B	Daddy'sAprilJoy	1:02^{1} H		
Four Furlongs		Lion Cavern	:48^{4} B	Evelyn's Pal	1:04^{2} B	**Seven Furlongs—1:20^{2}**	
Admirably	:51^{2} B	Malayan	:49^{3} B	Frisco Gold	1:01 Hg		
American Rye	:50^{3} B	Miner's Mark	:47^{4} H	Goldnthmthrhlls	1:01^{4} Hg	Tinchen'sPrince	1:27^{2} B

L BAKAN went the 1/4 in 24, and galloped out in 100. BERKLEY FITZ was humming. SEATTLE ORE holds form MINER'S MARK in on edge.

Berkley Fitz — **Ch. g. 4, by Graustark—Bird of Dawning, by Sea-Bird**

SMITH M E (187 46 26 25 .25) — **Br.—Lazy Lane Farms Inc (Va)**

Own.—Our Junco Stable — **Tr.—Monaci David (40 1 7 8 .03)** — **114**

Lifetime					
25 4 4 2	1993	7 1 1 1	$41,573
$161,571	1992	13 2 3 1	$105,820
	Turf	2 0 0 0	
	Wet	2 1 1 0	$40,744

7Jun93- 8Bel	fst 1 1/16	:46^{4}	1:11^{3}	1:43^{2}	3↑Handicap	—	4	2	3^{1}	4$^{3\frac{1}{4}}$	4^{15}	—	Krone J A	b 115	*1.60	— —	PurRumor112$^{3\frac{1}{4}}$KyContndr114^{13}SylvHond-GB113	Eased 4
22May93-14Suf	fst 1⅛	:47^{4}	1:12^{2}	1:51	3↑Bud Brdrs Cp	90	7	9	9$^{5\frac{1}{2}}$	9$^{4\frac{3}{4}}$	5$^{3\frac{1}{2}}$	5$^{5\frac{1}{2}}$	Alvarado F T	LB 114	5.30	93-14	BrnMth112$^{1\frac{3}{4}}$SnppyLndng114$^{3\frac{1}{2}}$Alytn116	Wide 2nd turn 10
13May93- 8Bel	fst 1 1/16	:46	1:10^{1}	1:40^{4}	3↑Alw 46000	107	7	3	3^{1}	2^{hd}	2^{1}	2^{1}	Smith M E	117	6.80	97-02	WestbyWest117^{1}BerkleyFitz117$^{14\frac{1}{4}}$Fbrshm117	2nd best 7
1May93- 8Aqu	fst 1	:46^{1}	1:10^{2}	1:36	3↑Alw 46000	92	4	3	5$^{2\frac{1}{2}}$	6^{4}	6^{5}	3$^{6\frac{3}{4}}$	Antley C W	117	7.90	77-27	Prmit117$^{5\frac{3}{4}}$RglConqust117^{1}BrklyFitz117	Steadied 1/2 pl 7
15Apr93- 8Aqu	fst 1	:46^{1}	1:10	1:34^{4}	3↑Alw 32500	89	1	4	3^{2}	4^{4}	4$^{4\frac{1}{2}}$	4$^{7\frac{1}{2}}$	Antley C W	119	4.40	82-18	Autorot117$^{1\frac{3}{4}}$SnppyLndng117^{nk}CoolsCrystl119	Steadied 5
27Mar93- 8GP	fst 1 1/16	:47^{2}	1:13	1:47	Alw 30000	95	5	5	5^{9}	4$^{3\frac{1}{2}}$	1$^{\frac{1}{2}}$	1^{6}	Krone J A	L 112	*1.30	75-30	BrklFt112^{6}ImprlGld114^{4}Shf'sFrstDnc113	Drftd in, drvg 7
10Feb93- 9GP	fst 1⅛	:48	1:12^{3}	1:51^{1}	3↑Hilarious H	84	7	2	2$^{\frac{1}{2}}$	3$^{\frac{1}{2}}$	7^{7}	7^{11}	Ferrer J C	L 112	5.30	70-24	Boots'nBuck111^{hd}Czr111^{no}ArchiesLughtr114	Gave way 8
6Sep92- 7Bel	fst 1 1/16	:46^{3}	1:10^{4}	1:42^{2}	3↑Alw 31000	82	5	3	3^{2}	3^{2}	4$^{3\frac{1}{2}}$	4$^{8\frac{1}{2}}$	Krone J A	b 113	*1.90	81-12	Polonium113^{4} Jacksonport113$^{2\frac{3}{4}}$ Yaros113	Wide, tired 8
2Aug92- 6Sar	fm 1 3/16 Ⓣ	:47^{2}	1:11^{4}	1:54^{1}	3↑Alw 31000	79	8	2	2$^{2\frac{1}{2}}$	5^{3}	8$^{5\frac{1}{4}}$	10$^{9\frac{3}{4}}$	Day P	112	8.70	87-04	ShrthGlory117^{nk}King'sGnt117$^{\frac{1}{2}}$Puchnto117	Forced pace 11
18Jly92-11Mth	fst 1 1/16	:46^{1}	1:10^{3}	1:42	Long Branch	80	5	1	1$^{3\frac{1}{2}}$	1$^{\frac{1}{2}}$	2^{5}	4$^{15\frac{1}{4}}$	Migliore R	L 114	2.00	84-12	Scudn114$^{13\frac{3}{4}}$PistolsndRoses122$^{\frac{3}{4}}$Munchn'Nosh114	Tired 8

LATEST WORKOUTS ●Jun 3 Bel 4f fst :45^{4} H ●May 8 Bel 3f fst :34^{1} H

Berkley Fitz was coming off a second place finish to *West By West* and a fifth place finish in a 100,000 stakes race at Suffolk Downs. On June 3, *Berkley Fitz* worked a incredible 45$\frac{4}{5}$ handily. In the next chapter, one will see how effective that work really was. In any event, *Berkeley Fitz* was then entered on June 7 in a $46,000 Handicap, off his impressive work-out. *Berkley Fitz* was never involved, not even finishing the race in a four horse field.

Berkley Fitz was then rested and entered in the same exact race on June 20. Coming off of this dismal performance, not many decided to wager on him. The four year old colt won by three lengths, covering the mile and one-eigth in a quick 148$\frac{4}{5}$. Even though *Berkley Fitz*'s work was only at a ½ mile, it still took too much out of this colt. It definitely showed on June 7. As an owner of horses, I already think like an owner or trainer when handicapping, but those who are not have to question why anyone would blow a horse out so hard when he is running a distance race. I could understand if the horse was preparing for a sprint, but for a distance runner, one would think stamina work would be best. Even when racing at a distance like today, they would not even be going 45³⁄₅ during the actual race. It would just be too fast. In any event, it led to a terrific payout of $23.20 on June 20.

Class Hat — B. g. 3(May), by Baldski—Hat Brim, by In Reality

ANTLEY C W (64 6 10 13 .09) — $35,000 — Br.—Mangurian Mr–Mrs H T Jr (Fla)

Own.—Triumviri Stable — Tr.—Hough Stanley M (6 1 1 1 .17) — 117

Lifetime 4 1 0 0 $7,865 — 1993 4 1 0 0 $7,865 — 1992 0 M 0 0

10May93- 3Bel	fst	6f	$:22^1$	$:46^3$	$1{:}12^2$	3↑Md 30000	65	1	3	1½	1½	1 1½	1^2	Krone J A	111	6.20	78-16	ClassHat111^{2}Polacsek115^{2½}PeekAttheLdies115	Driving	14
29Apr93- 9Aqu	fst	6f	:22	$:45^3$	$1{:}11^4$	3↑Md 35000	62	5	6	4 3½	3 2½	3 3½	4 6¾	Davis R G	122	*2.80	76-19	SlpThPnch118^{4¼}RtrntAccnt122^{1½}MthCr122	Lacked rally	9
19Feb93- 3GP	fst	7f	$:22^3$	$:46^2$	1:25	Md 50000	50	1	5	1½	1 1½	4 4½	9^{13}	Ramos W S	116	9.50	65-17	SyChsGorg116½DJ'sRinbow116^{6½}Jck'sHop116	Gave way	11
10Feb93- 1GP	fst	6f	:22	$:45^4$	$1{:}12^3$	Md 45000	52	3	5	5 5½	4 5½	6 5¼	8 5¼	Krone J A	118	2.90	73-17	HlldHndsm118^{no}Mr.Tth120^{1¾}ImprlShd116	Wide into str	11

LATEST WORKOUTS ●Apr 27 Bel 4f gd $:48^3$ H — Apr 21 Bel 3f fst $:36^2$ H — Apr 9 Bel tr.t 4f fst $:47^2$ H — Mar 30 GP 3f fst :38 B

In the next two examples, *Class Hat* and *Dr. Ron Miller* both worked days before their race. In the case of *Class Hat*, this three year old gelding was making only his third career start. Stanley M. Hough, *Class Hat*'s trainer drilled *Class Hat* a half mile on a good track in 48³⁄₅ handily on April 27. On the 29th of that same month, *Class Hat* was entered in an maiden claiming $35,000 contest. *Class Hat* ran an even race with no closing kick losing by 6³⁄₄ lengths as the 2.80-1 favorite. With no further workouts, *Class Hat* was entered on May 10. This performance was a little different: *Class Hat* led all the way, returning its followers a $14.40 payout.

Dr. Ron Miller — B. g. 6, by Announcer—Faithfully, by Lothario

$5,000 — Br.—Emport C J (NY)

Own.—Outlaw Biker Stable — Tr.—Grabowski John A (37 11 10 4 .30) — 117

Lifetime 55 5 7 5 $43,509 — 1993 5 2 0 1 $5,753 — 1992 24 2 3 2 $8,412 — Turf 8 0 0 0 $2,425 — Wet 9 0 3 0 $13,258

15May93- 2GS	fst	5½f	:22	$:45^2$	$1{:}04^3$	3↑Clm 5000	58	8	5	3½	3^2	4^4	3 5¾	Torres C A	Lb	117	2.80	83-17	Loykn117^{nk}Prsidnt'sChoic117^{5½}Dr.RonMllr117	No lt bid	9
1May93-10GS	fm	1^{70} ⓣ	$:46^4$	1:12	1:43	3↑Alw 8000s	47	2	7	5^4	4 5½	7^{16}	9 20¼	Barrera G	Lb	117	28.60	64-14	AmricnHonor117^{6½}Grnvill117^{4}WldEydBn117	Flatn'd out	11
23Apr93- 2Pha	gd	6f	:23	$:46^3$	$1{:}11^4$	3↑Clm 4000	68	3	5	1 1½	1^5	1^4	1 3¼	Castillo R E	Lb	119	*1.40	82-21	Dr.RnMllr119^{3¼}ShltrdMn109^{nk}FGnrl119	Bobbled st., drv	5
17Apr93- 4Del	fst	6f	$:22^3$	$:46^3$	$1{:}11^4$	3↑Clm 3750	69	8	2	1^1	1½	1½	1½	Barrera G	Lb	120	6.70	88-16	Dr.RonMllr120½OnthRodJck115^{8}LoghbrghLn122	Driving	10
7Apr93- 7Del	fst	6f	:23	$:47^2$	$1{:}14^1$	3↑Clm 3500	42	1	4	4¾	4^2	4 5½	5 4¾	Castro S R^7	Lb	113	3.40	71-28	McAv122^{hd}GnMmbr122^{4}ThrtyEghtCds122	Needed rally	9
12Dec92- 4Beu	sly	6f	$:23^1$	$:47^1$	$1{:}14^1$	3↑Clm 3000	25	6	11	11 6½	12^{12}	12^{11}	12 14¾	Miranda V	LBb	114	21.40	59-33	Optimn116^{nk}Angioplsty116^{2½}ChiefThief114	Never close	12
15Nov92- 4Beu	fst	1^{70}	$:47^4$	$1{:}13^4$	1:44	3↑Clm 3000	–0	11	8	9^3	11^{13}	11^{35}	11 38¾	Stannard G S	LBb	114	22.30	44-12	Lisa's Dan116^{nk} AmenWardy116^{no}CoolWater111	Outrun	11
7Nov92- 6Beu	sl	6f	$:23^3$	$:47^4$	$1{:}13^2$	3↑Clm 3000	43	8	10	6^1	3½	6 4½	5^6	Stannard G S	LBb	114	33.10	72-22	EysSoFlshy115^{2}GrcosFllw119^{1}JstfrChrstn116	No threat	12
23Oct92- 4Beu	fst	6f	$:22^2$	$:45^2$	$1{:}11^1$	3↑Clm 3000	26	7	8	6^6	7^{11}	10^{14}	10 13¾	Stannard G S	LBb	114	13.10	75-11	SprngLn116^{nk}JstfrChrstn115^{1}Trry'sLstBy119	Gave way	11
11Oct92- 4Beu	fst	6f	$:22^3$	:46	1:11	3↑Clm 3250	50	8	7	7 5¾	8 6¾	8^9	7 6½	Stannard G S	LB	116	14.90	83-11	HopNoMo114½EysSoFlshy115½SpringLn116	No menace	11

LATEST WORKOUTS Apr 6 GS 3f fst :37 Bg

Dr. Ron Miller's story is slightly different. On April 7, *Dr. Ron Miller* was making his first start of his '93 campaign. On April 6, at Garden State, *Dr. Ron Miller* worked three furlongs from the gate. This workout appeared to be additional work, but the backing he received at the betting windows made this workout legitimate. Also, if his connections wanted to submit an additional workout they would have posted it at Delaware. *Dr. Ron Miller* worked out of the gate, and then was shipped down to Delaware. This was just too much for this six year old gelding as he finished fifth, beaten by four and three-quarter lengths at odds of 3.00-1. After ten days off, *Dr. Ron Miller* moved slightly up in company from 3,500 to 3,750. April 17 was a winning day, as this gelding led every step of the way to a one-half length victory and returned $15.40 for a win payout. His next start was also a winning one, this one by three and one-quarter lengths at the claiming $4,000 level paying $4.80.

Maraud is the exact opposite of all the previous examples, showing how patience after a workout really pays off.

Maraud — **Ch. c. 4, by Sunny's Halo—Alpha Flight, by Oxford Flight**

NO RIDER (—) — **Br.—Wolff A Don (WVa)**

Own.—Hauman Eugene E — **Tr.—Hushion Michael E (20 7 2 4 .35)** — **117**

Lifetime	1993	9	1	0	3	$26,040
26 5 0 8	1992	11	2	0	4	$32,283
$82,781	Turf	1	0	0	0	$350
	Wet	5	1	0	1	$17,311

24May93-	6Bel	fst	7f	$:22^2$	$:45^2$	$1:22^3$	Clm 75000	**86**	7	3	$3^{2\frac{1}{2}}$	2^1	4^3	$3^{8\frac{3}{4}}$	Leon F^7		106	2.60e	81-22	LookAhd$116^{1\frac{1}{4}}$DrummondLn$116^{7\frac{1}{2}}$Mrud106	Lacked rally	8
15May93-	8Bel	fst	6f	$:22^2$	$:45^3$	$1:10^1$	3↑Handicap	**83**	7	6	4^1	4^{nk}	$5^{1\frac{1}{2}}$	$5^{4\frac{1}{2}}$	Bisono C V		109	9.80	84-17	FrndlyLovr$112^{1\frac{1}{2}}$Curbx$114^{2\frac{3}{4}}$DrummondLn120	Wide, trip	7
23Apr93-	6Aqu	fst	1	$:47$	$1:12^2$	$1:37^1$	Clm c-35000	**93**	4	3	$3^{2\frac{1}{2}}$	2^{hd}	$1^{1\frac{1}{2}}$	$1^{1\frac{1}{2}}$	Chavez J F		117	4.70	78-21	Maraud$117^{1\frac{1}{2}}$ Crafty Cash$112^{5\frac{3}{4}}$LordCardinal117	Driving	6
23Apr93-Claimed from New Atrium Stable, Marini Thomas Trainer																						
5Apr93-	4Aqu	fst	7f	$:22^4$	$:45^3$	$1:22^1$	Clm 45000	**75**	7	2	$5^{2\frac{1}{2}}$	$4^{1\frac{1}{2}}$	5^5	$5^{13\frac{3}{4}}$	Chavez J F		113	4.30	79-14	SenorCielo$115^{6\frac{3}{4}}$CrftyGolden$115^{\frac{3}{4}}$LeRisky115	Four wide	7
25Mar93-	2Aqu	gd	$1\frac{1}{16}$	⊡$:47$	$1:11^3$	$1:43^1$	Clm 47500	**91**	8	2	$3^{2\frac{1}{2}}$	2^1	4^4	6^3	Bisono C V^5		110	15.60	86-21	PayMeTody113^{nk}StudyHrd$117^{1\frac{3}{4}}$CostTooMuch117	Tired	8
3Mar93-	4Aqu	fst	1^{70}	⊡$:47^1$	$1:11^3$	$1:42^1$	Clm 47500	**96**	4	4	$4^{2\frac{1}{2}}$	3^1	1^{hd}	$3^{3\frac{1}{4}}$	Bravo J		115	31.60	88-23	I'm Sky High119^2StudyHard$113^{1\frac{1}{4}}$Maraud115	Bid, wknd	9
17Feb93-	1Aqu	gd	6f	⊡$:22^4$	$:45^4$	$1:10^1$	Clm 50000	**79**	2	6	$5^{2\frac{1}{4}}$	2^2	3^3	$4^{3\frac{1}{4}}$	Santagata N		117	8.30	89-09	ArgylLk$117^{1\frac{1}{4}}$SoldSnny$117^{1\frac{1}{4}}$AllSmrts112	Saved ground	6
25Jan93-	1Aqu	fst	$1\frac{1}{16}$	⊡$:46$	$1:12^3$	$1:45$	Clm 65000	**82**	3	4	3^3	2^1	3^6	$3^{10\frac{1}{2}}$	Santagata N		117	11.40	69-27	EsternBrve113^6I'llTkeStnd$117^{4\frac{1}{2}}$Mrud117	Drftd, bumpd	5
15Jan93-	7Aqu	my	6f	⊡$:22^4$	$:46^3$	$1:10^4$	Alw 34000	**75**	3	6	$5^{3\frac{1}{2}}$	$5^{2\frac{3}{4}}$	$5^{5\frac{1}{2}}$	$4^{8\frac{1}{2}}$	Santagata N		117	13.00	80-17	TheGretM.B.117^{nk}PnsionFrud$119^{\frac{3}{4}}$Vrmont117	No threat	7
21Nov92-	8Lrl	fst	6f	$:22$	$:45^1$	$1:09^3$	3↑Alw 23000	**82**	5	5	$6^{6\frac{1}{2}}$	5^6	3^5	3^5	Johnston M T	L	115	6.20	88-17	Blue Wolf$122^{1\frac{1}{4}}$ Lost Dutchman$122^{3\frac{3}{4}}$Maraud115	Rallied	6

LATEST WORKOUTS **May 9 Bel 4f fst :51 B** **●Apr 16 Bel tr.t 3f fst $:34^3$ H**

Maraud worked 3 furlongs in a snappy 34⅗ handling on April 16 and then took a week off before returning to the racetrack. *Maraud* was being extended from 7 furlongs to a mile and dropped from claiming $45,000, where he finished 5th beaten by 13¾ lengths and put into $35,000 claimers. This adjustment proved to be a winning combination on April 23. Maraud returned a solid $11.40 in the process.

Good trainers know that if they work their horses too close to the starting date it will affect performance. The normal pattern is two days before a horse runs. Many trainers will work three furlongs, just blowing them out down the stretch to keep them sound and on their toes. Closer than two days to the race date and any longer than 3 furlongs in distance is a tip to bettors to stay away. Also, one must look at the horse's previous workout pattern to make adjustments. For example, certain horses may run well off of a five furlong workout.

Comparing Workouts

8

When a horse runs well off a particular workout, it is good to go back and use that as a tip-off to others that may have worked comparatively well at the same time. I do not mean if one horse works 58 handily and wins, then the other who worked 58²/₅ handily will win, but he might have an advantage because of the performance of the other. Perhaps this next example will be clearer.

Horse A—51¹/₅ B
Horse B—52³/₅ B
Horse C—50²/₅ B
Horse D—51²/₅ B
Horse E—48 B
Horse F—53 B
Horse G—50²/₅ B
Horse H—47⁴/₅ B
Horse I—51 B
Horse J—51⁴/₅ B

Listed above are ten workouts. In this example, Horses E and H obviously worked better than the rest. This would not be obvious if we were talking about two stakes horses and the rest were $5,000 claimers. We are basing this on the premise that all horses are on a comparable level.

Horses E and H did work better and the rest have no excuses. As we learned in chapter 4, this angle is just the opposite.

PHILADELPHIA PARK – Track Fast

Three Furlongs						
Big Whip	:37² B	Snow Gamble	:38 B	Gold Shaker	:48³ Bg	FmosProspctor 1:02² B
Cruzan Clipper	:36² B	Sweet and Neat	:40 B	Its Been Fun	:51 B	Joe's Sleepy 1:02⁴ B
Dance of Fire	:39³ B	Time for Real	:38⁴ H	**Must Be Us**	:48² **Bg**	Liz's Large Step 1:03² B
Daren't Doubt	:39 B	Willy V A Hit	:39³ B	Privilegio	:51³ B	Lustful Dancer 1:03⁴ B
Dropp 'em	:38³ B	**Four Furlongs—** :45		So Close	:52 B	Miss Star Verse 1:02 Bg
Jack Winter	:38³ B	David'sLiniment	.48³ Bg	Son of Captain	:48⁴ B	Mt. Tirzah 1:03⁴ B
Jacuze Joe	:35⁴ **Bg**	Distinctive Girl	:50³ B	Talc Show Host	:19³ B	Northern Sur 1:03 B
Keepuseysomm	:38² B	Elegant Rose	:49² B	Vacation Bound	50 B	Reet Petite 1:01 B
King Kazar	:38 B	Erv's Duck	:49³ B	Wind OtheWest	.49 B	**Six Furlongs—1:08¹**
Patty Sunshine	:38³ B	Frozen Reef	:54 B	**Five Furlongs—** :56²		**Fawino** 1:15² **Bg**
Saratoga Wave	:36 Bg	Gallapiats Song	:49² B	Aiming High	1:02² B	MyOtherBrother 1:18² B
		Gavelin To	.51⁴ B	**Bench**	1:00⁴ B	

FAWINO continues (6f) to look sharp.

From our example in chapter 3, *Bench* completed a nice exacta with a 4-5 shot after working longer than he was running. If we look back at *Bench's* bullet workout on June 9, we see that *Bench* worked 100⁴/₅ breezing and *Reet Petite* worked 101 breezing. The other eight horses who worked ⅝ of a mile could not even come close, with only one horse coming within a second of *Reet Petite's* workout. These two stood out from the rest. In the 1st race, *Bench* finished second and *Reet Petite* was slated to go in the sixth race of the same day. Normally, as I have stressed in the past chapters, workouts are used as an addition to our handicapping. If a horse is in over his head, the best workout is not going to make him win. *Reet Petite* was a first time starter, so that was all we had to handicap with. With the performance of *Bench*, and after seeing the competition *Reet Petite* was facing, he was a sensible play. *Reet Petite* won the sixth race by seven and three-quarter lengths in an impressive 111 flat for the six furlongs, paying $6.40 in the process.

race #	dist fur.	trk con	race type	value of race	wnrs time	runners
6	6.00	FST	F3UM	$14,500	1:11.02	11

horse name	fp	lngths	wt	pp	earned	odds	claim
Reet Petite	1	7 3/4	114	2	$8,700	2.20	

```
Maudlin -- Nap Trap by Silent Screen
                Owner  : PARKER MELANIE
                Trainer: RICHARDSON GREG
                Jockey : MATZ N
Queen Mum             2  7 3/4 114  5      $2,900  5.00           062793PHA06
                Owner  : HILD SHARON L
                Trainer: HILD GLENN L
                Jockey : VERGE M E
Elegant Rose          3  8 1/2 115  4      $1,595 42.00           062793PHA06
                Owner  : RAWSON WALLACE C
                Trainer: EDER RICHARD A
                Jockey : CECIL K Y
More Witch            4  9      114  1        $870 17.40          062793PHA06
                Owner  : LOTT JESSIE D
                Trainer: LOTT WOODROW C
                Jockey : LLOYD J S
Joyfull Michelle      5  9 1/4 109  7        $435  2.00           070193PHA07
                Owner  : NUSS ROBERT
                Trainer: CRANFIELD ERNEST
                Jockey : UMANA J L
Enoughness            6 10 1/2 115  3          $0  6.00           062793PHA06
                Owner  : JOSELSON STANLEY I
                Trainer: SWENTKOWSKI ROBERT
                Jockey : HAMPSHIRE J F JR
Lady Georgene         7 15      122  9          $0 11.50          062793PHA06
                Owner  : MARIA JOHN J
                Trainer: MARIA JOHN J
                Jockey : BLACK A S
Royal Confusion       8 18 1/4 114  6          $0 26.00           062793PHA06
                Owner  : TZANDIS JAMES
                Trainer: ROGERS J MICHAEL
                Jockey : AGUILA G E
Madame Generale       9 20 1/2 122  8          $0 80.60           062793PHA06
                Owner  : COLE MRS CARLTON
```

PHILADELPHIA PARK – Track Fast

Three Furlongs				
Absolut Sterling :411 B	Boomeranged :521 B	Naturally Eval :504 B	Earsie 1:01 Bg
Aldon Justin :363 B	Castanya Nepal :50 Bg	OneHappySailor :521 B	Jacuzi Jo 1:021 B
Cataract Jones :372 B	Chargeittodddy :50 B	OnebllTwostriks :503 B	John Franklin 1:001 H
Fuzzy Slippers :371 B	Cool Blu Hue :494 B	PaintedWarning :512 B	Maudsleigh 1:023 B
Here'stotheLdis :372 B	Crowberry :491 B	PremierDiplomt :492 B	Neat'n'trim 1:012 B
Icy Don :394 B	DncingforMissy :512 B	Rock'nRollMdm :492 B	Norrey 1:051 B
Marriage Vow :392 B	**Do You Kow Me :461 Hg**	RuleroftheNight :51 B	North Well 1:013 B
Mito's Red Ed :354 B	DremofChmpgn :502 B	Sancerre :541 B	Omr'sConnction 1:012 B
Outlaw Squaw :393 B	DrumsofVictory :50 B	Seattle Native :484 B	Rainbow Right 1:001 Bg
Private Morning :411 B	Encase :523 B	Snow Gambol :494 B	RuggedAttitude 1:001 B
Regal Ball :382 B	Foretake's Ninf :492 B	StageDoorChief :501 B	Sister George 1:014 B
Saddle theWind :363 B	Hail Performer :492 Bg	U. S. Voyage :492 Bg	Tassi Bell 1:021 B
Saratoga Wave :371 B	Hidden Dignity :521 B	Vedor :492 B	Trap Jae 1:054 B
Talented Pitate :363 B	Hollywood Zeus :464 H	Witche's Star :531 B	Video Magic 1:011 B
Vlerie'sProspect :344 Bg	Junkaroo :493 B	Zappy :482 B	Wild Lady A 1:054 B
Four Furlongs— :45	Kohinoor's Ace :48 Bg	**Five Furlongs— :562**	**Six Furlongs—1:081**
	Lady Georgine :511 B	Always AGroom 1:034 B	A One Sandy 1:183 Bg

Always Dipping	:54 B	Lanamatt	:492 B	Bad Gerty	1:013 B	**Roodle**	1:18 B
Apache Hellfire	:512 B	Michael Josh	:503 B	Becky'sBirthday	1:034 B	**Seven Furlongs—1:211**	
As de Timeless	:514 B	MississppBound	:481 B	**Blushing Julian**	**:592 H**	Awfully Busy	1:303 B
Bald Robbery	:492 B	MsMndofHrOwn	:493 B	Country Sky	1:031 B	Burst of Stars	1:314 B
Bluesbforsunris	:49 B	Mumbles	:524 B	Don's Don's Pal	1:042 B	**Joey's First Jove**	1:272 B

BLUSHING JULIAN (5f) stays sharp and ready. MAUDSLEIGH (5f) improves. RAINBOW RIGHT (5f) and RUGGED ATTITUDE (5f) very sharp gate effort in company.

Do You Know Me broke her maiden by eight lengths in her first start in a maiden special weight contest. When we looked up his workout, we noticed that *Hollywood Zeus* worked 464/5 handily over four furlongs, just 3/5 slower than *Do You Know Me*. No one that day did better than 48 breezing besides those two. Forty-five horses worked that day, and this shows how these two stood out. *Hollywood Zeus* finished first in his next start at Philadelphia Park. In that claiming $8,000 race, *Hollywood Zeus* won by two and one-half lengths in 111 flat, equaling his best time ever.

Mannett and *Summon Thee* were spotted rather quickly because they received comments for their performances together. *Mannett* made his '93 debut on May 18 in a Philadelphia Park Allowance $14,000 race. The track came up muddy as it did in his maiden win, and *Mannett* did the same on this day, returning $23.00 to his supporters. *Mannett* covered the six panels in 1104/5, winning by a neck.

PHILADELPHIA PARK — Track Fast

Three Furlongs		Turning Pro	:371 B	Review Readers	.50 B	Polynesian Gold	1:03 B
Annie Brat	:382 B	**Four Furlongs— :45**		Silver Force	:493 B	**Summon Thee**	1:002 B
Big Sham	:391 B	Castlesinthesnd	:49 B	Unlucky Me	:501 B	Tanzania	1:014 B
Buckshooter	:392 B	EvrybodyDncnw	:493 B	**Five Furlongs— :562**		Two Brains	1:023 B
Diagnostic	:363 B	Go Voom	:501 B	Affirmaivea	1:024 B	Wings of Clay	1:023 B
Dundeeablo	:401 B	Gold Coaster	:504 B	Chargeittodddy	1:023 B		
ExecutivEdition	:391 B	Gold Letter	.514 B	Chelsea'sChnce	1:05 B		
Frozen Dew	:382 B	Gold Pop's	:51 B	DevonshireToff	1.042 B	**Six Furlongs--1:081**	
Kodari	:392 B	Highest Call	:511 B	Lady Georgene	1:033 B		
Pete the Chief	:372 B	Miss Star Verse	:533 B	**Mannett**	1:002 B	Mumbles	1:163 B
Privilegio	:37 B	Night Flyer	:493 B	Outlaw Squaw	1:033 B	Sunrise Willie	1:161 B
Sultry Princess	:401 B	**Potomac View**	:483 Bg	Passel	1:013 B	**Win Right Win**	1:144 B

POTOMAC VIEW (4F) went evenly from the gate, out (5F) in 1:02 2/5 B. MANNETT & SUMMON THEE (5F) worked very well together. WIN RIGHT WIN (6F) looked sharp.

Summon Thee, Mannett's working partner, made his debut off a three month layoff on May 24. *Summon Thee* was entered in a claiming $7,500 event. He was also entered in this company in February, where he finished ninth. Clearly overmatched, he ran a dismal tenth, beaten by fourteen and three-quarter lengths. On May 31, *Summon Thee* was dropped to claiming $4,000 level. With this drop, he was in the perfect position to win. There is nothing lower than claiming $4,000, and the clockers had to think something of this animal. No matter what, *Summon Thee* was definitely worth a shot now that he was dropped to a level where he could compete. He responded with a three and one-half length victory, returning $10.80. His next start was also victorious, and so was his next start after that. This victory, his third in a row, came in Allowance $17,500 company.

Mannett 1990 RO colt, by Hatchet Man 71 -- Starrett 81, by Halo 69

Breeder: Hemlock Ridge Stables

(SPR=94)

1993 in USA and Canada:

date	trk race#	dist furl	trk con	race type	value of race	wt	pp	fp	lngths	earned	wnrs time	claim price	# rn
0609	MTH03	6.00	FST	3UAL	25,000	111	02	01	1/2	15,000	1:12.0		07
	1st Mannett								2nd Isoroyal				
	3rd Kabala												
	Owner: Hemlock Ridge Stables												
	Trainer: Pollara Frank L												
	Jockey: Bravo J												
0518	PHA07	6.00	MUD	03AL	14,000	116	03	01	NK	8,400	1:10.4		07
	1st Mannett								2nd Storm Harvest				
	3rd Thaumaturge												

1992 in USA and Canada:

date	trk race#	dist furl	trk con	race type	value of race	wt	pp	fp	lngths	earned	wnrs time	claim price	# rn
1029	PHA07	6.00	FST	02AL	14,980	120	09	06	7 1/2	0	1:11.1		09
	1st No Name Dancer								2nd Sham's Groom				
	3rd Packhouse Road												
1009	MED07	6.00	SY	02M	18,700	118	03	01	1 1/2	11,220	1:11.2		12
	1st Mannett								2nd Castelli Street				
	3rd Savvy Sammy												
0906	MTH01	6.00	FST	02M	19,800	118	11	04	5	792	1:11.2		11
	1st But Oh My Dear								2nd Wading Castelli				
	3rd Mr Rodi												

Summon Thee 1989 GR colt, by Summing 78 -- Hie Thee 75, by Drone 66

Breeder: Ralph Gilster, Jr.

(SPR=87)

1993 in USA and Canada:

date	trk race#	dist furl	trk con	race type	value of race	wt	pp	fp	lngths	earned	wnrs time	claim price	# rn
0626	PHA08	8.32	FST	3UAL	17,655	116	02	01	3/4	9,900	1:42.3		07
	1st Summon Thee								2nd Heavy Medal Man				
	3rd Perfect Witness												
	Owner: Ferri Loreto												
	Trainer: Pollara Frank L												
	Jockey: Pennisi F A												
0611	PHA01	8.50	FST	3UCL	6,955	116	04	01	11	3,900	1:45.2	5,000	06
	1st Summon Thee								2nd Keen Marine				
	3rd Impressions												
0531	PHA03	8.32	FST	3UCL	5,000	116	01	01	3 1/2	3,000	1:45.0	4,000	07
	1st Summon Thee								2nd Rams Ace				
	3rd Encase												
0524	PHA06	7.00	FST	3UCL	7,260	116	10	10	14 3/4	0	1:24.0	7,500	12
	1st Rob Gelb								2nd Gallant Tower				
	3rd Knave of Hearts												
0220	PHA06	6.50	FST	4UCL	6,000	116	11	09	10 3/4	0	1:18.4	7,500	12
	1st Higher Threshold								2nd St. Vivan (ARG)				
	3rd Threshold Boy												

Tracking workouts is one thing, but when one sees one or two horses that are superior, he has to watch them closely, as they deserve more consideration. Once again, these horses have to be placed where they can win, as we saw with *Summon Thee*. When one see two workouts stick out, he knows as a handicapper that it has nothing to do with the track, because the rest would have been just as competitive. Also, the more horses that work out, the easier one will be able to get a read on the horse he is handicapping.

Comments

9

This chapter will be divided into four sections. The first will use examples to explain what a comment is and which ones are more important than others. The second will show how comments show their profitability with no handicapping. This section will provide an example of all comments from Philadelphia Park on April 16 to June 16 and their profits. The third will tell how to use comments effectively. The final section will give an example using comments that will knock your socks off.

As we have suggested, workouts are necessary to keep a horse fit or training toward that fitness. A comment is a few words about a particular horse that has worked impressively to the "clockers". By "clockers," I am speaking of the *Daily Racing Form* clockers who are in charge, whose responsibility it is to time all workouts. The comments are a bonus and are only written when a horse looks impressive to the clockers. Since we cannot always watch the workouts ourselves, we must put our trust into the *Daily Racing Form* clockers. These clockers time hundreds of workouts each day. When they notice a horse working impressively, they note it and it is passed on to the handicapper. If the handicapper is willing to take the time to use this information properly, it will definitely be profitable. Some days there could be 100 workouts and no comments. Discipline is required in selecting and noticing impressive and only impressive workouts. The farther the workout, the more impressive a comment is. Anyone could blow out in 35, but not many in 112.

Now that we know where they come from and why comments are there, we should learn how to use them. All comments here are for horses that have worked very well except at Delaware, where they give comments for good performances as well as bad.

In the next couple of pages we offer a list of comments that are written frequently by the *Daily Racing Form's* Clockers. The reason for this is to show how to differentiate comments and how to spot plays where we would wager more and receive greater profits.

Below are some examples showing differences in comments from a great comment to an okay one.

A) *Worked from the gate*

B) *Broke very well from the gate*

This might not sound like much, but the emphasis written in the second example may lead to more money bet and a greater return. If I were handicapping a horse and the horse received a comment as in example "B," I would think more of this horse, and probably would wager more. Remember, all the comments used in this chapter are in a two month time span where the clockers have given both types of comments out. If the track one is handicapping consistently gives out the one comment and not the other, one cannot think less of comment "A," if that is the only one the clockers are writing.

A) *Worked together*

B) *Were both full of run while working in company*

It is obvious that we can see the difference between the two and the emphasis on both horses in the second example. I would definitely think the two in example "B" were in better condition and looked tremendously better than the pair in example "A".

Before I list all of the comments and consideration grades, I'll give a few examples of comments from Delaware, the only track on the east coast to give a bad comment.

- "Not Much"
- "Tired after ⅜ in 35²/₅"
- "Learning"
- "Showed Little"
- "Bore Out"
- "Needs More"

All of these comments are bad, but if the horses that received these comments show improvement, they could be playable. In example three and five, "Learning and "Bore Out," these comments might have referred to a baby who is training slowly and may be improving. To play this horse, we would have to have a positive comment written about it.

The worst of the bunch are examples two and six. Example two shows the demise of a particular horse after ⅜ of a mile. For a clocker to notice, the horse had to slow down tremendously. This horse will probably be bet, because she shows early speed and then quits. By tracking this comment, one could throw these horses out when encountered in betting a race. In example six, the comment "Needs More," the lowest comment given, means that at this point the clockers feel that this horse could not even compete in claiming $4,000, the lowest level on the track. These horses should be immediately thrown out.

Remember, all comments show a horse is ready to perform and should be wagered upon. Some are more important then others, and they should be given more emphasis, but, if a horse is given a comment from this list or a list that one compiles from his home base track, this horse should be noted as a horse that is playable.

* - Great
    * - "Horse A bested Horse B"
    * - "Is ready for a top effort"
    * - "Is coming around nicely for a good effort"
    * - "Full of run"
    * - "Looked sharp, going"
    * - "Turned in the work of the day"
    * - "Was very impressive"
    * - "Sharp blowout"
    * - "Broke very well from the gate"
    * - "Went super, gallop out in"

* - "Sharp"
* - "Went very well"
* - "Went impressively"
* - "Finished strong"
* - "Sharp outing"
* - "Impressively urged"
* - "Was on the muscle"
* - "Stays super sharp"
* - "Stays sharp and ready"
* - "Very sharp gate effort in company"
* - "Was full of run, galloped out in"
* - "Is on his toes"
* - "Easily the best"
* - "Showed impressive speed with"
* - "Continues to sparkle"
* - "Went together with early speed"
* - "Worked very well together"
* - "Very sharp in company"
* - "Turned in a lively move"
* - "Best of others"
* - "Blistering"
* - "Is on edge for a top effort"
* - "Impressed trackside observers"
* - "Looks promising"
* - "Opened some eyes"
* - "Both turned some nice efforts"
* - "Were both full of run while working in company"
* - "Vibrantly"

** - Good
   ** - "Worked well out of the gate"
   ** - "Prep breeze"
   ** - "Easy breeze from the gate"
   ** - "Is getting ready for the turf season"
   ** - "Went well"
   ** - "Finished well"
   ** - "Went easily"
   ** - "Continues to run well"
   ** - "On the improve"

** - "Easily"
** - "In hand"
** - "In hand with"
** - "Looks good"
** - "Turned in a nice effort"
** - "Maintains good form"
** - "Went the last $\frac{1}{4}$ in"
** - "Was hard held"
** - "Donned blinkers"
** - "Maintains fitness"
** - "Urged bullet"
** - "Showed good speed"
** - "Worked evenly"
** - "Flashed early speed"
** - "Showed good speed throughout"
** - "Briskly"
** - "Mildly"
** - "Looks ready"
** - "Was going easily"
** - "Finished full of run"
** - "Was merely galloping"
** - "Continues to train smartly"
** - "In hand ready"
** - "Finished with good energy"
** - "Training impressively"
** - "Is sittin on ready"
** - "Sizzled"
** - "Is in fine fettle"
** - "Wore blinkers in his sharpener"

*** - "OK"
    *** - "Easy blowout"
    *** - "Has good speed"
    *** - "Had a useful work"
    *** - "Had a very easy trial"
    *** - "Worked together"
    *** - "Went nicely"
    *** - "Went usefully"
    *** - "Is showing some progress"

Here are all of the comments from Philadelphia Park from April 16 to May 18. All of the horses below have received comments with results of their next race next to their names. At the end of the listing, we have compiled statistics to show how these comments work in relation to the horse's race after the workout.

April 16, 1993

- * Good Beat 100¹⁄₅ HG   2nd by ½ at odds of 4.60 - 1 on 5-9
-   Threshold Boy 101⁴⁄₅ B   8th by 25 at 11.40 - 1 on 5-7
-   Batling Blades 112³⁄₅ B   4th by 5 1/4 at 5.70 - 1 on 4/27
- * Spanish Hollow 111⁴⁄₅ HG 6th by 11 at 4.80 - 1 on 5/1

April 17

- * Artful Pleasure 100²⁄₅ B 2nd by 2½ at 3.10 - 1 on 4/27

April 19

- * Rare Silence 34³⁄₅ H   1st by 3³⁄₄ at 4.00 - 1 on 5/7
- * Pewter Cowboy 100¹⁄₅ BG Had not competed

April 20

- * Blushing Julian 59²⁄₅ H 7th by 8½ at 6.80 -1 on 5/5
-   Maudsleigh 102³⁄₅ B   Competed at different track
-   Rainbow Right 100¹⁄₅ BG 1st by 3 at 3.10 - 1 on 5/16
-   Rugged Attitude 100¹⁄₅ BG 2nd by 2¼ at 4.00 - 1 on 5/10
  Next Start - 1st by 4³⁄₄ at 24.60 - 1 on 5/31

April 21

-   Lil Em N' Em 52 B   1st by 5³⁄₄ at 1.60 - 1 on 6/17
- * Tia Conchita 101¹⁄₅ B   3rd by 10¼ at .90 - 1 on 5/15
-   Close The Tepee 103³⁄₅ B No such animal
-   Heavens Parade 103 B   4th by 5 at 3.90 - 1 on 5/4

April 22

- * Esther In Nepal 35²⁄₅ B 4th by 3³⁄₄ at 7.00 - 1 on 4/26
-   Falcon Delight 117 B   6th by 12¼ at 3.30 - 1 on 4/25
  Next Start - 1st by Neck at 13.50 - 1 on 6/11

April 24

- - * Surely Youngest 47²/₅ B 3rd by 2³/₄ at 10.40 - 1 on 4/27
- - * Jimmy Who 114 B   7th by 21³/₄ at 20.40 - 1 on 5/3

April 25

- - * The Corn Doctor 46⁴/₅ B Didn't run
- - * Willow Star 59³/₅ HG   3rd by 4¹/₄ at 5.30 - 1 on 4/30
- - * Silver Force 113³/₅ H   3rd by 3 at 1.10 - 1 on 5/15

April 26

- - * Fawino 48⁴/₅ B   1st by 7¹/₄ at .50 - 1 on 5/4
- - * Don't Call Me Mary 112⁴/₅ 1st by 6 at 1.10 - 1 on 5/9
- - * Smiling Scot 112⁴/₅ HG   6th by 5¹/₂ at 8.30 - 1 on 5/8

April 27

- - * Bid Strong 114⁴/₅ BG   2nd by ³/₄ at 13.10 - 1 on 6/11

April 28

- -   Frozen Dew 35¹/₅ B   1st by 2 at .90 - 1 on 5/1
- -   Rob Gelb 35¹/₅ B   3rd by 1³/₄ at 4.00 - 1 on 5/4
- - * Spanish Hollow 34¹/₅ B Already noted above
- -   Do You Know Me 100²/₅ B 1st by 6¹/₂ at 1.00 - 1 on 5/18
- -   Premier Diplomat 100³/₅ Already noted above
- -   Blushing Julian 111⁴/₅ B Already noted above

April 29

- -   Admiral B. 58³/₅ HG   Didn't run

April 30

- - * Maxataway 47⁴/₅ BG   Didn't run
- - * Alden's Tribute 100¹/₅ H 7th by 13¹/₂ at 7.20 - 1 5/14
- -   Tender Ice 101 B   Competed at a different track
- -   Review Readers 130⁴/₅ B 9th by 24¹/₄ at 29.90 -1 on 5/31

May 1

- * Vacation Bound 46²/₅ HG 10th by 17¹/₂ at 22.30 -1 on 5/9
- * Ursula's Ruler 114 HG   Competed at a different track

May 2

- * Cool Fragrance 35³/₅ B 1st by 3³/₄ at 4.60 - 1 on 5/18
- Copper Man 100²/₅ B 2nd by ¹/₂ at 8.20 - 1 on 5/8

May 3

- Emerald's Mine 37¹/₅ B 3rd by a Head at 1.60 - 1 on 5/7
- Ack's Champ 50³/₅ B 4th by 6¹/₂ at 28.00 - 1 on 5/14
- * Clever Nick 47⁴/₅ B 3rd by 2³/₄ at 10.30 - 1 on 5/9

May 4

- The Last Crusade 38³/₅ B Didn't run
- * Visual Signal 48 BG   Competed at a different track

May 5

- I'm Your King 48¹/₅ B 1st by 2 at 14.90 - 1 on 6/21
- Wahael 48¹/₅ H   Competed at a different track

May 6

- * Joyfulle Michelle 35 B 3rd by 8³/₄ at 2.50 -1 on 5/9
- Joey's First Jove 36³/₅ B 2nd by 1¹/₄ at 1.40 - 1 on 5/8
- Lakeside Park 101²/₅ BG Competed at a different track

May 7

- * Radagundo 35¹/₅ B   Didn't run
- * Don Regal 48 BG   No such horse
- * I'llthinkaboutit 101¹/₅ B Competed at a different track

May 8

- * Glimmering Crest 59 H 4th by 4¹/₂ at 10.00 - 1 on 5/28
- * Seattle Native 115 B Competed at a different track

May 9

- Mississippi Bound 59¹/5 BG 7th by 19 at 7.00 - 1 on 5/29

May 10

- * Potomac View 48³/5 BG   5th by 10¹/2 at 10.00 - 1 on 6/6
- * Mannett 100²/5 B   1st by a Neck at 5.60 - 1 on 5/18
- * Summon Thee 100²/5 B   1st by 3¹/2 at 4.60 - 1 on 5/31
- * Win Right Win 114⁴/5 B   Didn't run

May 11

- Precious Priss 59³/5 HG Competed at a different track
- R.M.'s Girl 116²/5 B   2nd by 3¹/4 at 7.40 - 1 on 5/16

May 12

- * Premier Diplomat 58²/5 B   4th by 6¹/2 at .50 - 1 on 5/31

May 13

- * Clayton's Nobility 59³/5 H 3rd by 1¹/2 at 2.00 - 1 on 5/22

May 14

- Desert Hit 47⁴/5 H   3rd by 3 at 25.70 - 1 on 6/11
- * There For Fortune 59⁴/5 H 2nd by 1 at 2.40 - 1 on 5/21

May 15

- * Mr. Rosario 100 HG   Competed at a different track
- * Secret Calvary 112⁴/5 H 1st by 2³/4 at 2.70 - 1 on 5/23

May 16

- * Win Right Win 114³/5 B Didn't run
- Wolf Luck 115²/5 B   7th by 8¹/4 at 14.70 - 1

Avg. Winning Price
15 Winners $217.20 Total Mutuals Average - $14.48

Avg. Place Odds
8 Horses   Average - $5.53 Odds

Avg. Show Odds
10 Horses   Average - $6.03 Odds

A big mistake a lot of handicappers will make with handicapping comments and blacktype workouts will be to assume that since the horse had the best work of the day at that distance, he looked the best and received a comment. This could not be farther from the truth. During April 16 and June 16, a total of 259 horses received a blacktype workout, and only 44, or 17 percent, received a comment.

As I stated earlier about results without handicapping, nothing says more than these statistics. If you put $20 to win on every comment, you would have received $2,090.00, while betting $1,140.00 for a profit of $950.00 in a one month period. If you had wagered across the board on each horse, your profits would have increased dramatically. Also, of the 52 comments, there were 15 wins, or 29 percent, a percentage which is close to the percentage of winning favorites. The winning prices are, as follows: $10.00, $8.20, $51.20, $5.20, $29.00, $3.00, $4.20, $3.80, $4.00, $11.20, $31.80, $13.20, $11.20, $15.40, $7.40, $8.40—only four favorites of 15 winners, not bad considering all the favorites are batting almost the same average. Out of these 52 comments, 33, or 63 percent, finished in the money. This, too, is close to the percentage of favorites in the money. The comments are averaging odds of $6.18 - 1 compared to the favorites, who are usually between 4–5 and 9–5. The success of comment betting is tremendous. You will notice a difference in winnings the first time you try it. In the next example, you will see why some of these winners were successful and how this added factor will greatly increase your profits.

The next four examples in this section, called "Using Comments Effectively," all come from Philadelphia Park, in the time period discussed earlier in this chapter.

Rare Silence is a five year old colt who shipped up from Turfway Park and was ready to make his debut after a sparkling three furlong blowout in 34³/₅ handily. *Rare Silence* received a comment for this workout: *Rare Silence* "Sharp Blowout".

At Turfway Park, *Rare Silence* was currently running in claiming $6,250 and $5,000. He finished 4th, then 7th, and then was dropped to claiming $4,000 company at Philadelphia Park.

PHILADELPHIA PARK – **Track Fast**

Three Furlongs		Four Furlongs— :45		Wizzy	:47² B	Pewter Cowboy	1:00¹ Bg
Irish Incite	:39⁴ B	Feriado	:50¹ B	Five Furlongs— :56²		Royal Cinch	1:00³ B
Pasta n'Peas	:38¹ B	LnchAChowChw	:51³ B	Amberfax	1:03⁴ B	Valiant Emzee	1:04 B
Perfect Witness	:38² B	LemmonPepper	:50³ B	Aye Blue	1:06¹ B		
Rare Silence	:34³ H	Persuasive	:50 B	Diagnostic	1:00² B	Seven Furlongs—1:21¹	
Rob Gelb	:36² B	Round My Door	:48³ B	Don'tfightoverme	1:00¹ B		
Sir Robert Jr.	:36 Bg	Sitting On Top	:48 Bg	I'm Maxine	1:06¹ B		
Water Skipper	:37⁴ B	St. Haven	:47⁴ H	Mr. Excellerator	1:00³ B	Direct Approach	1:29 B

RARE SILENCE (3F) sharp blowout. PEWTER COWBOY (6F) broke very well from the gate.

Rare Silence 1988 DK B/ colt, by Rare Brick 83 -- Classic Silence 75
by Silent Screen 67

Breeder: Pope McLean & Art Baumohl

(SPR=86)

1993 in USA and Canada:

date	trk race#	dist furl	trk con	race type	value of race	wt	pp	fp	lngths	earned	wnrs time	claim price	# rn
0606	PHA07	6.50	FST	3UCL	6,000	122	10	09	11	0	1:19.1	7,500	11

1st Maybe On Monday   2nd Mommy's Faster
3rd Glib
Owner: Aubrey Racing Stable Ltd
Trainer: Bearden Wayne
Jockey: Petersen J L

| 0507 | PHA02 | 6.00 | FST | 3UCL | 4,500 | 116 | 02 | 01 | 3 3/4 | 2,700 | 1:11.3 | 4,000 | 09 |

1st Rare Silence   2nd Old Key
3rd A One Sandy

| 0213 | TP 08 | 8.00 | MUD | 4UCL | 6,200 | 115 | 03 | 07 | 27 1/2 | 0 | 1:41.1 | 5,000 | 12 |

1st Rowing Club   2nd Lucky Forbes
3rd Billy Genn

| 0101 | TP 03 | 9.00 | FRZ | 4UCL | 7,200 | 115 | 05 | 04 | 7 1/4 | 360 | 1:54.3 | 6,250 | 08 |

1st Adversarial   2nd Mr. Nice Sky
3rd Double Stink

1992 in USA and Canada:

date	trk race#	dist furl	trk con	race type	value of race	wt	pp	fp	lngths	earned	wnrs time	claim price	# rn
1216	TP 04	8.00	MUD	3UCL	7,900	116	01	03	1 1/4	790	1:41.4	8,000	08

1st Lost Cannon   2nd Thousand Palms
3rd Rare Silence

| 1205 | TP 02 | 6.50 | FST | 3UCL | 10,200 | 111 | 04 | 06 | 22 1/2 | 0 | 1:20.3 | 12,500 | 09 |

1st Downtown Clown   2nd Sky Tracer
3rd Krugerrand

```
1118 CD 04  6.00  FST  3UCL   14,700 116 05 08 10 1/2      0 1:11.2 13,500 11
     1st   Allen Charge                    2nd  Rollo's Chet
     3rd   Jumping Johnny
0925 TP 06  6.50  FST  3UCL   10,600 111 06 06 10 1/4      0 1:16.2 12,500 09
     1st   Sharkey                         2nd  Hatcher Hill
     3rd   Irish Jack
0913 TP 07  6.00  FST  3UCL   10,600 116 02 06 11 1/4      0 1:10.2 12,500 12
     1st   Hatcher Hill                    2nd  Akrokerami
     3rd   Apalana
0826 ELP08  8.00  FST  3UCL   11,000 112 07 08 30        110 1:37.0 16,000 08
     1st   Jon Juan                        2nd  Evergreen Ridge
     3rd   Frankies Pride
```

Rare Silence was sent off second choice in the six furlong sprint and galloped clear in the stretch to win by 3¾ lengths. *Bankers Holiday*, the even money favorite, finished 8th, beaten by 12 lengths. *Rare Silence* returned a mutual of $10.00, to all supporters and workout experts. Workouts and comments can give the handicapper a much needed edge before the race. Why not take advantage of them?

The next two examples show horses that have worked together and carried these good workouts successfully to the winners' circle. The first pair are experienced colts that have been coming off long layoffs, the other pair consists of a colt and a filly that were making their career debuts. Nevertheless, all four horses were not consistently running at the workout time. This shows that the clockers did do a fine job in spotting horses that are in top condition and ready to make their return or debut.

Mannett and *Summon Thee* both worked five furlongs in a snappy 100 2/5 breezing.

PHILADELPHIA PARK — Track Fast

Three Furlongs		Turning Pro	:371 B	Review Readers	:50 B	Polynesian Gold	1:03 B
Annie Brat	:382 B	**Four Furlongs—**	:45	Silver Force	:493 B	**Summon Thee**	1:002 B
Big Sham	:391 B	Castlesinthesnd	:49 B	Unlucky Me	:501 B	Tanzania	1:014 B
Buckshooter	:392 B	EvrybodyDncnw	:493 B	**Five Furlongs—**	:562	Two Brains	1:023 B
Diagnostic	:363 B	Go Voom	:501 B	Affirmaivea	1:024 B	Wings of Clay	1:023 B
Dundeeablo	:401 B	Gold Coaster	:504 B	Chargeittodddy	1:023 B		
ExecutivEdition	:391 B	Gold Letter	:514 B	Chelsea'sChnce	1:05 B		
Frozen Dew	:382 B	Gold Pop's	:51 B	DevonshireToff	1:042 B	**Six Furlongs—1:08**1	
Kodari	:392 B	Highest Call	:511 B	Lady Georgene	1:033 B		
Pete the Chief	:372 B	Miss Star Verse	:533 B	**Mannett**	1:002 B	Mumbles	1:163 B
Privilegio	:37 B	Night Flyer	:493 B	Outlaw Squaw	1:033 B	Sunrise Willie	1:161 B
Sultry Princess	:401 B	**Potomac View**	:483 Bg	Passel	1:013 B	**Win Right Win**	1:144 B

POTOMAC VIEW (4F) went evenly from the gate, out (5F) in 1:02 2/5 B. **MANNETT & SUMMON THEE (5F)** worked very well together. **WIN RIGHT WIN (6F)** looked sharp.

Mannett was the first to run. This occurred on April 18 in an allowance $14,000 contest at six furlongs. *Mannett* was checked twice in the stretch in his only allowance appearance, but seemed to fit with this company. On October 10, 1992, *Mannett* did break his maiden in his second start of his career in a Maiden Special Weight contest.

Manne t 1 9) :(colt, by Hatchet Man 71 -- Starrett 81, by   Halo 69

Breed(r: ie⅄ ck Ridge Stables

(SPR=9)

1993 in USA and Canada:

date	trk race#	dist furl	trk con	race type	value of race	wt	pp	fp	lngths	earned	wnrs time	claim price	# rn
0609	MTH03	6.00	FST	3UAL	25,000	111	02	01	1/2	15,000	1:12.0		07
	1st Mannett								2nd Isoroyal				
	3rd Kabala												
	Owner: Hemlock Ridge Stables												
	Trainer: Pollara Frank L												
	Jockey: Bravo J												
0518	PHA07	6.00	MUD	03AL	14,000	116	03	01	NK	8,400	1:10.4		07
	1st Mannett								2nd Storm Harvest				
	3rd Thaumaturge												

1992 in USA and Canada:

date	trk race#	dist furl	trk con	race type	value of race	wt	pp	fp	lngths	earned	wnrs time	claim price	# rn
1029	PHA07	6.00	FST	02AL	14,980	120	09	06	7 1/2	0	1:11.1		09
	1st No Name Dancer								2nd Sham's Groom				
	3rd Packhouse Road												
1009	MED07	6.00	SY	02M	18,700	118	03	01	1 1/2	11,220	1:11.2		12
	1st Mannett								2nd Castelli Street				
	3rd Savvy Sammy												
0906	MTH01	6.00	FST	02M	19,800	118	11	04	5	792	1:11.2		11
	1st But Oh My Dear								2nd Wading Castelli				
	3rd Mr Rodi												

Mannett was then entered in an allowance race at Philadelphia Park, and the track also turned up sloppy, as it did when *Mannett* broke his maiden. Mannett came flying home in the slop to win by a neck, paying $14.40.

Summon Thee 1989 GR colt, by Summing 78 -- Hie Thee 75, by   Drone 66

Breeder: Ralph Gilster, Jr.

(SPR=87)

1993 in USA and Canada:

date	trk race#	dist furl	trk con	race type	value of race	wt	pp	fp	lngths	earned	wnrs time	claim price	# rn
0626	PHA08	8.32	FST	3UAL	17,655	116	02	01	3/4	9,900	1:42.3		07
1st	Summon Thee								2nd	Heavy Medal Man			
3rd	Perfect Witness												
Owner:	Ferri Loreto												
Trainer:	Pollara Frank L												
Jockey:	Pennisi F A												
0611	PHA01	8.50	FST	3UCL	6,955	116	04	01	11	3,900	1:45.2	5,000	06
1st	Summon Thee								2nd	Keen Marine			
3rd	Impressions												
0531	PHA03	8.32	FST	3UCL	5,000	116	01	01	3 1/2	3,000	1:45.0	4,000	07
1st	Summon Thee								2nd	Rams Ace			
3rd	Encase												
0524	PHA06	7.00	FST	3UCL	7,260	116	10	10	14 3/4	0	1:24.0	7,500	12
1st	Rob Gelb								2nd	Gallant Tower			
3rd	Knave of Hearts												
0220	PHA06	6.50	FST	4UCL	6,000	116	11	09	10 3/4	0	1:18.4	7,500	12
1st	Higher Threshold								2nd	St. Vivan (ARG)			
3rd	Threshold Boy												
0130	PHA02	8.32	FST	4UCL	10,000	116	09	09	23 1/2	0	1:42.2	14,000	09
1st	Executive Edition								2nd	Pasta n' Peas			
3rd	Ikhnatoon (IRE)												

Summon Thee, the other half, debuted on May 24 in a claiming
$7,500 event. The last time Summon Thee was entered was in the
same company as May 24, finishing ninth of twelve, 10¾ lengths behind
the eventual winner. Even though *Summon Thee* was playable, the handicapper should use caution. With a workout of this caliber, one would
think that he had to improve upon that last start.

With these examples and the upcoming few, I am not trying to show
you how much you can make or how comments can win for you. I do not
have to show that you will pick up those points throughout this book. If
you handicap and make sure the horse you are betting will be able to win,
then you will see tremendous results.

Summon Thee didn't get involved, and deciding that tenth was a
good position for himself, he lost by 14¾ lengths. When *Summon Thee*
was dropped to a level where he could compete, as in the case on May
31 when he was placed in a claiming $4,000 competition, *Summon Thee*
responded with a three and ½ length victory, while returning his fol-
lowers $11.20. *Summon Thee* then responded with victories in claiming

$5,000 and an allowance $17,655 contest. This was his third victory in a row. He paid $15.40 and $6.00 in those victories, proving once again, when horses are placed in a winnable position, workouts will show their profits.

The other pair of examples deal with maidens who were looking to make their first starts of their careers.

PHILADELPHIA PARK – Track Fast

Three Furlongs								
Absolut Sterling	:411 B	Boomeranged	:521 B	Naturally Eval	:504 B	Earsie	1:01 Bg
Aldon Justin	:363 B	Custanya Nepal	:50 Bg	OneHappySailor	.521 B	Jacuzi Jo	1:021 B
Cataract Jones	:372 B	Chargeittodddy	:50 B	OnebllTwostriks	:503 B	John Franklin	1:001 H
Fuzzy Slippers	:371 B	Cool Blu Hue	:494 B	PaintedWarning	:512 B	Maudsleigh	1:023 B
Here'stotheLdis	:372 B	Crowberry	:491 B	PremierDiplomt	:492 B	Neat'n'trim	1:012 B
Icy Don	:394 B	DncingforMissy	:512 B	Rock'nRollMdm	:492 B	Norrey	1:051 B
Marriage Vow	:392 B	Do You Kow Me	:461 Hg	RuleroftheNight	:51 B	North Well	1:013 B
Mito's Red Ed	:354 B	DremofChmpgn	:502 B	Sancerre	:541 B	Omr'sConnction	1:012 B
Outlaw Squaw	:393 B	DrumsofVictory	:50 B	Seattle Native	:484 B	Rainbow Right	1:001 Bg
Private Morning	:411 B	Encase	:523 B	Snow Gambol	:494 B	RuggedAttitude	1:001 Bg
Regal Ball	:382 B	Foretake's Ninf	:492 B	StageDoorChief	:501 B	Sister George	1:014 B
Saddle theWind	:363 B	Hail Performer	:492 Bg	U. S. Voyage	:492 Bg	Tassi Bell	1:021 B
Saratoga Wave	:371 B	Hidden Dignity	:521 B	Vedor	:492 B	Trap Jae	1:054 B
Talented Pitate	:363 B	Hollywood Zeus	:464 H	Witche's Star	:531 B	Video Magic	1:011 B
Vlerie'sProspect	:344 Bg	Junkaroo	:493 B	Zappy	:482 B	Wild Lady A	1:054 B
Four Furlongs—	:45	Kohinoor's Ace	:48 Bg	**Five Furlongs—**	:562	**Six Furlongs—**	1:081
Always Dipping	:54 B	Lady Georgine	:511 B	Always AGroom	1:034 B	A One Sandy	1:183 Bg
Apache Hellfire	:512 B	Lanamatt	:492 B	Bad Gerty	1:013 B	Roodle	1:18 B
As de Timeless	:514 B	Michael Josh	:503 B	Becky'sBirthday	1:034 B	**Seven Furlongs—**	1:211
Bald Robbery	:492 B	MississppBound	:481 B	Blushing Julian	:592 H	Awfully Busy	1:303 B
Bluesbforsunris	:49 B	MsMndofHrOwn	:493 B	Country Sky	1:031 B	Burst of Stars	1:314 B
		Mumbles	:524 B	Don's Don's Pal	1:042 B	Joey's First Jove	1:272 B

BLUSHING JULIAN (5f) stays sharp and ready. MAUDSLEIGH (5f) improves. RAINBOW RIGHT (5f) and RUGGED ATTITUDE (5f) very sharp gate effort in company.

Rugged Attitude was the first of the two to hit the track, and he responded, running second, finishing 2¼ lengths off the lead.

Rainbow Right was next and decided to run in the same class as *Rugged Attitude*, claiming $8,000. After seeing the performance that *Rugged Attitude* displayed, *Rainbow Right* should be a solid play at the same level. If the comment said *Rugged Attitude* and *Rainbow Right* worked in company, then the emphasis would be a lot less, but since the Daily Racing Form's clockers made a point to say that both looked very sharp, this gives us the confidence to go ahead and wager.

Rainbow Right covered the six furlongs in 113³/₅, winning by three lengths. She also came right back at Monmouth to run second in a claiming $10,000 event.

PHILADELPHIA PARK May 16, 1993

race #	dist fur.	trk con	race type	value of race	wnrs time	runners
2	6.00	FST	F03MCL	$4,500	1:13.02	9

horse name	fp	lngths	wt	pp	earned	odds	claim	most recent trk/race #
Rainbow Right	1	3	122	5	$2,700	3.10	$8,000	062993MTH04

Far Out East —— Friendly Folly by Steve's Friend
        Owner   : OUR FARM INC
        Trainer: IWINSKI ALLEN
        Jockey : MADRIGAL R JR

Wise Baroness	2	3	117	3	$900	2.80	$8,000	063093MTH10

        Owner   : REID ROBERT E JR
        Trainer: REID ROBERT E JR
        Jockey : HOMEISTER R B JR

Grams Thrill	3	7 3/4	122	2	$495	9.80	$8,000	062693ATL04

        Owner   : LINK O WAYNE
        Trainer: ALTMAN ROBERT D
        Jockey : TORRES C A

Forty Two Special	4	9 1/4	122	7	$270	34.50	$8,000	061893PHA02

        Owner   : KOONTZ KATHERINE & MAC JAC II
        Trainer: SNYDER FLOYD W
        Jockey : CAPANAS S

Regal Pro	5	9 1/2	122	4	$135	1.60	$8,000	061193PHA02

        Owner   : MINASSIAN ZEKE
        Trainer: WEINHOLD JEFFREY D
        Jockey : LLOYD J S

Jocarm	6	12 1/2	122	1	$0	6.60	$8,000	061793PHA09

        Owner   : HILD SHARON L
        Trainer: HILD GLENN L
        Jockey : BLACK A S

Tawny Evening	7	17 1/2	122	6	$0	71.10	$8,000	061593MTH03

        Owner : CAMMEYER JOHN N
        Trainer: RUSSO FRANK P
        Jockey : ARROYO E R

An Extra Million	8	21 3/4	113	9	$0	45.40	$7,000	061293PHA02

        Owner   : BOORSE HERBERT C
        Trainer: RIEGLER MARY P
        Jockey : CECIL K Y

Castanya Nepal	9	25 1/2	122	8	$0	21.30	$8,000	061793PHA09

        Owner   : LINWOOD STABLES
        Trainer: IMPERATORE MICHAEL
        Jockey : D'AGUSTO J G

Meanwhile, *Rugged Attitude* was ready to make his second start, and moved up to a Maiden Special Weight event. About 80 percent of the time, I would disagree and dislike this move, but one has to evaluate the trainer to get a read on what he is trying to do. A good trainer might move a horse up after the second place performance, because he feels the horse will be able to move up and win against better horses and be rewarded with a higher purse. A bad trainer will want to believe he has something better and be afraid he is going to lose him in a claiming race, instead of letting him run where he can win.

Rugged Attitude jogged in this higher company, and, in the process, returning a whopping $51.20.

```
PHILADELPHIA PARK May 31, 1993

          dist   trk    race        value of   wnrs
  race #  fur.   con    type            race    time    runners
  ----    ----   ----   ----       ---------   -----    -------
   4      6.50   FST    3UM        $19,575    1:18.04      11
                                                                   most recent
  horse name            fp  lngths wt   pp    earned   odds  claim   trk/race #
  -----------           --  ------ --   --    ------   ----  -----   ---------

Rugged Attitude          1   4 3/4 113   7    $11,745  24.60         070193PHA09
Burts Star --- Rough Eagle by L'Aiglon
               Owner  : OUR FARM INC
               Trainer: IWINSKI ALLEN
               Jockey : PETERSEN J L
Sir Robert Jr            2   4 3/4 113   9    $3,915   11.90         062193PHA07
               Owner  : FALLON MARTIN L
               Trainer: FALLON MARTIN L
               Jockey : SOMSANITH N
Range Baron              3   7 1/4 116  10    $2,153   12.20         061893PHA07
               Owner  : RITCHIE OLGA B
               Trainer: MERCER THOMAS F
               Jockey : BLACK A S
Romantic Encounter       4   7 1/2 108   6    $1,175   45.60         070293PHA06
               Owner  : TRIN-BROOK STABLES INC
               Trainer: ST LEWIS URIAH
               Jockey : BISONO J
Earsie                   5  10 1/2 113   3      $587   12.60         061893PHA07
               Owner  : PESARIDAN STABLES
               Trainer: BROOME EDWIN T
               Jockey : RYAN K
Contending               6  13     114   1        $0    5.40         062893DEL01
               Owner  : DANEY MRS BERNARD R
               Trainer: BONIFACE J WILLIAM
               Jockey : COLTON R E
Tar Men                  7  14 1/2 116  11        $0   10.20         053193PHA04
               Owner  : LIZ TREE STABLE
               Trainer: ROBBINS CHARLES R
               Jockey : LANDICINI C JR
```

Mr Brownwood	8 19	113	5	$0	19.40	053193PHA04
Owner : MURPHY ROBERT L						
Trainer: REID MARK J						
Jockey : JOCSON G J						
Hagecius	9 19 3/4	113	4	$0	17.50	061993PHA01
Owner : WEYMOUTH MRS EUGENE E						
Trainer: WEYMOUTH EUGENE E						
Jockey : MOLINA V H						
Tod's Zeus	10 19 3/4	114	8	$0	84.70	062193PHA07
Owner : GREENBURG MURRAY M						
Trainer: CRANFIELD ERNEST						
Jockey : LLOYD J S						
R. D. Golden Land	ff	122	2	$0	0.70	062793PHA01
Owner : DOMMEL ROBERT W						
Trainer: ROWAN STEVE E						
Jockey : MADRIGAL R JR						

In the next section is an example of a horse that had received multiple comments. This horse was working back into shape, coming from an operation. The horse, *Cody's Key*, has been consistently placed in stakes competition. I was present for this horse's return to the races, and was there because of his workouts and saw the opportunity to make a nice score.

Cody's Key was ready to make his '93 debut on May 15. This was exactly eight months from his last race. *Cody's Key*, while working toward this, race posted workouts of 58 handily on April 29 and 112²/₅ on May 4. Both of these workouts received comments.

BELMONT PARK — Track Fast

Three Furlongs

A.k.a. Candy	:35³ H
American Rye	:38³ B
Ferociously	:35¹ H
Jim's Best Boy	:36³ B
Love 'n Glory	:37¹ Hg
Pigeon Pea	:37 B
Press On Jesse	:36¹ H
ShareMyFntsies	:37¹ Hg
Slate Six	:36³ B
Talking to Delta	:38³ B

Four Furlongs

Alyten	:49¹ B
Athleague	:49 B
BrronVonBlizen	:50¹ B
Be Haven	:48 H
Big Sur	:51² B
Bold RosaLined	:48 H
Chambolle	:50 B
Crackedbell	:48¹ H
DefenseSpnding	:48¹ H

ExplosiveMatch	:51³ Bg
Fly So Free	:48³ B
Flying Cherub	:48³ H
Grady's Star	:49 B
High Policy	:49³ B
Knight On Call	:49¹ B
Kris's Kiss	:49 B
MrryMeMrryMe	:48² B
Miner's Halo	:48⁴ B
Miss Turlington	:47 H
One D. Flawless	:50 B
Ozan	:48¹ H
Permit	:49³ B
Press Card	:49 B
Private Light	:48⁴ B
Raise A Carter	:47⁴ H
Regal Display	:48³ B
Rinka Das	:49¹ B
RoscommonClln	:49² B
RoscommonPrd	:49 B
Sal's Flower	:50 B

Stoney Wolf	:47⁴ H
Talk Politics	:49² B
Tiara Miss	:49⁴ B
Toe Loop	:49 B

Five Furlongs— :56¹

Abi Yo Yo	1:00³ H
Carsey's Pal	1:00 H
Cody's Key	:58 H
Digging In	:59 H
Distinctive Hat	1:01 Hg
Ghazi	1:03³ B
Half A Hope	1:02 B
Hot Slew	1:01¹ H
Ivory Dreams	1:01⁴ H
Miss Lynell	1:02 H
Miss Panchita	1:02² H
Moss Pond	1:02 B
MyLittleDnielle	1:02 Hg
My Mogul	1:00 H
Promised Relic	1:02³ B
Real Irish Hope	1:00 H

Stellenbosch	1:03³ B
Step Out Front	1:02² B
Suken Fleet	1:02 Hg
Tarq	:58³ H
Tricky Catman	1:00 H
Tropical Waters	1:03 B
Very Tricky	1:02⁴ B
Waitforthebeep	1:03³ B
Well of Gold	1:02³ B
Wet Reel	1:01² B
Yuseppa	1:02 H

Six Furlongs—1:07⁴

Appropriately	1:19 B
Gold Medal Girl	1:18⁴ B
Pretty Firm	1:16¹ B
Special Agent	1:13³ Hg

Seven Furlongs—1:20²

Melamy Jeseli	1:29³ B

1 Mile—1:33

Dr. Alfoos   :48¹ B   Steel Power   :49³ B   Saltanic Smile   :59⁴ H   Dream So Real 1:40² Hg

RAISE A CARTER (4F) and **STONEY WOLF (4F)** worked in company. **CODY'S KEY (5F)** opened some eyes. **DISTINCTIVE HAT (5F)** bested **SUNKEN FLEET (5F)**. **TARQ (5F)** finished up strong. **MELAMY JESELI (7F)** had a useful trial.

BELMONT PARK – Track Fast

Three Furlongs						
American Rye	:37 B	Alyten	:47³ H	Pure Rumor	:47³ H	Personal Bid	1:04¹ B
Bland	:38 B	Bless Our Home	:52² B	**Rosenose**	:47 H	Rain Alert	1:01¹ B
Desert Warning	:36⁴ B	**Cannon Row**	:47 H	Secret Rullah	:48² B	**Springal**	:59² H
Eden Isle	:38³ B	Carr Heaven	:50² B	SelectiveSurgry	:49³ B	Stantorian	1:00 H
Fly So Free	:35¹ B	Classy Mirage	:52 B	Setta	:51² B	Watrals Charm	1:04² B
Forest Tiger	:35¹ H	Crnshw'sCornor	:50¹ B	Sham's Gold	:52³ B	White Man	1:01 H
GrindstoneRidg	:38 B	Current Impact	:50² B	Star Guest	:47¹ H	**Six Furlongs—1:07⁴**
Lauries Cup	:38 B	Dan Shot	:48³ B	Stero Casette	:47³ H	Abi Yo Yo	1:15³ B
LivingVicriously	:39² B	Fighting Jet	:47⁴ H	**Stoney Wolf**	:48⁴ H	Big Leap	1:13⁴ H
Mountain Trapp	:39³ B	Groomed toWin	:48³ H	What A Doris	:50⁴ B	ChampagneAffir	1:13⁴ H
Personal Choice	:36⁴ B	I've GotPromise	:47¹ H	**Five Furlongs— :56¹**		**Codys Key**	1:12² H
Potentilla	:38³ B	Intriguing	:51³ B	AugustusSprngs	1:00⁴ H	Half A Hope	1:17¹ B
Reawakening	:37 B	Ivory Dreams	:47³ H	CaptainCutious	1:00³ B	Irish Doctor	1:14² B
Ridge Road	:36³ H	Jazz Doctor	:49⁴ B	Chambolle	1:05 B	Majestic Hawk	1:14¹ B
Sand Lick	:38 B	Jazzy Carr	:49³ B	Estedor	1:01¹ H	Russian Tango	1:14⁴ B
Smart Weed	:38 B	Magic Street	:51 B	**Hilbys BriteFlite**	:59² H	Share the Glory	1:15³ B
Strolling Along	:34⁴ H	One D' Flawless	:49¹ B	Home oftheFree	1:01⁴ H	State Dancer	1:15² B
Talking to Delta	:37² B	Play WithHooch	:49 B	KazuminaSpring	1:00⁴ H	Well of Gold	1:16 B
Four Furlongs		Port of Silver	:49³ B	Moyer	1:00² H	Yuseppa	1:16¹ B
		Pres Card	:51 B	OurShoppingSpr	1:00⁴ H		

FLY SO FREE (3f) galloped out in :47. **SPRINGAL (5f)** is in form. **CODYS KEY (6f)** looks good.

As *Cody's Key* came into the paddock, he was very nervous, and, by the way he looked, he was washed out. It was obvious that the trip to the paddock did not agree with this four year old colt.

His behavior made me very wary, and I bet cautiously and not nearly as much as I planned on.

He did not run a lick, trailing all of the way, and I knew that, with a race under his belt, he would run better. The workout proved he was fit and ready, but he was just too nervous and high strung to compete on this day.

On May 29, *Cody's Key* was entered in the Roseben Handicap. Before the first race, Gary Contessa (*Cody's Key's* trainer) walked *Cody's Key* in the paddock to get him use to the surroundings. After seeing this, I knew that *Cody's Key* was a play on this day. The reason I felt this way was because Gary obviously knew the horse could win, and he knew that the reason for his previous failure was because he was washed out and too nervous.

He never looked back in the Roseben Handicap, winning by a head and returning $64.20. This example is for all the handicappers who believe that you do not get big prices with workouts.

BELMONT PARK May 29, 1993

ROSEBEN H. -G3

race #	dist fur.	trk con	race type	value of race	wnrs time	runners
8	6.00	FST	3USTK	$85,500	1:09.04	6

horse name	fp	lngths	wt	pp	earned	odds	claim	most recent trk/race #
Codys Key	1	HD	108	5	$51,300	32.10		070493BEL05
Corridor Key -- Go Thither by Cabin								
Owner : SHEERIN RAYMOND T								
Trainer: CONTESSA GARY C								
Jockey : CHAVEZ J F								
Sunnybutcold	2	HD	111	6	$18,810	6.90		070493BEL05
Owner : CARROLL DONALD J								
Trainer: MONACI DAVID								
Jockey : FERRER J C								
Slerp	3	HD	118	4	$10,260	1.10		052993BEL08
Owner : RICHIE ALLAN L								
Trainer: HESS ROBERT B								
Jockey : SANTOS J A								
Now Listen	4	2 1/2	116	2	$5,130	3.40		070393HOL08
Owner : JUDDMONTE FARMS								
Trainer: FRANKEL ROBERT								
Jockey : SMITH M E								
Shuttleman	5	10	113	1	$0	3.90		052993BEL08
Owner : BIRRIEL JOSE A JR								
Trainer: HOUGH STANLEY M								
Jockey : KRONE J A								
Majesterian	6	10 3/4	113	3	$0	5.40		062893BEL08
Owner : MERIWETHER JOHN W								
Trainer: FREEMAN WILLARD C								
Jockey : DAVIS R G								

All of these examples in this chapter led to one thing: if you use workouts with handicapping, you will win at the track. Comments tell the obvious. If a horse works out and is noticed, he is worth a extra look and is usually in a playable situation. If the clockers are saying that a particular horse looks very good and is in great condition, one must decide whether to take advantage of it. The answer was obvious in the previous example of betting all of the comments at Philadelphia Park. The example shows the consistency of the clockers to notice only horses that are fit and ready. In the next two chapters we will show examples of two different tracks that cannot be trusted as well as Philadelphia Park.

Knowing Which Comments and Track To Trust

10 A comment is a bonus to the handicapper and a re-
ward to a horse for looking sharp during his workout.
After reading this book, one will still have to test the
track he is betting at and see if they are giving the
right information and horses that are consistently
running well.

At Calder, 144 comments were given out between April 16 and
June 16. Of these comments, 99 were multiple listings of the same
horses, or 69 percent. When this occurs, it usually means that there is a
group of horses that dominates the track, and the clockers seem to give
these horses comments over and over. As you look through the listings
below, you will notice certain horses will have three to four comments.
The *Daily Racing Form's* clockers seem to be giving them a comment before they work out. At tracks like Belmont, Monmouth, and Philadelphia,
one will rarely see a horse get two comments, never mind three or four.
Below is a listing of those horses. The dashes represent repeat entries.

Sir Stephen Michael
- Tunecke Charlie
Cinderella
Debbie's Bliss

Walkie Talkie
- Gentle Patrick
Niki B Mine
I'm A Badman
- Boot's N' Buck
- Tunecke Charlie
- Forever Whirl
- Star Jolie
Midnight Cookie
More Freedom
Fortunate Wish
Fanny's Frolic
Humbugaboo
- Pistols and Roses
- Fight for Love
Confidence is High
- Absent Russian
Bujama
- Star Jolie
Track Gossip
- Forever Whirl
- Gipsy Countess
Spectacular Tide
- Pistols and Roses
- Sambacarica
- Ponche
- Best in Sale
Panacho's Choice
- Coolin It
- Star Jolie
Halftime Dancer
Gator Coed
- Super Doer
- The Vid
- Forever Whirl
- Fight For Love
- Pistols and Roses
- Pride Prevails
Spinning Round

- San Imagination
  Peaceful Appeal
- Proud Runner
- Tunecke Charlie
  Real Bucks
- Always Silver
- Coolin It
- Aspen Fortune
- The Vid
- Franklin Me
  Northern Trend
- Forever Whirl
- Ponche
- Pistols and Roses
- A Demon A Day
  Beyond Description
- Boot's N Buck
- Proud Runner
  Let Them Eat Cake
- Always Silver
- Gipsy Countess
- Lady Sonata
- Groomstick
- Inside Connection
  Starion
  Fun Finger - AR
- Franklin Me
- Forever Whirl
- Sambalarica
- Always Silver
- San Imagination
- Pride of Burkann
  Reissaurus
- Carterista
- Proud Runner
  Archie Laughter
  Signor Valery
- Magal
- Gentle Patrick

- Always Silver
  Jackie Wackie
- Super Doer
- Not Surprising
- Ponche
- A Demon A Day
  Swedaus
  Delta Lady
- Gipsy Countess
- Lady Sonata
- Magal
- Sambacarioca
- Absent Russian
- Forever Whirl
- The Vid
- Pride Prevails
- Best in Sale
  Faultness Singer
- Super Doer
- Hidden Tomahawk
  Oh My Blue Boy
  Fortune Forty Four
- Absent Russian
- Magal
  Jamie's Boy
- Pride of Burkman
  Striding Star
- D.J. Cat
- Not Surprising
- Inside Connection
- Always Silver
- Proud Runner
- Ponche
- Hidden Tomahawk
- Supah Gem
- Aspen Fortune
  Air Mike
- Gilded Trial
- Groomstick

Barging Through
- Franklin Me
- Carestia
My Luck Runs North
Aly T
Doyouseewhatlsee
- Always Silver
Silver Maggie
- Pistols and Roses
Island Delay
- Super Doer
- Hidden Tomahawk
- Supah Gem
- Proud Runner
- Ponche
- Gilded Trial
Ma Bird Too
- D.J. Cat
Full of Stuff
- Carterista
- Magal
- Best in Sale
- Pistols and Roses
- Always Silver

As one can see above, many names have been repeated quite often. Though it may be expected of stakes horses to receive a comment, there is no way that they can be razor sharp every time they hit the track. In any two month period, a horse will work out an average of five to six times. Below are some of the horses that have received multiple comments, with the number of times each worked out:

Forever Whirl	6
Always Silver	7
Pistols and Roses	6
Ponche	5
Proud Runner	5
Magal	4

For the reasons listed above, one can see why the comments at Calder might not be as trustworthy as those at other tracks. It is important to evaluate the track one is handicapping to see if the comments will work for him. Even if some of the horses listed above are stakes animals, it is an injustice to the handicapper, because it is not a true read on those other horses.

Who Deserves Comments

11

Chapter 10 dealt with the handicapping problem that develops when tracks give the same horses an abundance of comments. Those horses may not deserve the recognition they are receiving every time. In this chapter, we are going to discuss how, at certain tracks, comments can be more detrimental than profitable. The problem, as shown below at Delaware, is that too many horses receive comments. In Chapter 10, we saw a listing of the comments from Philadelphia Park. There were 259 bullet workouts during that time period, and only 44 of these bullet workouts were given comments. At Delaware, in the same time period, there were 193 bullet workouts and 211 comments. These statistics show that the clockers are not looking as closely as they should. When they are timing these workouts and looking at the workers, they are not zooming in on what is important and their boundaries are too broad; thus, everyone looks good. Although Delaware's comments may be good, we might not be able to trust them.

DELAWARE PARK – Track Fast

Three Furlongs		Four Furlongs		Pommel	:51 B	Can't Rule	1:05² B
All Desire	:37³ B	Beauty Supply	:51 B	Prince Ivy	:51 B	Class Spring	1:04 H

Do You Believe	:40 B	Blush On	:49¹ Bg	Saberano	:51 B	Palacade	1·04² B
Forgotten Ally	:36 B	Center CityMiss	:50 B	Songs of Praise	:49⁴ B	**Polar Promise**	1:03¹ B
Pugahman	:38 B	ChillKtExpditon	:49¹ B	Truly Striking	:51 B		
Sophie	:37 B	My Cut	:50¹ B	Visioness	:50¹ B		
Sweet Bear	:36³ B	**Pleasure Vent**	:49 B	**Five Furlongs—**	:56¹		

FORGOTTEN ALLY (3f) ready. PLEASURE VENT (4f) improving. POLAR PROMISE (5f) shows promise.

DELAWARE PARK — Track Fast

Three Furlongs							
Do You Believe	:38 B	Trademebem	:38 B	Itchen	:50¹ B	Visioness	:49¹ B
High Force	:35⁴ B	You Aughta	:39² B	Lotta Liberty	:50³ B	Western Peak	:50³ B
LittleTouchn'Go	:39¹ B	**Four Furlongs**		Maudie Mine	:51 B	**Five Furlongs—**	:56¹
Northern Gun	:36¹ H	Brightons Double	:47⁴ H	Mrs. Highness	:50¹ H	April Strike	1:02¹ B
Summit One	:39² B	Filch	:49¹ H	Pommel	:50¹ B	BumpAlongLne	1:03¹ B
		Hypoxia	:49¹ B	Rippleton Road	:50³ B	Got the Point	1:04² B

HIGH FORCE (3f) easily, out in :49 1/5. BRIGHTONS DOUBLE (4f) out in 1:03 1/5 with D. Rice up. APRIL STRIKE (5f) sharp.

DELAWARE PARK — Track Fast

Three Furlongs						Six Furlongs—1:08¹	
EmeraldEssence	:37 B	Dahar's Charm	:51⁴ B	A Top Brandy	1·04⁴ B		
Irish Eminence	:36³ B	Embassy Mill	:50 B	Blue Summer	1:02² Bg		
Walking Single	:40¹ B	Faviano	:51 B	Count OnAFight	1:05 Bg	Chantose	1:14² Hg
Four Furlongs		Hazel's Liberty	:48¹ Hg	Looking Home	1:05 Bg	Miss Mallary	1:20¹ H
Bob's Cormorant	:47² B	Journeys Crest	:51⁴ B	Saucy Mist	1:01⁴ B	Silent Duchess	1:14⁴ Bg
Cup O'brew	:49² B	Truchster	:50⁴ B	**Sherlock Slew**	1:01 B	The Gimmic	1:20³ B
		Five Furlongs—	:56¹	Speedy Lover	1:01 B	Tidal Surge	1:15¹ Bg

BOB'S CORMORANT (4F) as expected. FAVIANO (4F) H. Alexander up. HAZEL'S LIBERTY (4F) first 3/8 :35 4/5. BLUE SUMMER (5F) on the improve. SAUCY MIST (5F) remains sharp. SHERLOCK SLEW (5F) briskly with SPEEDY LOVER. CHANTOSE (6F) to watch for. SILENT DUCHESS (6F) sharply trained.

As one can see in the above workouts, most of Delaware's comments usually coincide with bullet workouts. It seems that the Delaware clockers think that if the horse worked the best time, he looked good. The bottom line is that a comment is something that a horse earns, and it is apparent that the clockers at Delaware and Calder are too generous, and this can be more damaging then profitable to the handicapper. However, I am only using Delaware and Calder as examples. They are not the only tracks that have these problems. You will have to evaluate the track located closest to you and make your own judgment on the quality of the comments.

Working Great and Not Getting a Comment

12 This chapter should not be confused with the last. When horses work tremendously fast and do *not* get a comment, this works dramatically the *opposite* way. Stay away from these horses.

April 20	Bowie	Open Account	113 H
20	Hialeah	River Clare	35³/₅ HG
22	Hialeah	One Up On You	35 H
23	Philadelphia	Tender Ice	35¹/₅ B
23	Keenland	Crafty Digger	46²/₅ B
24	Belmont	Groovy Green	46⁴/₅ H
25	Pimlico	Senior Scoot	34²/₅ H
25	Belmont	Start A Fight	58⁴/₅ H
26	Belmont	Fifth Business	59²/₅ H
26	Philadelphia	Toy Won	34²/₅ BG

All of the workouts above are very good and competitive, but with a workout this good and no comment, one has to be very cautious. If the trainer is good and legit, then I would consider playing, but I cannot stress enough the need to be careful if a horse works out that fast and does not look good enough to get a comment. This says to me that he was all-out in his workout. I do not want to play those horses. All of the examples have been selected in a period of six days and are from six different tracks, showing that this could happen all over. Also, the time period of six days shows how often this can occur.

Open Account 1990 CH filly, by Thirty Eight Paces 78 -- Amanti 79
                                                      by   Anticipating 71

Breeder: William R. Harris

(SPR=76)

1993 in USA and Canada:

date	trk race#	dist furl	trk con	race type	value of race	wt	pp	fp	lngths	earned	wnrs time	claim price	# rn
0626	LRL11	7.00	FST	F3UM	16,700	113	05	02	2 1/4	3,255	1:27.0		10
	1st Good Apple								2nd Open Account				
	3rd Rahraja												
	Owner: Harris William R												
	Trainer: Bailes W Robert												
	Jockey: Delgado A												
0613	LRL07	6.00	FST	F3UM	16,700	113	02	03	5	1,705	1:12.0		10
	1st Salutetheplaygirl								2nd Code's Blossom				
	3rd Open Account												
0601	PIM03	9.00T	FRM	F3UM	17,700	113	05	06	27 1/4	330	1:53.4		10
	1st Glory Mood								2nd My Marchesa				
	3rd Gemini's Gem												
0515	PIM01	8.50	FST	F35M	17,100	108	04	03	9	1,815	1:44.4		08
	1st Ygerne								2nd Anyone's Daughter				
	3rd Open Account												
0425	PIM12	9.00T	YLD	F35M	17,400	113	03	05	7	495	1:55.3		09
	1st Rosalie's Charm								2nd Tanks Spark				
	3rd Glory Mood												
0404	PIM03	8.50	FST	F35M	17,700	113	08	02	3	3,465	1:48.0		10
	1st Prettyfineandmine								2nd Open Account				
	3rd Bet the World												
0325	PIM03	6.00	FST	F35M	16,400	114	09	05	11 3/4	465	1:13.2		09
	1st Fleet Broad								2nd Ygerne				
	3rd Latin Prospect												
0215	LRL02	6.00	FST	F03M	15,900	119	04	05	9 1/2	465	1:12.1		08
	1st Somebody Else								2nd Raggae D. Anne				
	3rd Contradanza												

1992 in USA and Canada:

date	trk race#	dist furl	trk con	race type	value of race	wt	pp	fp	lngths	earned	wnrs time	claim price	# rn
0716	LRL05	5.50	FST	F02M	16,100	119	06	02	3/4	3,100	1:07.0		08
	1st Carnirainbow								2nd Open Account				
	3rd Beckys Bread												

River Clare 1991 CH colt, by Irish River (FR) 76 —— Lady of Arathorn 87
                                                    by Stage Door Johnny 65

Breeder: Nursery Place & M. Rayberg

(SPR=64)

1993 in USA and Canada:

date	trk race#	dist furl	trk con	race type	value of race	wt	pp	fp	lngths	earned	wnrs time	claim price	# rn
0629	MTH05	5.00	FST	02MCL	10,000	114	01	04	5 1/4	500	1:00.0	28,000	09

1st Private Enough   2nd Gifted Son
3rd Sonny's Bruno
Owner: Krakower Lawrence J
Trainer: Taylor Ronald J
Jockey: Lopez C

| 0616 | MTH01 | 5.00 | FST | 02MCL | 10,000 | 114 | 01 | 03 | 9 1/2 | 1,200 | 1:00.1 | 30,000 | 07 |

1st Duelling Knight   2nd Carry a Rose
3rd River Clare

| 0429 | HIA03 | 3.00 | FST | 02M | 16,800 | 118 | 07 | 06 | 5 3/4 | 140 | :32.2 | | 09 |

1st Bye Guys   2nd Frank Knew
3rd El Chiquito

One Up On You 1989 B filly, by Premiership 80 —— L'Engone 77, by L'Enjoleur 72

Breeder: Franks & Fernung

(SPR=80)

1993 in USA and Canada:

date	trk race#	dist furl	trk con	race type	value of race	wt	pp	fp	lngths	earned	wnrs time	claim price	# rn
0623	MTH08	8.50T	FRM	F3UAL	19,000	121	05	07	22 3/4	190	1:43.0		08

1st Uptown Show   2nd Living On Credit
3rd Motel Amiss
Owner: Paez Carlos E
Trainer: Paez Carlos E
Jockey: Pennisi F A

| 0611 | ATL08 | 5.50T | FRM | F3UCL | 9,000 | 119 | 03 | 05 | 4 1/2 | 90 | 1:04.2 | 32,000 | 07 |

1st Tip's Terror   2nd Ms. Copelan
3rd Ruthies Reason

| 0529 | GS 08 | 8.00T | FRM | F3UAL | 14,000 | 116 | 09 | 02 | 1 1/2 | 2,660 | 1:37.4 | | 09 |

1st Palace Revolt   2nd One Up On You
3rd Goldfinch

```
0520 HIA08  5.50T FRM F3UCL      16,800 113 01 01  2 3/4  11,200 1:04.2 65,000 07
1st  One Up On You                        2nd  Current Gossip
3rd  Copelan's Cachet
0516 HIA11  6.00  FST F3UAL      15,000 116 03 03  1      1,950 1:12.3         06
1st  Sugar Pike                           2nd  Panama Hattie
3rd  One Up On You
0506 HIA07  6.00  FST F3UAL      18,000 116 02 03  7 1/2  1,650 1:11.3         10
1st  Nikki B. Mine                        2nd  Panama Hattie
3rd  One Up On You
0425 HIA03  7.00  FST F4UAL      15,000 116 05 04 10 1/2    750 1:25.2         08
1st  Ensignette                           2nd  Sugar Pike
3rd  Appeal to Glory
0413 HIA03  7.00  FST F4UCL      12,000 115 01 06 20 1/4    100 1:24.3 22,500 06
1st  My Angel Maryon                      2nd  Druid Woman
3rd  Staticelectricity
0404 HIA06  8.50T FRM F4UAL      18,000 116 02 08 12        150 1:44.2         09
1st  Capote's Princess                    2nd  Authentic Heroine
3rd  Top Roberto
0205 GP 08  6.00  SY  F4UAL      24,000 114 06 09 16 1/4    200 1:11.4         10
1st  Silent Knight                        2nd  Graceful Glory
3rd  My Middle Name
```

Tender Ice 1989 CH colt, by Northern Ice 80 —— Tender Note 79
                                            by Rube the Great 71

Breeder: Barbara Rickline & Matthew Dinan

(SPR=15)

1993 in USA and Canada:

date	trk race#	dist furl	trk con	race type	value of race	wt	pp	fp	lngths	earned	wnrs time	claim price	# rn
0620	PEN01	8.32	FST	45MCL	5,700	117	03	05	14 1/2	171	1:47.1	9,000	08

1st Part of the Gang   2nd Putzdadoma
3rd McAmber
Owner: Zellman Donna
Trainer: Maxey Carl L
Jockey: Gonzalez L M

| 0606 | PEN02 | 6.00 | FST | 35MCL | 3,500 | 112 | 03 | 04 | 9 1/4 | 210 | 1:15.1 | 4,500 | 11 |

1st Alexandria   2nd Miney Mo
3rd Heather's Lord

| 0522 | PEN01 | 8.32 | FST | 35MCL | 5,500 | 115 | 02 | 06 | 22 1/4 | 0 | 1:44.3 | 10,000 | 07 |

1st Odysseus   2nd Sense of Iron
3rd Calling Your Bluff

| 0426 | PHA09 | 5.00 | SY | 3UMCL | 6,000 | 120 | 04 | 08 | 8 1/2 | 0 | 1:01.2 | 10,500 | 08 |

1st Carlisle Star   2nd Run Hibby Run
3rd Speakin Out

```
0220 PHA02  6.00  FST   4UMCL    4,500 122 12 12 25 1/2       0 1:14.1  8,000 12
     1st  Crack Shot                   2nd  Inaugural Ball
     3rd  Broadripple
0130 PHA01  8.32  FST   4UMCL    5,000 122 06 07 34           0 1:44.0  8,000 07
     1st  Transfer                     2nd  Dublin Diplomacy
     3rd  Suitor
0117 PHA01  6.00  FST   4UMCL    4,500 122 09 11 21 3/4       0 1:13.0  8,000 12
     1st  Ten Oaks Pilot               2nd  Jake's Tuition
     3rd  Beau Hollow
0103 PHA10  5.50  FST   4UMCL    6,000 122 02 09 14 1/2       0 1:05.2 12,500 11
     1st  Hollywood Screen             2nd  Pellstar
     3rd  Counter Question
```

1992 in USA and Canada:

date	trk race#	dist furl	trk con	race type	value of race	wt	pp	fp	lngths	earned	wnrs time	claim price	# rn
1123	PHA03	5.50	MUD	3UMCL	6,000	119	08	ff		0	1:06.4	12,500	08
	1st Costly Emerald								2nd Smokey's Song				
	3rd Clifford Park												
1107	PHA11	6.00	FST	3UMCL	4,500	119	08	10	25 1/2	0	1:13.4	8,000	11
	1st Not in Line								2nd Painter Pete				
	3rd Okinori												

Crafty Digger 1990 CH colt, by Crafty Prospector 79 —— English Miss 81
                                               by London Company 70

Breeder: Hendricks Venture Farms Ltd.

(SPR=94)

1993 in USA and Canada:

date	trk race#	dist furl	trk con	race type	value of race	wt	pp	fp	lngths	earned	wnrs time	claim price	# rn
0406	KEE08	7.00	FST	03STK	84,400	113	04	05	9 1/2	2,532	1:21.1		08
	LAFAYETTE S.--G3 (75,000A)												
	1st Cherokee Run								2nd Poverty Slew				
	3rd Williamstown												
	Owner: Hendricks Randall												
	Trainer: Broussard Joseph E												
	Jockey: Perret C												
0320	FG 09	8.50	SY	03STK	300,000	114	11	05	4 1/2	9,000	1:44.4		13
	LOUISIANA DERBY--G3 (300,000A)												
	1st Dixieland Heat								2nd Offshore Pirate				
	3rd Tossofthecoin												

```
0223 FG 57  8.18  FST  03AL      15,000 115 01 01   1 1/4    9,000 1:40.0          06
     1st  Crafty Digger                        2nd   Ground Force
     3rd  Gold Angle
0116 FG 10  6.00  FST  03STK     32,475 113 01 07  6              0 1:11.3          09
       BLACK GOLD H.-O (30,000A)
     1st  Premier Cheer                        2nd   Tonkas Mean Streak
     3rd  No Name Dancer
```

1992 in USA and Canada:

date	trk race#	dist furl	trk con	race type	value of race	wt	pp	fp	lngths	earned	wnrs time	claim price	# rn
1231	FG 10	6.00	FST	02STK	33,175	116	02	12	10 1/4	0	1:11.2		13

```
       SUGAR BOWL H.-O (30,000A)
     1st  Tonkas Mean Streak                   2nd   Bobbidy Bob
     3rd  Jest in Orbit
```

| 1218 | FG 09 | 6.00 | FST | M02AL | 13,500 | 119 | 01 | 01 | 4 1/2 | 8,100 | 1:11.2 | | 06 |

```
     1st  Crafty Digger                        2nd   Premier Cheer
     3rd  Hill of Fame
```

| 1030 | HAW06 | 6.00 | FST | 02M | 14,000 | 119 | 02 | 01 | 1 1/4 | 8,400 | 1:13.1 | | 07 |

```
     1st  Crafty Digger                        2nd   South Wind Blowin'
     3rd  Star Turner
```

Groovy Green 1990 CH colt, by Groovy 83 -- Shades of Green 78
                                               by   Secretariat 70

Breeder: Paula J. Tucker

(SPR=58)

1993 in USA and Canada:

date	trk race#	dist furl	trk con	race type	value of race	wt	pp	fp	lngths	earned	wnrs time	claim price	# rn
0627	BEL05	8.50T	FRM	3UM	25,500	114	06	03	1/2	3,060	1:43.4		10

```
     1st  Lee's Suitor                         2nd   Stellar Hawk
     3rd  Groovy Green
     Owner:   Live Oak Plantation
     Trainer: Kelly Patrick J
     Jockey:  Samyn J L
```

| 0620 | BEL05 | 8.50T | FRM | 3UM | 25,500 | 114 | 03 | 05 | 6 3/4 | 0 | 1:41.2 | | 12 |

```
     1st  Peter And                            2nd   Secretary Brady
     3rd  Alytonka
```

| 0605 | BEL10 | 8.50T | GD | 3UM | 25,500 | 114 | 05 | 05 | 13 | 0 | 1:44.0 | | 10 |

```
     1st  Jodi's the Best                      2nd   Nobiz Like Showbiz
     3rd  Luciano P.
```

```
0521 BEL05  7.00  FST  3UM     23,500 122 03 06 24          0 1:24.0        07
     1st  Carsey's Pal                 2nd  Western Forte
     3rd  Private Plan
0509 BEL03  6.00  FST  03M     23,500 122 02 09 15 1/4       0 1:10.2        11
     1st  Red River Gorge             2nd  Carsey's Pal
     3rd  Jason Dean
```

Senior Scoot 1990 DK B/ colt, by Buckfinder 74 -- Costly Doll 86
                                         by Key to the Mint 69

Breeder: T. M. Evans

(SPR=89)

1993 in USA and Canada:

date	trk race#	dist furl	trk con	race type	value of race	wt	pp	fp	lngths	earned	wnrs time	claim price	# rn
0521	DEL05	6.00	FST	03AL	8,300	116	01	01	1	4,980	1:12.3		05

1st Senior Scoot   2nd Unseated
3rd Vegas Hustle
Owner: Mudge Edmund T IV
Trainer: Bernier Louis D Jr
Jockey: Rocco J

0429	PIM06	6.00	FST	03AL	16,800	117	02	05	7 3/4	495	1:11.0		07

1st Punch Line   2nd Ask Questions
3rd Trump Mahal

0412	PIM07	8.50	GD	03AL	19,100	114	05	03	3 1/4	2,035	1:46.3		08

1st Glide Home   2nd Fleeting Symmetry
3rd Senior Scoot

0330	PIM07	8.50	GD	03AL	18,500	114	04	03	5 3/4	2,035	1:47.0		08

1st Snooky's Taylor   2nd Fleeting Symmetry
3rd Senior Scoot

0318	LRL07	7.00	FST	03M	15,800	120	06	01	3 1/2	8,835	1:26.2		07

1st Senior Scoot   2nd Laughteristhekey
3rd Rocky Prospector

0306	LRL07	6.00	FST	03M	16,400	120	08	02	4 1/2	3,255	1:10.2		09

1st Mighty Game   2nd Senior Scoot
3rd Super Memory

0220	LRL07	7.00	FST	03M	16,100	120	01	03	1 3/4	1,705	1:26.0		08

1st Woodliketobe   2nd Laughteristhekey
3rd Senior Scoot

0202	LRL05	6.00	FST	03MCL	12,300	120	03	02	3/4	2,415	1:13.0	25,000	10

1st Midlantic   2nd Senior Scoot
3rd Belinter

Start a Fight 1989 CH colt, by Fight Over 81 —— Raise a Belle 71
                                            by Raise a Native 61

Breeder: Hobeau Farm

(SPR=84)

1993 in USA and Canada:

date	trk race#	dist furl	trk con	race type	value of race	wt	pp	fp	lngths	earned	wnrs time	claim price	# rn
0625	BEL05	6.00	FST	4UCL	19,500	113	04	07	14 1/2	0	1:11.1	30,000	08

1st I'll Take a Stand   2nd Red Hot Red
3rd Quickest Blade
Owner: J M Dee Stable
Trainer: Odintz Jeff
Jockey: Toscano P R

date	trk race#	dist furl	trk con	race type	value of race	wt	pp	fp	lngths	earned	wnrs time	claim price	# rn
0501	AQU02	7.00	FST	4UCL	17,500	115	02	07	10 1/4	0	1:24.4	22,500	07

1st Lord Cardinal   2nd Alex's Candy
3rd Two Wise

| 0410 | AQU02 | 6.00 | FST | 4UCL | 17,500 | 115 | 02 | 03 | 3 1/4 | 2,100 | 1:10.1 | 22,500 | 06 |

1st Two Eagles   2nd Top the Record
3rd Start a Fight

| 0224 | AQU07 | 6.00 | FST | 4UCL | 18,000 | 112 | 06 | 03 | 7 3/4 | 2,160 | 1:11.0 | 25,000 | 08 |

1st Exploding Rainbow   2nd Midnight Sunny
3rd Start a Fight

| 0113 | AQU04 | 6.00 | SY | 4UCL | 18,000 | 112 | 05 | 04 | 2 1/2 | 1,080 | 1:11.3 | 25,000 | 08 |

1st I've Got Mine   2nd Pay Me Today
3rd Mashriq

| 0106 | AQU04 | 6.00 | GD | 4UCL | 20,000 | 106 | 07 | 03 | 1 3/4 | 2,400 | 1:10.2 | 30,000 | 07 |

1st Roscommon Proud   2nd Golden Cloud
3rd Start a Fight

1992 in USA and Canada:

date	trk race#	dist furl	trk con	race type	value of race	wt	pp	fp	lngths	earned	wnrs time	claim price	# rn
1218	AQU03	6.00	MUD	03CL	18,000	117	10	02	1 3/4	3,960	1:11.3	25,000	11

1st Easy Going A. J.   2nd Start a Fight
3rd Otto Beit

| 1213 | AQU03 | 6.00 | SY | 03CL | 20,000 | 117 | 05 | 05 | 7 1/4 | 0 | 1:12.4 | 35,000 | 06 |

1st Sunshine Magic   2nd Jingle Ice
3rd Mashriq

| 1116 | AQU02 | 7.00 | FST | 03CL | 22,000 | 113 | 01 | 08 | 24 1/2 | 0 | 1:22.4 | 45,000 | 08 |

1st Norphlet   2nd Cool Quaker
3rd Eastern Brave

| 1106 | AQU01 | 6.00 | MUD | 3UAL | 28,000 | 115 | 04 | 02 | 3 1/2 | 6,160 | 1:10.0 | | 05 |

1st Preporant   2nd Start a Fight
3rd Carried Interest

Fifth Business 1989 CH colt, by Majestic Light 73 —— Shushin 80, by Wajima 72

Breeder: William B. Sturgill

(SPR=79)

1993 in USA and Canada:

date	trk race#	dist furl	trk con	race type	value of race	wt	pp	fp	lngths	earned	wnrs time	claim price	# rn
0616	BEL06	8.50	FST	4UCL	16,500	117	02	07	25	0	1:43.4	17,500	07

1st Red Scamper   2nd   Sailing On Aprayer
3rd Diamond Anchor
Owner: Sommer Viola
Trainer: Martin Frank
Jockey: Davis R G

| 0523 | BEL01 | 7.00 | FST | 4UCL | 19,500 | 117 | 02 | 06 | 18 1/2 | 0 | 1:23.3 | 35,000 | 07 |

1st Two Eagles   2nd   Carr's Pleasure
3rd Ocean Splash

| 0505 | BEL01 | 8.00 | FST | 3UAL | 30,500 | 119 | 03 | 05 | 11 | 0 | 1:33.4 | | 05 |

1st Colonial Affair   2nd   Hannibal Lecter
3rd Grampa Jack

1992 in USA and Canada:

date	trk race#	dist furl	trk con	race type	value of race	wt	pp	fp	lngths	earned	wnrs time	claim price	# rn
0828	SAR01	9.00	FST	03CL	22,000	117	05	03	3 1/4	2,640	1:50.3	35,000	07

1st Sparkling Sky   2nd   Home Base
3rd Fifth Business

| 0814 | MTH08 | 8.50 | MUD | 03CL | 15,000 | 115 | 01 | 03 | 3 1/4 | 1,800 | 1:45.1 | 40,000 | 07 |

1st Wild Dante   2nd   Lord Wollaston
3rd Fifth Business

| 0802 | MTH05 | 8.50T | GD | 03STK | 40,000 | 115 | 05 | 07 | 15 3/4 | 400 | 1:43.4 | | 09 |

    RESTORATION S.-O (40,000A)
1st Bidding Proud   2nd   Cobblestone Road
3rd Coax Stardust

| 0712 | MTH07 | 8.00T | FRM | 3UAL | 18,000 | 112 | 05 | 08 | 9 1/2 | 180 | 1:36.1 | | 08 |

1st Bondi   2nd   Super Modest
3rd Freight Bill

| 0616 | CD 08 | 8.50 | FST | 03AL | 31,620 | 115 | 02 | 05 | 10 3/4 | 0 | 1:44.2 | | 06 |

1st Hold Old Blue   2nd   Eastern Affair
3rd Hold the Truth

| 0530 | CD 09 | 9.00T | YLD | 03STK | 55,300 | 112 | 06 | 04 | 6 | 2,765 | 1:49.4 | | 07 |

    JEFFERSON CUP S.-L (50,000A)
1st Senor Tomas   2nd   Coaxing Matt
3rd Black Question

| 0517 | CD 09 | 8.50T | FRM | 03AL | 31,350 | 115 | 04 | 04 | 3 1/4 | 1,973 | 1:42.3 | | 08 |

1st Apart   2nd   Senor Tomas
3rd Late Surge (IRE)

Toy Won 1990 DK B/ filly, by Air Forbes Won 79 -- Toy Gun 84, by Hagley 67

Breeder: Lambholm & Roy S. Lerman

(SPR=75)

1993 in USA and Canada:

date	trk race#	dist furl	trk con	race type	value of race	wt	pp	fp	lngths	earned	wnrs time	claim price	# rn
0504	PHA08	6.00	FST	F3UAL	18,725	113	04	06	11 3/4	0	1:11.3		06

1st   Finish On Top   2nd   Landomakebeaulieve
3rd   Ri's Rondezvous
Owner: Dommel Robert W
Trainer: Rowan Steve E
Jockey: Colton R E

date	trk race#	dist furl	trk con	race type	value of race	wt	pp	fp	lngths	earned	wnrs time	claim price	# rn
0403	PHA10	6.00	MUD	FO3STK	27,400	122	03	06	15		0	1:12.2		06

CROCUS S.-O (25,000A)
1st Wild Lady A.   2nd   Shananie's Dancer
3rd   Sharp Reef

| 0318 | GS 08 | 6.00 | GD | F3UAL | 14,000 | 112 | 02 | 06 | 15 1/2 | 140 | 1:11.3 | | 06 |

1st Practical Susan   2nd   Finish On Top
3rd   Flowerforalexandra

1992 in USA and Canada:

date	trk race#	dist furl	trk con	race type	value of race	wt	pp	fp	lngths	earned	wnrs time	claim price	# rn
1115	PEN09	6.00	FST	FO2STK	49,825	119	05	01	10	29,895	1:11.3		10

BLUE MOUNTAIN FUTURITY-OR (35,000A)
1st Toy Won   2nd Carnival Caper
3rd Nofa's Polish Star

| 1022 | AQU08 | 7.00 | FST | FO2STK | 113,200 | 119 | 02 | 05 | 16 | | 0 | 1:24.4 | | 06 |

ASTARITA S.-G2 (100,000A)
1st Missed the Storm   2nd Dispute
3rd Statuette

| 1003 | BEL08 | 6.00 | FST | FO2STK | 53,700 | 118 | 04 | 03 | 5 | 6,444 | 1:10.4 | | 08 |

PERSONAL ENSIGN S.-L (50,000A)
1st Missed the Storm   2nd Family Enterprize
3rd Toy Won

| 0907 | PHA08 | 6.00 | GD | FO2STK | 26,400 | 118 | 05 | 02 | 1 1/2 | 5,280 | 1:11.2 | | 07 |

CRITICAL MISS S.-O (25,000A)
1st Carnirainbow   2nd Toy Won
3rd Lasque

| 0810 | PHA08 | 5.00 | FST | FO2AL | 17,545 | 119 | 05 | 01 | 6 1/4 | 11,745 | :58.2 | | 08 |

1st Toy Won   2nd Ray's Lindy
3rd Medieval Anne

```
0711 PHA08  5.00T FRM FO2STK     26,400 115 04 05  2 1/2      792 1:00.0        06
        BUDDLEIA S. OR (25,000A)
     1st   Fired Heater                    2nd   Ray's Lindy
     3rd   Vacation Bound
0620 PHA03  5.00  FST FO2M       13,500 118 10 01  5 1/2    8,100  :59.2        10
     1st   Toy Won                         2nd   Medieval Anne
     3rd   Station House
```

These workouts are performed at all types of distances and would suggest to the average player that the horses are razor sharp. The experienced handicapper will throw these horses out and use this to his advantage instead of being suckered in like most bettors. Remember: the public makes the favorite. If we disagree, so be it! The average bettor is not an indepth handicapper, and will bet on what is printed under the horse's name. An experienced bettor will read into that information and do the required research to make it worthwhile.

Working Under a Different Name

CHAPTER 13 Everyone who bets and owns a horse wants his horse to win, but most also seek a big price, where the owner could make a nice score at the windows. For the bigger stables, it is hard to disguise a good horse without hurting his potential when preparing to run. If a trainer was to work a horse very slowly, he would receive a bigger price than if the horse were working bullets, but this method might hinder the horse during training and conditioning.

So how does a trainer try to pull this off without doing any damage?

It is relatively simple: train as you would normally train but under a phony name.

Ben Perkins Jr. and Sr. are very well respected trainers on the East Coast, especially with two year old maidens. There is not much that does not perform well that this team lets loose at first asking. By now, the reader must be scratching his head trying to figure out how in the world he would be able to find out if a horse is working under a phony name. When trainers work their horses under a different name, they usually change only one or two letters to make it seem that it was a mistake by the clockers.

On June 2, *Pagofire*, a Ben Perkins Sr. trainee, was entered and had no posted workouts to her credit. It was obvious that she was working under a different name, and the hardest thing was to find what name and when.

MONMOUTH PARK – Track Fast

Three Furlongs		Four Furlongs						
Amazing Face	:37³ B	Artful Minister	:49 B	Reslleant Kris	:48 H	Screen Trial	1:04¹ B
BlssdFromAbov	:37⁴ B	Big Red Kisses	:52 B	Sinagua	:49 B	Staticelectricity	1:01² H
Code Home	:40 B	Corporate Killer	:49³ B	Wedding Jitters	:49 B	Toy Maker	1:02³ B
Dander Man	:40 B	Cozzene's Wish	:48 B	**Five Furlongs— :56¹**			
Diadora Pine	:37⁴ B	Dew Keeper	:50 B	Barbados	1:04³ B	**Six Furlongs—1:07⁴**	
Firstflagtofly	:37¹ B	Dixie Lite	:47² H	**Burning Chestnut**	:59² H	Billy Romantico	1:16 Bg
Inga's Bo	:37³ B	Halo Fire	:49⁴ B	Concord'sFutur	1:02⁴ B	C.c. Romer	1:14⁴ B
Justinthefastlne	:39¹ B	Island Dash	:49⁴ B	Dixie Brat	1:02³ B	Chief Quick Pay	1:16 Bg
Kerby's Slew	:37² B	**Jeffery Who**)	:47 H	Entroski	1:05² B	**Concorde'sRvng**	1:15 B
Medical Record	:38² B	Jet Above	:48⁴ B	Ever So True	1:02² B	**Concorde's Tune**	1:13³ H
Pleasant Delima	:37³ B	King Kaleia	:52 B	Hai Anxiety	1:04² B	Coupon Kind	1:15² Hg
Sacred Honor	:40 B	Lustily	:49 B	Isoroyal	1:01² H	Little Gold	1:16³ Bg
Seven Layer	:37¹ B	Magic ofVictory	:50⁴ Bg	Juke Box Jackie	1:02 B	Mon Montreaux	1:16¹ B
Shananie Lane	:38² B	Maison de Rev	:49³ B	Karon Smile	1:02 Bg	North Again	1:14² Hg
Such AProspect	:39³ B	Native Times	:49⁴ B	LeGrndPrincess	1:03³ B	Play for Play	1:14² Hg
Sunny Angel	:37³ B	Never SayNever	:49⁴ B	Luramore	1:02³ B	Snow Gently	1:16¹ B
Things to Come	:37⁴ B	Ranch Folly	:47¹ H	Motel Madness	1:02 B	Sociably Johnny	1:15¹ Hg
U.s. Loyalty	:40 B	RecklessDremer	:51⁴ B	Nt'sMgicMomnt	1:01⁴ Hg	Society Billy	1:15 Hg
				PleseDon'tRing	1:02³ Bg	Vrythoughtofyo	1:16¹ Bg

COZZENE'S WISH (4F) was impressive galloping out in 100; BURNING CHESTNUT (5F) was full of run: CONCORDE'S TUNE (6F) was going nicely with jockey J. Bravo in the irons. Additional workouts: 5/13, track fast, MERRI TALES (3F) 36 2/5 B, FROZREN FUNDS (4F) 48 2/5 B, ENTROSKI (5F) 105 2/5 B.

On May 14, *Pagofire*, or *"Halofire"*, as entered for a workout, worked four furlongs in a modest 49⅘ breezing.

MONMOUTH PARK – Track Fast

Three Furlongs							
Avie's Magic	:39² B	Discreet Groom	:52 B	Sunny Angel	:51² B	StalwartPlesure	1:02 Bg
Basques Ad	:36³ B	Dixie Light	:49² Bg	Tell Margie	:50 B	Star Victory	1:04⁴ B
Big Red Kisses	:37³ Bg	Doc N Trope	:49² B	Tricky Six	:50² B	StateStreetDori	1:03² B
Castietta	:38² B	Double Onery	:50² B	Unlimitdpotntil	:49 Bg	Staticelectricity	1:00³ H
Chief Outlaw	:37⁴ Bg	Egar Salute	:49¹ B	ValiantVlentine	:49³ B	**Sunny Cookie**	1:00¹ H
ChristmsVirgini	:37 B	Fight Ain't Over	:48 H	Wedding Jitters	:49 Bg	TinaciousTiffny	1:00² H
Cinnamon Cake	:36 B	Five Star Dance	:50² Bg	Work Sheet	:52 B	Tony Tower	1:05 B
CouldThisBMgc	:39² B	Flowers of Evil	:50 B	**Five Furlongs— :56¹**		Topnotcher	1:05² B
DarnedAlarming	:37 B	Glori Halo	:49³ B	Arborcrest	1:02 B	TropiclGentlmn	1:00³ H
Dehere	:37² B	Graceful Glory	:48 H	Birthday Blues	1:03⁴ B	TurbulantCareer	1:00³ H
Gallant Wolf	:36³ B	Green Martian	:49⁴ B	Booster Club	1:04⁴ B	Ugotnochoice	1:01⁴ Hg
HappytoBeAlive	:37³ B	IKnowYoCnDnc	:51⁴ B	Bright Arrow	1:01⁴ H	Vimandvigor	1:04⁴ B
Holly Bugs	:37⁴ B	Island Dash	:48² Hg	Bye Union Ave	1:01² H	Wild Dante	1:04² B
Honor Princess	:36 B	Jeffery Who	:49¹ B	CapabilityQueen	1:03² B	Yeckly	1:02¹ B
Irish Skater	:37¹ B	Koluctoo's Lori	:49 B	Count NewYork	1:03³ B		
JacquesbeQuick	:36 B	Land At War	:48² H	Coupon Scott	1:06 B	**Six Furlongs—1:07⁴**	
Jersey Gold	:36 Bg	Lori's Passion	:49 Bg	Cup of Cheers	1:02 B	Artful Lodger	1:17 B
King Kalea	:36⁴ Bg	Luciente	:50³ B	Danny Rose	1:03 B	Billy Romantico	1:17 B
		Lustily	:48¹ Hg	Delores MyLove	1:01² B	Chief Quick Ay	1:17 B

MajesticChrism	:38² B	Madura Villa	:49¹ Bg	Entroski	1:02³ B	Coupon Kid	1:17² B
Master Disaster	:36² Bg	Miss Bondi	:48⁴ B	Every So True	1:01³ B	Dance Track	1:20 B
MonyOnMyMnd	:37² B	Miss Speckles	:48⁴ B	Evil Hear	1:02 B	Devasted Glory	1:18 B
Neon's Delight	:35⁴ Bg	Motel Amiss	:49³ B	Felt Blue	1:00⁴ H	Funinthesun	1:15⁴ B
Northern Fir	:39 B	My Protege	:49³ Bg	FiveStarBaggge	1:04³ B	Gail's Falcon	1:14⁴ H
Pickled Road	:36² B	Nt'sMgicMomnt	:51 N	Fling	1:03 B	Hai Anxiety	1:17² B
Royal Passion	:38 B	Night Trap	:48¹ H	For CharitySake	1:04 B	Hotel Madness	1:16 B
Savanna Danna	:36³ B	Onery Castle	:49² B	FortyNineSmils	1:04² B	Jazz Legend	1:15 B
Southern Anna	:35 H	Orvietto	:52 B	Forza Pireti	1:02³ B	Joy of Lite	1:17⁴ B
Sunday Lady	:36¹ H	Parella Fella	:47⁴ Hg	Fran's Folly	1:02³ B	Jukebox Jackie	1:16³ B
Total Kaos	:38² B	Pego Fire	:48³ Bg	FrnksPersusion	1:02⁴ B	Mon Montreaux	1:18 B
Tru Mac	:38³ B	Pixie's Greatest	:48⁴ B	Friends R Us	1:02 B	North Again	1:18³ B
Two Timer	:36⁴ Bg	Political's Half	:48⁴ B	Girvannie	1:02¹ B	Play for Play	1:20 B
Want toBeAlive	:38⁴ B	Premier Jumbo	:51¹ B	Gone Visiting	1:03³ B	PridelssRosmry	1:17 B
WesternSavings	:37⁴ B	Pretty Mama	:49¹ B	Here's John	1:07 B	Six Ways	1:14³ B
Four Furlongs		Prosque Isle	:52 B	JailHouseLwyer	1:03 B	Snow Gently	1:18 B
Acary	:51² B	Quick Kayo	:49³ Bg	Lura More	1:01² B	Sunny Sidekick	1:16² B
Afternoon Star	:49¹ Bg	Red Square	:51³ B	Mangeta Mark	1:03³ B	Sure Gone	1:17² B
Amazing Face	:51² B	Resilient Kris	:50³ B	My Treasure	1:01³ B	Sweet Beast	1:17² B
Arieas	:48³ H	Rocky Marshu	:50³ B	Normandy Belle	1:02 Bg	These Dreams	1:18³ B
Arion's Wish	:51¹ B	Ruffner	:51 B	Overheated	1:05² B	Touch of Love	1:15² B
Babe's Honor	:50³ B	Rule Breaker	:50 B	Peb	1:01⁴ H	Twilightslstglm	1:16 B
Beno's JodyTwo	:50² B	Ruth's Revenge	:52 B	Proud Pete	1:05⁴ B	VrythoughtofYo	1:16³ B
Butter Cream	:48⁴ B	Sacred Honor	:48² Hg	Proud Plebian	1:03³ B		
Callmemrtibbs	:49 B	Sender Spender	:48 H	Ready Alarm	1:06 B	**Seven Furlongs**	
Caro Lure	:48⁴ B	Shiela'sRevenge	:48⁴ B	Relay Action	1:01³ Hg		
Coxie Home	:48² Hg	Shouldn'tSyNvr	:48¹ H	Seurot	1:03¹ B	Bankok Star	1:32 B
Crafty Afel	:48⁴ B	Sinagua	:51 B	Sharp Tracy	1:03 B	Basket Leave	1:29³ B
Crazy and Wild	:48⁴ B	Sisiman Cove	:48² Hg	Sir Angel	1:02⁴ B	LieutenntDunbr	1:30 B
Cryjinsky!	:54 B	Sizeable Perk	:49 B	Sky Box	1:04 Bg	Randomly	1:30 B
Daisho	:51² B	Spanish Kiss	:50¹ B	Society Billy	1:06 B	Red Ritual	1:32 B
Dew Keeper	:50¹ B	Special Illusion	:52¹ B	Sound Design	1:03³ B	Tasteful T. V.	1:28 H

FIGHT AIN'T OVER and GRACEFUL GLORY (4F) worked nicely in company. PARELLA FELLA (4F) was full of run from the gate. SUNNY COOKIE (5F) was impressive. TINACIOUS TIFFANY (5F) galloped out in 1:14. GAIL'S FALCON (5F) finished strong.

Eight days later, she also worked four furlongs, but this time as *"Pegofire"*. *"Pegofire"* or *Pagofire* breezed in 48³/₅ from the gate, the fastest breezing workout either from the gate or not. The workout might seem okay on paper, but no one came close when coming out of the gate.

MONMOUTH PARK – Track Fast

Three Furlongs							
Battleship Cove	:38² B	Ashley's Boy	:50 B	Pickled Road	:49² B	My Lady Lynn	1:01² B
Captain C.	:37 B	Back Nine	:51 B	Political Half	:54 B	Patriot Dancer	1:05 B
Danazatiz	:38² Bg	BadabingBdbng	:48⁴ B	PremirCommnd	:48¹ B	Pego Fire	1:02 Bg
Five Star Dance	:39³ B	Bonnie Kate	:51 B	Royal Josh	:52³ B	Reckless Place	1:05 B
For CharitySake	:36² B	Bound for Dixie	:49¹ Bg	Royal YardStick	:52 B	Shouldn'tSyNvr	1:03 Bg
JustBetwnFrind	:38² B	Charblade	:51 B	Sabin Major	:49² Bg	Sinague	1:03³ Bg
Keys Idle	:37 B	Code Home	:50 Bg	Sajakal	:48³ H	Slip MetheWord	1:02³ Bg
Koluctoo's Lori	:36 B	Copelan'sCharm	:50 Bg	SantIsMySister	:48² B	Solo Kris	1:05¹ B
La La Honey	:36³ B	Deputy Jam	:53 Bg	Savannah Style	:51² B	Super Nip	1:01² H
Living On Credit	:35³ B	Ever So True	:47³ Hg	Seven Layers	:48⁴ H	Tasteful T. V.	1:01¹ H
Madura Villa	:36⁴ B	Favorable Tab	:50² Bg	So Long Waj	:49⁴ B	Tenacious Tiffany	1:00³ H
Me and theBoys	:36² B	Firstflagtofly	:49 B	Sterling Royalty	:50 B	Terry's Manner	1:05 B
Miss Con Court	:37¹ Bg	Gallant Warfare	:49¹ Bg	Such AProspect	:52 B	Tom Fitz	1:07 B
Mr. Rodi	:35⁴ Bg	HappytoBeAlive	:49² B	Sweet Bobby B.	:52 B	**Six Furlongs—1:07⁴**	
		Here's John	:50 B	Three Timer	:49 Bg	Afleets Gold	1:16 B

Nine Loves	:38² B	Island Dash	:49⁴ Bg	Toro Weed	:49 Bg	Billy Romantico	1:15 B
No Gold	:39³ Bg	Karama Tales	:51² B	U. S. Loyalty	:50² B	Bold Con	1:16² B
Silver Willow	:37² B	Keratold	:51² B	Ugotnochoice	:50¹ Bg	Coupon Scott	1:17 B
Spanish Edition	:37¹ B	Key theNursury	:49⁴ Bg	Wedding Jitters	:49 Bg	FamilyEnterprise	1:12 H
Sunday Lady	:38³ B	King Kalea	:52 Bg	**Five Furlongs**	:56¹	Felt Blue	1:17 B
Sunny Cookie	:36² B	King WorldLady	:51³ B	BellaVistaRoma	1:06 Bg	Lil Gold	1:18 B
Texas Music	:38 B	Long Clover	:49 B	Belle's Rider	1:03² B	MjesticMoment	1:17 B
Timeforathrill	:37¹ B	Lustlly	:49¹ Bg	CapabilityGreen	1:02 B	Nat's My Love	1:15² B
Timely Warning	:35⁴ B	MoneyofthMind	:51 Bg	Dusty Screen	1:01² H	PrestigousDncr	1:16 B
WhimsiclMlody	:36³ B	Mr. Frizz	:47⁴ H	Friends R. Us	1:02³ Bg	RuannRuannDn	1:14 H
WolfPackLeder	:36² B	Mylo	:49⁴ B	Good for Poppy	1:01¹ Hg	Touch of Love	1:14⁴ B
Four Furlongs		Neon's Delight	:49¹ Bg	Major Way	1:03³ B	**Seven Furlongs**	
Abduct	:50 B	North Again	:49² B	Merri Tales	1:02 B	Bye Union Ave.	1:29² B
Another Appeal	:50² B	Onery Josh	:49⁴ B	Michael's Angel	1:03 B	Danny Rose	1:30 B

TIMELY WARNING (3F) was going easy: **SANTA IS MY SISTER (4F)** galloped out in 101: **TENACIOUS TIFFANY (5F)** turned in a nice effort with jockey N. Santagata up; **FAMILY ENTERPRISE (6F)** was full of run. Fractions: 22 3/5, 34 3/5, 46, 59 and galloped out in 128 4/5. Additional workouts: 5/22 **THREE TIMER (3F)** Fst 36 4/5 BG; **CAPABILITY GREEN (5F)** Fst 103 2/5 B.

On May 28, also under the name of *"Pegofire,"* Perkins worked this two-year-old filly at five furlongs in an easy 102 breezing from the gate. Another work that could not be touched by any one coming out of the gate.

June 3's paper, which is available on June 2, displayed all of *Pagofire's* workouts.

MONMOUTH PARK – Track Sloppy

Three Furlongs		National Kid	:37 B	Wave Form	:39 B	Get Long Gold	1:04² Bg
CndlelightDinnr	:37 B	Pappa Way	:36³ B	**Four Furlongs**		Thrilla inManilla	1:02³ Bg
Dinner Affair	:37² B	Quick Courage	:36³ B	Call Me Guy B.	:51² B	Viola D.	1:04 B
Easy Buck	:37² B	Slady Roberto	:35⁴ B	Kirby Slew	:54 B		
Esmerldo'sGem	:37² B	Timber Ghost	:35 B	Lost Another	:51 B	**Six Furlongs**—1:07⁴	
Front Line	:35⁴ B	TowerofWisdom	:39 B	Lucky She'sMine	:49¹ Bg		
Lynn'sNotebook	:37 B	Via Search	:38⁴ B	**Five Furlongs**—	:56¹	All the Honor	1:16 B

Additional workouts: May 14, track fast, **PAGOFIRE (4f)** :49 4/5 b. May 22, track fast, **EXPERT PLAY (4f)** :47 4/5 hg and **PAGOFIRE (4f)** :48 3/5 b. May 28, track fast, **PAGOFIRE (5f)** 1:02 b. May 29, track fast, **EXPERT PLAY (5f)** 1:02 4/5 b. May 31, track fast, **DEFENIE POLICY–IR (3f)** :36 b. May 31, track fast, **SHAKE AND SHIVER (3f)** :38 1/5 b, **SLIM PAS SUEL (3f)** :37 b, **TSNAMI SPANGLER (3f)** :35 hg and **BARBADES (6f)** 1:30 b.

One might be wondering why a trainer would go through all of this trouble if the information is going to be available anyway. There are many reasons. First, if anyone follows workouts, he would see if these horses received blacktype comments. Also, the point is that 90 percent of all handicappers are content with the fact that the horse did not work out. They think that, if there are no workouts printed, then the horse must never have worked out. The announcer will tell the handicapper these workouts over the public address system, but at this point, how would one be able to handicap and look these workouts up? Finally, one would have to buy the next day's *Daily Racing Form* to find these additional workouts, and most handicappers do not buy this until the end of the day.

It did not matter too much, as *Pagofire's* greatness was noticed by the whole backstretch. She won by 11½ lengths and paid $4.80.

Peb is a three-year-old filly who has raced four times before making her Monmouth debut. *Peb* had been currently running in maiden special weight company at Garden State and Philadelphia Park. This class level was too high for *Peb* at Monmouth Park and she was dropped into the claiming ranks. *Peb* has been working under her name during all of his training, except one particular day on June 2. On this day, John Tammaro III decided to blow out *Peb* at three furlongs, but apparently used the name "*Jeb*". *Peb* or "*Jeb*" received blacktype for this blowout of 34³/₅, and the comment was listed under "*Jeb*". This would only be picked up by astute workout experts.

MONMOUTH PARK - Track Fast

Three Furlongs		Timer	:36² Bg	Northern Fir	:49 B	Dia Jora Pine	1:03³ B
Amarillo Slim	:4 Bg	Jolie	:35² B	Oncetherewswy	:49³ B	Fancy Teddy	1:03³ B
Ann's Angel	73 B	J. Kind	:37² B	Onery Josh	:49⁴ Bg	Frog Proof	1:03³ B
Bad Gerty	72 B	What's It'sFace	:35¹ B	Orestes	:48¹ H	High Decline	1:03 Bg
Basques Ad	5 B	Whstlngjcksmth	:36² B	Prospect Girl	:50¹ Bg	Holy Jill	1:02 B
Classic Ridge	:0 B	Yankee Express	:37 B	Regal Dawn	:49 B	Blooming cndnc	1:04⁴ B
Clever Rick	:52 H	**Four Furlongs**		Safe Shelter	:47³ B	Ingroove	1:01¹ Bg
Dancing forGold	:37 B	A Shaky Queen	:49² B	Savanna Danna	:49⁴ Bg	Mr. Minor	1:01 Hg
Daner Man	374 Bg	Ack Classy	:52 B	Siesta Sun	:50³ B	Onery Castle	1:01⁴ H
Danzig'sReward	372 B	Avie's Fancy	:52 B	Slew's Gold	:49 B	RoundingProof	1:06 B
Felt Blue	:36 B	Baby Pro	:50¹ Bg	Snomite	:50 B	Royal Ninja	1:03³ B
Fishy Business	:37² B	Benny theBlade	:48¹ B	Sweet Trick	:50 B	Screen Trial	1:00 B
Get the Rope	:26 B	Blue Dan You	:49⁴ Bg	Swinging Sis	:50 Bg	Sixteen to Come	1:05² B
Go Paradise	:38 Bg	Classic Guy	:51 B	TenaciousTiffny	:48 B	Syl	1:02² Bg
Jeb	:34³ H	Clean Wager	:50 B	These Dreams	:49⁴ B	ings to Come	1:03³ B
Jet Above	:39 B	Couldthisbmgic	:52 B	Tru Mac		**Six Furlongs—1:07**	
Lure'sChampion	:37 B	Crafty Belle	:49 B	Twenty Twenty		Andover Ally	1:17² Bg
Mango Man	:36³ B	Dance Track	:52² Bg	Ultimate Warrior	:50² B	Bloomn'goodTrl	1:16² B
Meadow Flight	:374 B	Elegant Lilly	:53 B	VigorousPrincss	:49 B	Bye Bye Brazil	1:17 Bg
MomentofGlory	:38² Bg	EuropeanWomn	:50² B	WaitingtoDance	:52 B	Concorde'sFinale	1:13³ H
Mundo Latino	:364 Bg	Great Gilly	:50³ B	Wild Zone	:49² B	Fleet Hoof	1:16¹ Bg
Parcial Day	:36¹ B	HappytoBeAlive	:49² Bg	Wilma Will	:53 B	Fling	1:14² H
Polarette	:37¹ B	I'm Wild	:49 B	**Five Furlongs**	:50¹	Tender Heart	1:14³ H
Roman Splasher	:38² Bg	Magick Top	:49⁴ B	Aspiring Proof	1:04³ B	ValiantVlentine	1:15 B
Royal Rue	:37¹ B	MamselleBbette	:51 B	Awfully Aloof	1:02 B	**Seven Furlongs**	
Sacred Honor	:36² Bg	MomntofSpring	:49⁴ B	BlssdFromAbov	1:03³ B	Brava Gianni	1:34 B
Scully's Secret	:38¹ B	Mr. Fitness	:51² Bg	BloomingBusnss	1:03¹ B	Seminar	1:34 B
Sioux Sweet	:37³ B	Nine Loves	:50¹ B	Cpote'sPrincess	1:02² B	Smart Time	1:27² H
Sister's Image	:38² Bg	Nine Plus	:50 B	Devilish Boy	1:02 B		

JEB (3F) was full of run. SAFE SHELTER (4F) was impressive. WOODS OF WINDSOR (4F) worked nicely on the turf. TENACIOUS TIFFANY (4F) galloped out in 101. CONCORDE'S FINALE (6F) turned in a nice effort. TENDER HEART (6F) is being kept on edge. Additional workouts: A SHAKY QUEEN 5/30 Mth (4F) Fst 49 2/5 B.

On June 4, just two days later, *Peb* was entered in a maiden claiming event with a tag of $25,000. This class level was still high, and the blowout obviously took too much out of *Peb*. She finished fifth.

Peb then came back on June 29 to gallop to a nine-length victory in the maiden claiming $10,000 ranks.

MONMOUTH PARK June 29, 1993

race #	dist fur.	trk con	race type	value of race	wnrs time	runners
3	6.00	FST	F3UMCL	$6,500	1:13.03	6

horse name	fp	lngths	wt	pp	earned	odds	claim	most recent trk/race #
Peb	1	9	106	6	$3,900	1.00	$10,500	062993MTH03
Exuberant —— Mrs. Bridges by Bold Effort								
Owner : BANTIVOGLIO ROBERT T								
Trainer: TAMMARO JOHN J III								
Jockey : HOMEISTER R B JR								
Dandy Denda	2	9	122	2	$1,300	2.20	$12,500	062993MTH03
Owner : FLATS N TROTS STABLE								
Trainer: QUARTAROLO ANTHONY T								
Jockey : WILSON R								
Miss Tarbec	3	9 3/4	113	3	$780	17.70	$10,500	062993MTH03
Owner : MER STABLE								
Trainer: RISPOLI JOSEPH N								
Jockey : GOBERDHAN C P								
Arabess	4	11	110	1	$390	11.80	$12,500	062993MTH03
Owner : STUDLEY NANCY & R								
Trainer: PREGMAN JOHN S JR								
Jockey : RUSSELL W B								
Lauren's Bird	5	12 1/2	113	5	$65	15.20	$10,500	062993MTH03
Owner : ALMOST IVY STABLE								
Trainer: CARROLL HENRY L								
Jockey : SANTAGATA N								
Big Ann Taylor	6	15 1/2	115	4	$65	3.60	$12,500	062993MTH03
Owner : LEVINE ROBERT L								
Trainer: LEVINE ROBERT L								
Jockey : BRAVO J								

Even though these examples paid low prices, they definitely point the way toward finding high payoffs. The first tipoff is when a horse has no workouts. The horse must have at least one workout, or he could not start. Having this knowledge the next time one handicaps a maiden race, before he throws out the horse with no workouts, he should look him up and see if he worked out under a different name. Remember, if the name is not exactly correct, the computer will not pick it up and it will think it is another horse.

Another factor to consider when evaluating first starters is their workout background. Some trainers have farms near race tracks. They work their maidens hard at the farm and then bring them to the track and give them an easy breezing workout with a time that does not stick out. Go figure.

Noel Hickey, for example, is an outstanding breeder-owner-trainer whose winning percentage is impressive at Arlington Race Track near Chicago. His farm is only a few miles from Arlington. On occasion, Hickey has been known to bring in a two year old and show only one modest workout at the track.

On August 23, 1993, for example, Hickey entered a first time starter in a maiden race, a two-year-old filly named *Red Hot Babe*. The *Babe* showed one workout—4f breezing in a moderate 50.52. He won by more than four lengths at eight to one.

$2 QUINELLA; $2 PERFECTA; $2 TRIFECTA WAGERING; 1ST HALF OF LATE DAILY DOUBLE

9TH **RACE** — *THE ARLINGTON-WASHINGTON LASSIE (Grade II)* Purse $150,000 Guaranteed

1 MILE

WIN	PLACE	SHOW

STAKES

FOR FILLIES, TWO-YEARS-OLD. (FOALS OF 1991) By subscription of $100.00 each horse (Early Bird), Friday, February 19, 1993, or $700.00 each horse (Final Nomination) on Saturday, August 7, 1993 (which also nominates you to the Palatine Breeders' Cup Stakes). Fee to accompany the nomination. Supplementary nominations of $10,000 may be made by Thursday, September 16, 1993, which includes entry and starting fee. Original nominations to pay $1,000 to pass the entry box and $1,000 additional to start, with $150,000 Guaranteed of which $90,000 to the winner; $30,000 to second; $16,500 to third; $9,000 to fourth and $4,500 to fifth. Weight: 119 lbs. This event will be limited to fourteen starters, with as many as six also eligibles. Preference will be to winners of Graded/Grouped Stakes (in order I-II-III), next preference: Highest lifetime earnings. Failure to draw into the race at scratch time cancels all fees. Trophy to the owner of the winner. Early Bird Nominations Closed February 19, 1993, with 140 nominations. Final Nominations Closed Saturday, August 7, 1993, with 19 nominations. Supplementary Nominations of $10,000 each were made for 2 horses.

ONE MILE

Track Record: Dr. Fager (4), 134 lbs; 1:32-1/5 (08-24-68)	Fastest Time In 1993: Count the Time (4), 119 lbs; 1:33.99 (08-26-93)

Pgm	Owner	Weight	Trainer

1	P.P. 8 Gina's Stables, Inc. (Virginia Singletary)		Donnie K. Von Hemel(132 15-17-23)
4-1▲	BLUE, gold 'G' and diamond frame, blue stripes on gold sleeves, blue cap		

Don Pettinger **ALYSTONE** 119
Gr.f.91, Turkoman-Tumstone by Best Turn
Jockey Stats (233 34-23-24)

| | | | | | | | | | | | 1993 | 2 | 1 | 1 | 0 | $14,600 | Turf | 0 | 0 | 0 | 0 | $0 |
| | | | | | | | | | | | 1992 | 0 | 0 | 0 | 0 | $0 | Off Track | 1 | 1 | 0 | 0 | $11,100 |

15Aug93 1AP sy 2 ⒻMsw20350 1 48.21 1:15.04 1:43.43 2/6 6 43½ 43½ 3nk 1hd Pettinger,DR 118 *.60 Alystone hd Burrows 1½ MyBelleChantel 19 Wide turn, drivi.
28Jul93 1AP ft 2 ⒻMsw19250 5½f 22.24 46.33 1:07.22 3/6 6 45½ 45½ 2² 2ns Pettinger,DR 118 4.00 Dynatane ns Alystone 6 Rasputin 6¼

Workouts: Sep.5 AP 7f ft 1:27.42 h   Sep.1 AP 4f m :51.04 b   Aug.25 AP 4f ft :49.43 b   Bred in Kentucky by R. & P. Tackett & C. Robertson

1a	P.P. 9 Thunderhead Farms (Bill & Margie Peters)		Donnie K. Von Hemel(132 15-17-23)
4-1▲	BLUE, blue 'P' on white diamond, white diamond braces, white diamond stripe on sleeves, blue cap		

Robert Lester **MARIAH'S STORM** ¹119
B.f.91, Rahy-Immense by Roberto
Jockey Stats (2 0-1-1)

| | | | | | | | | | | | 1993 | 2 | 1 | 1 | 0 | $14,910 | Turf | 0 | 0 | 0 | 0 | $0 |
| | | | | | | | | | | | 1992 | 0 | 0 | 0 | 0 | $0 | Off Track | 1 | 1 | 0 | 0 | $4,320 |

22Aug93 8AP ft 2 ⒻStk50000 6f 21.95 45.13 1:12.07 6/11 4 6⁴ 48½ 35½ 2½ Lester,RN 115 7.30 TraceysRock½ Mariah'sStorm2½ BayouPlans¾ Steady advance
01Jul93 3AKS sl 2 ⒻMsw8800 5½f 22.80 47.60 1:07.00 3/8 4 1hd 1¹ 1⁴ 1¹³ Lester,RN 120 2.80 Mariah'sStorm 13 ErnaMabel½ Backtolife 3 In hand, easily

Workouts: Sep.11 AP 5f ft 1:03.04 b   Sep.5 AP 7f ft 1:27.38 h   Sep.1 AP 4f m :52.27 b   Bred in Kentucky by Crescent Farm

2
15-1▲
K.C.Murray

P.P. 1 Queens Meadow (Sue Thomas)

WHITE, purple 'ST', purple stripes on sleeves, purple cap

Shawn Thomas(0 0-0-0)

KAUIA QUEEN   119
B.f.91, Gate Dancer-Toohappylorwords by Torsion

Jockey Stats
(1 0-0-0)

				1993	2	2	0	0	$7,320	Turf 0 0 0 0 $0
				1992	0	0	0	0	$0	Off Track 1 1 0 0 $3,000

03Sep939WDSgd 2   Alw5000   6f   22.20   46.20 1:13.00   9/9   1   4$1\frac{1}{2}$ 2^{hd} $1\frac{1}{2}$ 13$\frac{1}{2}$ Murray,KC   115   *1.20 KauiaQueen$^3\frac{1}{2}$ ExclusiveEnergy^{hd} WinterWheat$^6\frac{1}{2}$ Drew off, driving

17Jun93 5AKSft 2   [F] Msw8300   5f   22.60   47.40 1:00.80   5/10   10   9$9\frac{3}{4}$ 8^8 4^2 1^4 Valovich,CJ   118   9.20 KauiaQueen^4 MaximumEffort^1 MsAgrevation^{nk} Circld field, ridd out

Bred in Florida by Sue Thomas

3
10-1▲
Shane
Sellers

P.P. 3 Louis J. Roussel, Jr (lessee)

BLACK, gold cat, gold stars on sleeves, red cap

Robert Kelly(0 0-0-0)

MINORITY DATER   119
B.f.91, Kris S-Guadery by Golden Act

Jockey Stats
(558 105-99-82)

				1993	2	1	0	0	$13,377	Turf 0 0 0 0 $0
				1992	0	0	0	0	$0	Off Track 0 0 0 0 $0

22Aug93 8APft 2   [F]Stk50000   6f   21.95   45.13 1:12.07   2/11   11   11$8\frac{1}{2}$ 10^{22} 6^9 4$3\frac{1}{2}$ Guidry,M   115   7.00 TraceysRock^2 Mariah'sStorm$^2\frac{1}{2}$ BayouPlans$^3\frac{1}{2}$ Late rally, 5 wide

27May93 3APft 2   [F]Msw18700   4$\frac{1}{2}$f   23.17   47.39   53.68   4/7   7   6$4\frac{1}{4}$ 3$1\frac{1}{2}$ 1$1\frac{1}{2}$ Guidry,M   117   4.50 MinorityDater$^1\frac{1}{4}$ Candleberry$^1\frac{1}{2}$ Rene'sPride$^2\frac{1}{4}$ 6 wide, just missed

Workouts: Sep.16 AP 3f m :36.08 b(d)   Sep.8 AP 7f ft 1:28.02 h   Sep.1 AP 3f m :36.16 b   Bred in Kentucky by Jaime S. Carrion

---

4
12-1▲
Wigberto
Ramos

P.P. 4 Jim Tafel

ROYAL BLUE & GOLD diagonal quarters,blue bars on gold sleeves,royal blue & gold cap

(Tobin Doyle) Carl A. Nafzger(129 11-16-19)

LADY TORI (L*)   119
Dk.B./Br.f.91, Fappiano-Deviltante by Devil's Bag

Jockey Stats
(615 103-89-78)

				1993	3	1	0	0	$13,139	Turf 0 0 0 0 $0
				1992	0	0	0	0	$0	Off Track 0 0 0 0 $0

22Aug93 8APft 2   [F]Stk50000   6f   21.95   45.13 1:12.07   11/11   8   10$5\frac{1}{4}$ 7^{11} 5$9\frac{1}{2}$ 5$6\frac{1}{2}$ Ramos,W   115   20.50 TraceysRock^2 Mariah'sStorm$^2\frac{1}{2}$ BayouPlans$^3\frac{1}{4}$ Mild rally

05Aug93 7APft 2   [F]Msw19250   5$\frac{1}{2}$f   22.06   46.67 1:07.58   6/9   4   4$5\frac{1}{2}$ 5^6 2^1 1$\frac{1}{2}$ Ramos,W   118   3.30 LadyTori$^\frac{1}{2}$ SlewKittySlew^{nk} SweetMia$^\frac{1}{4}$ Angled out, gamely

22Jul93 4APft 2   [F]Msw19250   6f   23.20   47.35 1:06.08   6/11   5   6$3\frac{1}{4}$ 6$4\frac{1}{4}$ 6$4\frac{1}{2}$ 4$5\frac{1}{4}$ Ramos,W   118   9.10 ClarySage^4 ChattaCode$^2\frac{1}{2}$ Pointofcontention$^1\frac{1}{2}$ 5 wide stretch

Workouts: Sep.14 AP 5f sy 1:02.99 b   Sep.4 AP 4f ft :48.57 b   Sep.1 AP 4f m :49.90 b   Bred in Pennsylvania by Brushwood Stable

---

5
8-1▲
Earlie
Fires

P.P. 6 Mike Rutherford

ORANGE, blue hoops, blue bars on sleeves, orange cap

Tom Amoss(0 0-0-0)

PLAYCALLER (S)   119
Dk.B./Br.f.91, Saratoga Six-Delice by What a Pleasure

Jockey Stats
(522 89-61-56)

				1993	2	2	0	0	$27,960	Turf 0 0 0 0 $0
				1992	0	0	0	0	$0	Off Track 0 0 0 0 $0

28Aug93 8LaDft 2   [F]Stk35000   6f   21.97   45.38 1:11.35   8/11   6   9$4\frac{1}{4}$ 7^4 3^1 1^{hd} Ardoin,R   116   *2.00 Playcaller^{hd} Sonsearay^6 BoundingGladys^{hd} Up in final strides

11Aug93 10LaDft 2   [F]Msw11600   5$\frac{1}{2}$f   22.13   46.69 1:06.74   4/9   8   6$3\frac{1}{2}$ 4^2 1^1 1$2\frac{1}{2}$ Ardoin,R   119   *.70 Playcaller$^2\frac{1}{2}$ BlissfulAmerican$^2\frac{1}{2}$ LuckyLineage^{nk} Circled field, driving

Workouts: Sep.6 LAD 4 f :48.00   Aug.21 LAD 5 f 1:01.80   Aug.5 LAD 5 f 1:00.60   Bred in Texas by Mike Rutherford

---

6
6-1▲
Aaron
Gryder

P.P. 7 Ron Lance & Keith Asmussen

BROWN, white blocks, brown cap

Steven M. Asmussen   (101 10-14-14)

TRACEYS ROCK   119
Gr.f.91, Taylor's Falls-Rock Finder by Pass the Tab

Jockey Stats
(518 77-61-87)

				1993	3	2	1	0	$30,370	Turf 0 0 0 0 $0
				1992	0	0	0	0	$0	Off Track 0 0 0 0 $0

22Aug93 8APft 2   [F]Stk50000   6f   21.95   45.13 1:12.07   5/11   1   1$\frac{1}{2}$ 1$\frac{1}{2}$ 1^4 1$\frac{1}{2}$ Barton,DM   115   10.40 TraceysRock$\frac{1}{2}$ Mariah'sStorm$^2\frac{1}{2}$ BayouPlans$^3\frac{1}{4}$ Prevailed

24Jun93 6APft 2   [F]Msw18700   5f   22.41   45.95   58.93   3/10   1   1$\frac{1}{2}$ 1^1 1^3 1^3 Barton,DM   117   3.00 TraceysRock^3 RareReview$^1\frac{1}{2}$ QueenIsabella^3 Driving

10Jun93 4APft 2   [F]Msw18700   4$\frac{1}{2}$f   22.95   47.00   53.54   2/7   2   1   1^{hd} 2$\frac{1}{2}$ Barton,DM   117   13.10 Ayanka$\frac{1}{2}$ TraceysRock^6 TripleTake$^1\frac{1}{4}$ Dueled, just missed

Workouts: Sep.15 AP 4f m :53.21 b(d)   Aug.19 AP 3f gd :37.00 b   Aug.13 AP 5f ft 1:02.00 b   Bred in Texas by Ron Lance

---

Pgm	Owner	Weight	Trainer

7
15-1▲
Ray
Sibille

P.P. 10 Lee Sacks, Burton Glazov & Timothy J. Muckler

WHITE, blue dots and sleeves, white cap

(Jerry Gryczewski) Timothy J. Muckler(89 14-7-9)

ITSALOTTAHOUSE (S)   119
Ch.f.91, Tejano-Future by Nodouble

Jockey Stats
(356 30-35-41)

				1993	3	1	0	0	$15,680	Turf 0 0 0 0 $0
				1992	0	0	0	0	$0	Off Track 1 0 1 0 $11,100

29Aug93 7APsy 2   [F]Msw20350   6f   22.79   47.23 1:13.17   5/10   3   4$3\frac{1}{2}$ 3$2\frac{1}{2}$ 2$1\frac{1}{2}$ 1$9\frac{1}{2}$ Pettinger,DR   118   5.90 Itsalottahouse$^9\frac{1}{2}$ FastanSexy$^3\frac{1}{2}$ NileChant$^1\frac{1}{4}$ Drew off, in hand

18Aug93 2APft 2   [F]Mcl40000   5$\frac{1}{2}$f   22.83   46.95 1:05.88   3/7   7   7$7\frac{1}{4}$ 5^9 5$4\frac{1}{4}$ 2^{hd} Guidry,M   118   3.90 Pointofcontention^{hd} Itsalottahouse^1 PlayfulBay^4 Closed fast, missed

31Jul93 3APft 2   [F]Mcl30000   5$\frac{1}{2}$f   22.94   47.03 1:05.74   7/9   5   4^3 4$4\frac{1}{4}$ 4^5 2^6 Guidry,M   114   11.20 MissLizaJane^6 Itsalottahouse^2 PlayfulBay$^3\frac{1}{2}$ No match for winner

Workouts: Sep.16 AP 4f m :48.38 h(d)   Aug.26 AP 3f ft :37.05 b   Aug.15 AP 4f ft :53.09 b   Bred in Kentucky by Peter Blum & Highclere

---

8
10-1▲
Mark
Guidry

P.P. 11 Irish Acres Farm (P. Noel Hickey)

GREEN and GOLD halves, green shamrock on white sleeves, green and gold cap

(Doug Matthews) P. Noel Hickey(131 40-23-14)

RED HOT BABE   119
Ch.f.91, Fire Dancer-Poquita Fe by Apollo Streak

Jockey Stats
(668 103-94-95)

				1993	1	1	0	0	$11,000	Turf 0 0 0 0 $0
				1992	0	0	0	0	$0	Off Track 1 1 0 0 $11,100

29Aug93 4APsy 2   [F]Msw20350   6f   22.16   46.85 1:12.00   2/11   3   2^2 2^{hd} 1^3 1$4\frac{1}{2}$ Take,Y   118 b   8.90 RedHotBabe$^4\frac{1}{2}$ KaraokeKid^6 SlewKittySlew^2 Drew off well rated

Workouts: Sep.12 AP 5f ft 1:03.05 b   Sep.7 AP 6f ft 1:18.08 b   Aug.25 AP 4f ft :50.52 b   Bred in Canada by Irish Acres Farm

---

9
30-1▲
Garrett
Gomez

P.P. 12 Millard R. Seldin

PURPLE, white 'S', white bars on sleeves, purple cap

Charlie Livesay(15 1-1-2)

SLEW KITTY SLEW   119
B.f.91, Slew City Slew-Turn the Blade by Best Turn

Jockey Stats
(459 81-73-63)

				1993	4	0	2	1	$9,135	Turf 0 0 0 0 $0
				1992	0	0	0	0	$0	Off Track 2 0 1 1 $5,635

29Aug93 4APsy 2   [F]Msw20350   6f   22.16   45.86 1:12.00   4/11   5   8$7\frac{1}{4}$ 6^7 4$9\frac{1}{2}$ 3$10\frac{3}{4}$ Gomez,GK   118   *3.30^6 RedHotBabe$^4\frac{1}{2}$ KaraokeKid^6 SlewKittySlew^2 Closed willingly

19Aug93 3APmy 2   [F]Msw19800   6f   22.19   45.87 1:11.16   4/12   8   3^3 3^2 2^5 2^5 Barton,DM   118   7.20 SkippinUpbroadway^9 SlewKittySlew^{nk} Karnile^3 Saved ground

05Aug93 7APft 2   [F]Msw19250   5$\frac{1}{2}$f   22.06   46.67 1:07.58   7/9   6   5$5\frac{1}{2}$ 4^5 5^5 2$\frac{1}{2}$ Barton,DM   118   22.40 LadyTori$\frac{1}{2}$ SlewKittySlew^{nk} SweetMia$^\frac{1}{4}$ Swung wide, gaining

22Jul93 4APft 2   [F]Msw19250   6f   23.20   47.35 1:06.08   5/11   7   7$3\frac{3}{4}$ 8$5\frac{1}{2}$ 10^{12} 10$15\frac{1}{4}$ Barton,DM   118   17.40 ClarySage^4 ChattaCode$^2\frac{1}{2}$ Pointofcontention$^1\frac{1}{2}$ Failed to respond

Workouts: Sep.9 AP 7f ft 1:30.74 b   Aug.3 AP 3f ft :36.41 b   Jul.10 AP 5f ft 1:01.96 b   Bred in Kentucky by Millard Seldin

---

10
9-5▲
Joe
Bravo

P.P. 13 Candy Stable (Herb Moelis)

GRAY, black triangle, gray cap

Ben W. Perkins, Jr.(0 0-0-0)

SHAPELY SCRAPPER   119
Dk.B./Br.f.91, Fit to Fight-Awesome Promise by What Luck

Jockey Stats
(0 0-0-0)

				1993	3	1	2	0	$60,200	Turf 0 0 0 0 $0
				1992	0	0	0	0	$0	Off Track 0 0 0 0 $0

31Jul93 8MTHft 2   [F]Stk60000   6f   21.70   44.92 1:11.47   9/10   3   4$1\frac{1}{2}$ 3^2 2^5 2^2 Bravo,J   114   14.50 CatAttack^2 ShapelyScrapper^5 AttheHall^4 Rail trip, good effort

18Jul93 10MTHft 2   [F]Stk50000   5$\frac{1}{2}$f   22.34   46.34 1:06.79   4/7   6   5^4 4$\frac{1}{2}$ 2$\frac{1}{2}$ 2$1\frac{3}{4}$ Ferrer,JC   115   9.50 AttheHall$^1\frac{3}{4}$ ShapelyScrapper^3 MissBondi^{nk} 4w bid, no match

15Jun93 5MTHft 2   [F]Msw17000   5f   22.35   46.74 1:00.48   4/9   2   3^2 1$1\frac{1}{2}$ 1$5\frac{1}{2}$ 1$6\frac{1}{2}$ Ferrer,JC   117   8.80 ShapelyScrapper$^6\frac{1}{2}$ WeddingJitters^3 Patti'sGirl^2 Bid, driving

Workouts: Sep.15 AP 3f m :35.44 hg(d)   Bred in Kentucky by Hilary J. Boone, Jr.

11 P.P. 14 **Peter Strandwitz** **30-1▲** — **Michael B. Campbell(71 8-8-8)**

LIGHT BLUE, green cross sashes, green stars on sleeves, light blue cap

Eddie Zuniga — **GILLS ROCK** — **119** — **Jockey Stats (147 6-8-7)**

B.f.91, Cure the Blues-Task Force by Tap On Wood

1993	4	0	1	0	$4,224
1992	0	0	0	0	$0
Turf	0	0	0	0	$0
Off Track 2	0	1	0		$3,900

30Aug93	2AP my2	F Msw21450	1	47.32	1:12.91	1:39.64	1/8	8	87¾	88	2hd	22	Zuniga,JE	118	19.90	SweetMaryB.2 GillsRock2¼ MyLadyT.J.3½	Split horses, drifted
19Aug93	3AP my2	F Msw19800	6f	22.19	45.87	1:11.16	11/12	9	1215¾	1213¼	1212¾	713¾	Zuniga,JE	118	51.80	SkippinUpbroadwa9 SlewKittySlewnk Karnile2½	7 wide throughout
31Jul93	3AP ft 2	F Mcl35000	5½f	22.94	47.03	1:05.74	6/9	7	75¼	75¼	69	512	Zuniga,JE	118	36.90	MissLizaJane6 Itsalottahouse½ PlayfulBay3½	Steadied, in tight
10Jun93	4AP ft 2	F Msw18700	4½f	22.95	47.00	53.54	4/7	7		718¼	722¾	723¾	Guidry,M	117	8.00	Ayanka¾ TraceysRock8 TripleTake1½	Trailed throughout

Workouts: **Sep.10 AP 7f ft 1:31.76 b** **Aug.26 AP 3f ft :40.99 b** **Aug.17 AP 3f gd :39.04 b** **Bred in Virginia by Meadow Grove Farm, Inc.**

12F P.P. 2 **M E S Stable, Inc. (Nicholas J. Balodimas)** **30-1▲** — **(Kathy Stover) Eddie A. Cole(117 14-12-11)**

FUCHSIA, black dots, black dots on fuchsia cap

E. T. Baird — **POINTOFCONTENTION** — **119** — **Jockey Stats (272 29-19-37)**

Ch.f.91, Fit to Fight-Raise a Pocket by Raise a Native

1993	5	1	0	2	$12,895
1992	0	0	0	0	$0
Turf	0	0	0	0	$0
Off Track 0	0	0	0		$0

18Aug93	2AP ft 2	F Mcl40000	5½f	22.83	46.95	1:05.88	1/7	2	43	43	41¾	1hd	Baird,ET	118	2.80	Pointofcontentionhd Itsalottahouse½ PlayfulBay¾	Angled out, gamely
05Aug93	2AP ft 2	F Msw19250	5½f	22.66	46.91	1:06.66	5/7	2	42	32	22½	34½	Baird,ET	118	2.00	RecoveredGoods½ MyLadyT.J.4 Pointofcontention5½	Broke awkwardly
22Jul93	4AP ft 2	F Msw19250	5½f	23.20	47.35	1:06.08	11/11	3	42	41¾	32	33¾	Baird,ET	118	22.10	ClarySage1¼ ChattaCode2½ Pointofcontention1½	Contended, 4 wide
24Jun93	6AP ft 2	F Msw18700	5f	22.41	45.95	58.93	6/10	5	710	612	513	49½	Guidry,M	117	3.70e	TraceysRock3 RareReview3½ QueenIsabella3	Best stride late
10Jun93	4AP ft 2	F Msw18700	4½f	22.95	47.00	53.54	7/7	6		53¼	57¾	410¼	Baird,ET	117	*1.90	Ayanka¾ TraceysRock8 TripleTake1½	4 wide turn

Workouts: **Sep.16 AP 4f m :50.96 b(d)** **Sep.10 AP 7f ft 1:28.66 hg** **Aug.29 AP 5f m 1:01.97 h** **Bred in Kentucky by August Moon Farm**

13F P.P. 5 **J. Longfield & J. Ekezian** **30-1▲** — **Ernie T. Poulos(144 16-21-18)**

LIME GREEN, orange blocks, orange stripes on sleeves, orange cap

Randall Meier — **MY LADY T. J.** — **119** — **Jockey Stats (141 13-12-19)**

Ch.f.91, Tejano-Sharili by Gummo

1993	4	0	1	1	$6,185
1992	0	0	0	0	$0
Turf	0	0	0	0	$0
Off Track 2	0	0	1		$2,685

30Aug93	2AP my2	F Msw21450	1	47.32	1:12.91	1:39.64	5/8	4	32	54½	31½	34¼	Bourque,CC	118	7.00	SweetMaryB.2 GillsRock2¼ MyLadyT.J.3½	5 wide turn
19Aug93	3AP my2	F Msw19800	6f	22.19	45.87	1:11.16	2/12	7	76½	88½	58	513¼	Sterling,LJ Jr	118	5.40	SkippinUpbroadwa9 SlewKittySlewnk Karnile2½	Late rally, inside
05Aug93	2AP ft 2	F Msw19250	5½f	22.66	46.91	1:06.66	6/7	1	54	43½	33	2½	Sterling,LJ Jr	118	23.90	RecoveredGoods½ MyLadyT.J.4 Pointofcontention5½	Swung wide, bid short
22Jul93	4AP ft 2	F Msw19250	5½f	23.20	47.35	1:06.08	7/11	6	95¾	95	89	810¼	Sterling,LJ Jr	118	42.60	ClarySage1¼ ChattaCode2½ Pointofcontention1½	Erratic stretch

Workouts: **Sep.13 AP 5f ft 1:06.09 b** **Aug.28 AP 4f ft :51.50 b** **Aug.13 AP 5f ft 1:06.99 b** **Bred in Kentucky by Pillar Stud, Inc.**

(L) Treated with Furosemide; (L)* First time using Furosemide; (O) Off of Furosemide
& 1a - Gina's Stables, Inc. - Thunderhead Farms; Entry
Equipment Change: Lady Tori will race with blinkers on.

(F) DENOTES MUTUEL FIELD AND IS SO DESIGNATED BY TICKET #12. * 5 lbs. Apprentice Allowance
(S) DENOTES SUPPLEMENTARY NOMINATION.
Scratched: Karaoke Kid

Now obviously this kind of pattern suggests that *Red Hot Babe* had some stiff workouts away from Arlington that would not show in *The Racing Form*. Alert handicappers in Chicago have learned to pay attention to first time starters from Hickey even if the workouts aren't much at the track. Now that he has a public stable, Hickey should continue to do well with green horses.

We have stressed how important it is to know your trainers. It is also useful to know their training patterns. Try to determine if they bring horses to the track from their farm on a regular basis. That will help you more than all the Beyer speed ratings in the world.

Maidens

14 This area of handicapping is my specialty. Many times, I have been called the best maiden handicapper on the East Coast, and perhaps in the United States. This chapter will make you a lot of money if you read it carefully and use your noggin.

Here are my…

12 Keys to Handicapping the Maidens

1 - Looking Up Workouts
This is the most important angle in handicapping maiden races. If you learn anything from this book, I want you to learn to look up workouts and learn how to use the "Latest Workouts" page. Once one learns the benefits from the "Latest Workouts" page, he will be able to use it for all types of races. But be careful about trainers who bring in horses from their farms, as we noted before.

2 - Dissecting Breeding
Knowing which horses are currently producing is essential. Just because

certain sires were good runners does not mean the foals are doing well. You can pick up valuable bits of information about hot sires and cold sires from *The Racing Form* and, occasionally, from comments the track announcer makes regarding a winner. Some track announcers will mention that the winner is a brother or sister to stake winners. Useful information to tuck away for the next start.

3 - Workouts from Other Tracks

It is a challenge to find workouts that are performed at a different track and are not provided in the *Daily Racing Form*. These workouts might not be published, because the paper had to go to press. Always look at the next day's *Daily Racing Form* for additional workouts. This point will be made clear in an upcoming example.

4 - Class Edge over Field

Certain maidens will have an edge based on all-around class. Great workout, excellent breeding, and master handlers constitute all-around class.

5 - Watching the Board

This is one of the more obvious techniques used by most handicappers in maiden races. First time starter's money often finds "Hot Horses."

6 - Layoffs

Layoffs with maidens are usually caused by injuries. These injuries to two-year-olds are often minor. One should learn how to use this angle to your advantage either by throwing these horses out or by betting them.

7 - Consistency of Workouts

Many times, horses will have workouts spaced more than seven days apart. This usually means an injury is involved. Watch these horses closely.

8 - Two-to-Three Start Theory

The two-to-three start theory is very simple. If a maiden has not won after his second start, he is not playable. The only way we could possibly play a horse on his third start is if the particular horse had an excuse in one of those first two starts. Obviously, if a maiden race is compiled of horses that have all made more than three starts, this theory cannot be used. This theory is essential in maiden special weight races, where false favorites turn up.

9 - Bouncing Back

A maiden loses to a horse that goes on to win against better. The loser in that race could be "live". I will show you how to find such horses.

10 - Knowing Trainers, Owners, and Jockeys

Be aware! Every handicapper should know which trainer uses certain jockeys on a regular basis. If there is a maiden with great workouts and his trainer is not using his regular jockey, be careful.

11 - Maiden Claiming Races

Watch out for maidens that have impressive workouts and are in a claiming race. If these horses were that good, they would not be running for a tag.

12 - Maidens Who Do Not Win, But Are Still Bet Down

Certain maidens will always come close to winning but never win. They will continue to be bet down. I will show you how to eliminate these non-contenders and take advantage of throwing out the favorite.

Let's get going with some actual race examples!

Our first example deals with a common factor found in all maiden races and what astute handicappers live for: "Stupidity".

On July 2, Belmont offered the 87th running of Astoria Breeders Cup for two year old fillies at six furlongs. All who entered were winners, except for *Daily Routine*. This filly had made two unsuccessful tries in her short career.

```
8TH BEL CHART JULY 2, 1993   THOROUGHBRED
5 1/2 FURLONGS DIRT    PURSE $100,000 FILLIES 2 YEAR OLDS
THE ASTORIA BREEDERS' CUP. GRADE III. 22 NOMINATIONS.
ADDED.
VALUE OF RACE 96,700   VALUE TO WINNER 52,020   2ND 24,574   3RD 13,404
4TH 6,702
TOTAL PURSE: $111,700. $15,000 REVERTS BACK TO THE BREEDERS' CUP FUND.
MUTUEL POOL $185,657.00
EXACTA POOL $403,734.00
PICK SIX POOL $90,505.00
```

```
7 WENT
ST    1/4    3/8    STR    FIN
CASA EIRE (2) 2 114   7 O'BRIEN LEO
  5    7     7     1HD    1-2 3/4 SANTOS J A CONNAUGHTON BERNARD   17.10
SHE RIDES TONITE (2) 2 114   5 CONTESSA GARY C
  6    6HD   4HD   2HD    2-3/4 ALVARADO F T WINBOUND FARMS    19.50
DAILY ROUTINE 2 110   3 LAKE ROBERT P
  2    4HF   5HD   4--1    3-4    CHAVEZ J F ACKERLEY BROS FARM   13.20
CAMCORDER 2 112   6 MOTT WILLIAM I
  3    2-1HF 3HF   3HD    4-1    SMITH M E PERRY WILLIAM HAGGIN    0.30CTS
AYE BLUE (1) 2 113   2 MCKEE JOHN D
  4    3HF   6HF   7     5-2 1/4 LLOYD J S MCKEE JOHN D   16.60
INNOCENT BYSTANDER 2 112   1 FORBES JOHN H
  1    1HF   2HD   5HD    6-1 3/4 KRONE J A OLD BELLEVUE FARM   10.40
SAM'S IN CONTROL 2 112   4 SHAPOFF STANLEY R
  7    5HF   1HF   6HF    7     MAPLE E COHEN ROBERT B    6.10
OFF   4:34 START GOOD. WON DRIVING.
TIME 22 3/5   46 1/5   58 3/5   1:05 1/5   SHOWERY. TRACK: FAST.
7--CASA EIRE 36.20 13.80 15.800K
5-SHE RIDES TONITE 13.00 18.000K
3- DAILY ROUTINE 17.00
$2.00 EXACTA 7-5 PAID $355.00
$2.00 PICK SIX 5--6-1-6-5-7 (6 WINNERS 1 TICKET) PAID $50.909.00
5 WINNERS 40 TICKETS PAID $424.00
WINNER--B. F. 2, BY COMPLIANCE--CASARETTE, BY UPPER CASE
TRAINER-O'BRIEN LEO BRED BY SPIELMAN MICHAEL (NY)
SCRATCHED: NONE
OVERWEIGHTS- CASA EIRE (2), SHE RIDES TONITE (2), AYE BLUE (1)
DK    16:53
```

The main story, though, lies with *Camcorder*, a six length winner at five furlongs in her debut. For this reason, *Camcorder* was an overwhelming choice. *Camcorder* was the 3-10 favorite in the Astoria.

Why does stupidity come into play in this race?

If I am going to bet a 3-10 shot, she must be in top condition, and consistently running or working superbly. *Camcorder* fell way short of this expectation of mine and the public was betting off of the conditions of her first start and not her current condition.

4 **5 FURLONGS.** (.56¹) MAIDEN SPECIAL WEIGHT. Purse $23,500. Fillies. 2–year–olds. Weight, 117 lbs.

Coupled—Undaunted Miss and Prejudice Eyes; Wildest Creams and Amavalidhope.

Undaunted Miss	Ch. f. 2(Feb), by El Raggaas—Miss Bold Forli, by Forceten		Lifetime	1993 0 M 0 0
CHAVEZ J F (—)	Br.—Bonita Farm (Md)		0 0 0 0	
Own.—Warfield Kennard Jr	Tr.—Boniface J William (—)	**117**		
LATEST WORKOUTS	Apr 23 Del 4f gd :50¹ Bg			

Lori's Passion	Ro. f. 2(Apr), by Sabona—Culture Shock, by Restless Native		Lifetime	1993 0 M 0 0
BRAVO J (—)	Br.—Snowden William G (Ky)		0 0 0 0	
Own.—Spina Nicholas	Tr.—Spina Chuck (—)	**117**		
LATEST WORKOUTS	Apr 24 GS 3f fst :36¹ Bg Apr 20 GS 4f fst :49 Bg Apr 13 GS 3f fst :37¹ Bg Apr 6 GS 3f fst :37 B

Wildest Dreams	Dk. b. or br. f. 2(May), by Talc—Valentine Kiss, by Reflected Glory		Lifetime	1993 0 M 0 0
DAVIS R G (—)	Br.—Dianne Boyken (N.J.)		0 0 0 0	
Own.—NuEquestar Stable	Tr.—Rice Linda (—)	**117**		
LATEST WORKOUTS	Apr 30 Bel tr.t 4f fst :48³ H Apr 20 Bel tr.t 4f fst :48⁴ B Apr 14 Bel tr.t 4f fst :48 H Apr 8 Bel tr.t 4f fst :48² Hg

Amavalidhope	B. f. 2(Feb), by Valid Appeal—Amalie, by Bold And Brave		Lifetime	1993 0 M 0 0
MADRID A JR (—)	Br.—Stepp W Harley Jr (Fla)		0 0 0 0	
Own.—Stepp Harley W	Tr.—Rice Linda (—)	**117**		
LATEST WORKOUTS	●Apr 30 Bel tr.t 4f fst :47³ H Apr 24 Bel 3f fst :36¹ Hg Apr 15 Bel tr.t 4f fst :47³ Hg Apr 8 Bel tr.t 4f fst :48² Hg

World Predictions	Ch. f. 2(Jan), by World Appeal—Predictive, by Haveago		Lifetime	1993 1 M 0 1 $1,300
VELAZQUEZ J R (—)	Br.—Joseph Villella & Martha Villella (Fla)		1 0 0 1	
Own.—Firth Robert	Tr.—DiMauro Stephen L (—)	**117**	$1,300	
20Apr93- 5Kee fst 4½f :22⁴ :46² :52⁴	⑤Md Sp Wt	41 8 1	1hd 2² 35½	Peck B D	b 117	5.20	89-12 QnAthn117⁵SgrFtn117½WrldPrdcts117 Pace weakened 8
LATEST WORKOUTS	Apr 29 Bel tr.t 4f fst :49¹ B ●Apr 15 Kee 3f gd :35 Hg

Majestic Goose	B. f. 2(Feb), by Simply Majestic—Gander Crude, by Quack		Lifetime	1993 1 M 0 0
SANTOS J A (—)	Br.—Curtis C. Green (Ky)		1 0 0 0	
Own.—Blue Goose Stable	Tr.—Kelly Thomas J (—)	**117**		
20Apr93- 5Kee fst 4½f :22⁴ :46² :52⁴	⑤Md Sp Wt	29 3 8	87½ 78½ 69	Santos J A	L 117	2.90	86-12 QnAthn117⁵SrFtn117½WrldPrdcts117 Went to knees st 8
LATEST WORKOUTS	Apr 28 Bel 4f fst :48¹ H Apr 17 Kee 3f my :36 H Apr 12 Kee 4f fst :51² B Apr 8 Kee 3f fst :36³ B

Normandy Belle	B. f. 2, by Fit To Fight—French Flick, by Silent Screen		Lifetime	1993 1 M 0 0
KRONE J A (—)	Br.—Firman Pamela Mrs H (Ky)		1 0 0 0	
Own.—Firman Pamela H	Tr.—Pierce Joseph H Jr (—)	**117**		
22Apr93- 3Kee fst 4½f :22² :46⁴ :53²	⑤Md Sp Wt	35 5 8	76¾ 65 64¾	Perret C	117	3.00	87-08 Crafty and Evil117½OdieWest117²NewFe117 No factor 8
LATEST WORKOUTS	Apr 14 Kee 4f fst :48 Hg

Camcorder	B. f. 2(Mar), by Forty Niner—Video, by Nijinsky II		Lifetime	1993 0 M 0 0
SMITH M E (—)	Br.—Claiborne Farm & The Gamely Corp. (Ky)		0 0 0 0	
Own.—Perry William Haggin	Tr.—Mott William I (—)	**117**		
LATEST WORKOUTS	Apr 28 Bel 4f fst :48 Hg Apr 21 Bel 3f fst :39⁴ B Apr 12 Pay tr.t 4f fst :52⁴ B ●Apr 6 Pay tr.t 3f fst :38⁴ B

Also Eligible (Not in Post Position Order):

Prejudice Eyes	B. f. 2(Feb), by Deputed Testamony—Believing, by Believe It		Lifetime	1993 0 M 0 0
SHERIDAN E M (—)	Br.—Meadow Bridge Farm (Md)		0 0 0 0	
Own.—Boniface J William	Tr.—Boniface J William (—)	**117**		
LATEST WORKOUTS	Apr 28 Del 3f gd :38⁴ Bg Apr 21 Del 3f fst :37² Bg

When *Camcorder* made her first start, she had two works at Payson Park, a training track for Florida breds, and two at local Belmont.

Do not be deceived by the works at Payson Park; the works look slow, but very good, considering that Payson Park has a very deep base over its training track. She had an easy trial on April 21, and then a blowout on April 28 at four furlongs.

First of all, why a two month layoff? Angle #6 tells us that layoffs usually mean injuries, to which two-year-olds are very susceptible. Getting back to *Camcorder's* workouts, I would have to be convinced that this is the same horse that ran on May 5. In working for her second start, *Camcorder* had four workouts at Belmont. On June 6 at Belmont, *Cam-*

corder had a very good 36⁴⁄₅ breezing, but, then, twelve unexplainable days off. Twelve days off when one is bringing a horse back to the track and just when she started training back, I do not understand—unless of course the horse was hurting.

Camcorder obviously received an injury after the May 5 race and it might have been reaggravated after the workout on June 6. When Camcorder went back to the track starting with a work on June 18, her works were not as sharp, especially the workout on June 29, a horrible four furlongs breezing in 51²⁄₅. Usually when preparing for a race off a layoff as we have seen throughout this book, a trainer will just blow a horse out at three furlongs to keep him sharp. *Camcorder* had too many question marks for a 3-10 shot.

8

5 ½ FURLONGS. **(1.03) 87th Running THE ASTORIA BREEDERS' CUP (Grade III). Purse $100,000 Added ($75,000 added plus $25,000 Breeders' Cup Fund). Fillies. 2-year-olds. By subscription of $150 each which should accompany the nomination; $600 to pass the entry box; $600 to start with $75,000 added and an additional $25,000 from the Breeders' Cup Fund for Cup nominees only. The added money and all fees to be divided 60% to the winner, 22% to second, 12% to third and 6% to fourth. Breeders' Cup Fund monies also correspondingly divided providing a Breeders' Cup nominee has finished in an awarded position. Any Breeders' Cup Fund monies not awarded will revert back to the Fund. Weight: 118 lbs. Winners of two races of $35,000, an additional 2 lbs. Non-winners of a race of $50,000, allowed 3 lbs. Of a race of $35,000, 5 lbs. Of a race other than maiden or claiming, 7 lbs. Maidens, 9 lbs. This race will not be divided. Field will be limited to 14 starters. If more than 14 entries pass the entry box, preference will be given in the following order: Breeders' Cup nominated highweights; Breeders' Cup nominees, non-Breeders' Cup nominated highweights. Starters to be named at the closing time of entries. Trophies will be presented to the winning owner, trainer and jockey. Breeders' Cup nominees preferred. Highweights preferred Closed Wednesday, June 16, 1993, with 22 nominations.**

Innocent Bystander — Ch. f. 2, by Skip Trial—Sharp Maid, by Sharpen Up — Lifetime 1 1 0 0 $6,000 — 1993 1 1 0 0 $6,000
KRONE J A (217 39 26 33 .18) — Br.—Appleton Arthur I (Fla)
Own.—Old Bella... Farm — Tr.—Forbes John H (14 0 0 1 .00) — **112**
11Jun93- 1Mth fst 5f :23 :47² 1:00 ⒻMd 30000 62 6 1 1hd 1½ 11½ 13¼ Marquez C H Jr 115 10.20 81-25 InncntBystndr1153¼DcnTrp1176½ClnWgr112 D... 7
LATEST WORKOUTS Jun 28 Mth 4f fst :48³ B

Aye Blue — Dk. b. or br. f. 2(Apr), by Aye's Turn—Plowing Troy, by Polar Night — Lifetime 2 1 0 1 $9,420 — 1993 2 1 0 1 $9,420
LLOYD J S (—) — Br.—John D. McKee (W.Va.)
Own.—McKee John D — Tr.—McKee John D (1 1 0 0 1.00) — **112**
16May93- 5Pha ... :23² :47² :53² ⒻMd Sp Wt 56 3 2 1½ 14 14¾ Lloyd J S 118 2.90 94-20 Aye Blue1184¾ Sly Annie1186¾ Gliding Lady118 Handily 5
29Apr93- 3GS fst 4½f :23 :47¹ :53⁴ ⒻMd Sp Wt 23 1 6 46 36½ 33¾ Lloyd J S 117 17.90 92-16 Sixmore117¾HouseDivided1173AyeBlu117 Finished well 7

Daily Routine — Dk. b. or br. f. 2(Apr), by Well Decorated—From the East, by Gold and Myrrh — Lifetime 2 0 2 0 $10,340 — 1993 2 M 2 0 $10,340 — Wet 1 0 1 0 $5,170
CHAVEZ J F (205 39 27 15 .19) — Br.—Ocala Stud Farms (Fla)
Own.—Ackerley Bros Farm — Tr.—Lake Robert P (38 3 6 2 .08) — **110**
21Jun93- 5Bel my 5½f :22² :46 1:05 ⒻMd Sp Wt 63 4 3 32 33 23½ 25¼ Chavez J F 117 4.40 85-17 StrtgcMnvr1175¼DlyRtn1179WndrsFlyr117 Second best 8
12Jun93- 3Bel fst 5f :22² :46³ :59³ ⒻMd Sp Wt 57 4 3 42 31½ 31 22 Chavez J F 117 6.70 81-16 Sm'sInControl1172DilyRoutn1171½MoGrnd117 Willingly 7
LATEST WORKOUTS Jun 27 Aqu 3f fst :38¹ B Jun 17 Aqu 3f fst :37 B Jun 7 Aqu 4f fst :48⁴ Bg ●Jun 2 Aqu 5f fst 1:01¹ H

Sam's In Control — Dk. b. or br. f. 2(May), by Premiership—Wagers Delight-Ch, by Worldwatch — Lifetime 1 1 0 0 $14,100 — 1993 1 1 0 0 $14,100
MAPLE E (110 18 22 13 .16) — Br.—Cohen Robert B (NY)
Own.—Cohen Robert B — Tr.—Shapoff Stanley R (54 10 5 8 .19) — **112**
12Jun93- 3Bel fst 5f :22² :46³ :59³ ⒻMd Sp Wt 63 3 7 78¾ 54 41 12 Maple E 117 13.80 83-16 Sm'sInContrl1172DlyRtn1171½MGrnd117 Brk slow, drvg 7
LATEST WORKOUTS Jun 29 Bel tr.t 4f fst :49 H Jun 22 Bel tr.t 4f sly :48 B Jun 5 Bel tr.t 5f fst 1:03² B May 31 Bel tr.t 4f fst :51¹ B

She Rides Tonite

Ro. f. 2(Feb), by Stalwa   Hill Billy Dancer, by Never Bend Hill

ALVARADO F T (103 13 13 16 .13)
Own.—Winbound Farms
Br.—Mliffs.   rn Inc (NY)
Tr.—Contessa Gary C (30 3 3 2 .10)

	Lifetime	1993	1	1	0	0	$14,100
112	1 1 0 0						
	$14,100	Wet	1	0	0		$14,100

21Jun93- 3Bel my 5½f   :22³ :47² 1:06³   ⓒⒷMd Sp Wt   55 7 6 9¼ 8¾ 4¼ 1¼ Alvarado F T   117   8.90   82-17 ShRidsTont117¼OndFlor117³Tr'sTmpst117   Going away 9

LATEST WORKOUTS   Jun 30 Bel tr.t 3f fst :37 B   ●Jun 16 Bel tr.t 3f fst :36 H   Jun 9 Bel 5f fst 1:05 Bg   Jun 7 Bel 3f fst :37 Hg

---

Camcorder

B. f. 2(Mar), by Forty Niner—Video, by Nijinsky II

SMITH M E (243 56 34 35 .23)
Own.—Perry William Haggin
Br.—Claiborne Farm & The Gamely Corp. (Ky)
Tr.—Mott Willi   I (53 15 5 8 .28)

	Lifetime	1993	1	1	0	0	$14,100
112	1 1 0 0						
	$14,100						

5May93- 4Bel fst 5f   :22¹ :45² :57⁴   ⓒMd Sp Wt   69 7 5 1¹ 1¼ 1² 1⁶ Smith M E   117 *1.00   92-08 Cmcordr117⁶Lori'sPsson117¼Amvldhop117   doer. 7

LATEST WORKOUTS   Jun 29 Bel 4f fst :51² B   Jun 18 Bel 4f fst :49⁴ B   Jun 6 Bel 3f fst :36⁴ r

---

Casa Eire

B. f. 2, by Compliance—Casarette, by Upper Case

SANTOS J A (142 20 20 18 .14)
Own.—Connaughton Bernard
Br.—Spielman Michael (NY)
Tr.—O'Brien Leo (56 6 6 7 .11)

	Lifetime	1993	4	1	0	0	$1 750
.12	4 1 0 0						
	$14,750						

7Jun93- 5Bel fst 5f   :22⁴ :46³ 1:06³   ⓒⒷMd Sp Wt   62 6 1 1½ 1½ 1² 1⁴ Smith M E   117   4.70e 82-14 Casa Eire117⁴ Cynanite117¾ Buddy's Ga117   Dre off 9
26May93- 5Bel fst 5f   :22² :46³ :58³   ⓒⒷMd Sp Wt   — 1 1 — — — Smith M E   .17   2.10   — — Vivaling117⁴Cynanite117¾LikeThat117   wheeled, '.rdr 6
16May93- 3Bel fst 5f   :22³ :46² :59²   Md Sp Wt   36 7 4 5³¼ 5⁴¼ 5⁵¼ 6⁹¼ Velazquez J R   115   7.20e 75-15 Gliding Arrow118³ Lahint118ⁿᵏ CharlieC ssh119   Greenly 7
6Apr93- 3Kee fst 4½f   :22⁴ :47¹ :53⁴   ⓒMd Sp Wt   30 6 5   3¹¼ 3³ 45½ Feagin C O   117 15.40   84-07 CityJoyc117⁴⁰diWst117ⁿᵏSpphirBds117   Unseated rider 6

LATEST WORKOUTS   Jun 28 Bel 4f fst :48² H   ●Jun 21 Bel 5f sly 1:01 H   May 30 Bel 4f fst :49³ Bg   May 11 Bel 4f fst :48¹ H

If anyone told me that a 3-10 shot was going to run out of the money I would bet those races all day. Those are the races you dream about.

The winner, *Casa Eire*, had trouble in her first three starts and did win when she straightened out. She won against state breds, and that probably would have touted me off her. If one likes state breds, though, he would have caught a nice exacta. Learning how to throw favorites out that do not belong to be the favorite or favored at the odds will be very profitable. Even if one did not like anything in the race, then he should just stay away and not get suckered, as did the handicapper that picked *Camcorder*.

The first race at Belmont on June 23, 1993, offered a maiden special weight contest for five three year olds who were making their first starts. Here is my betting analysis.

This race brings into play Angle #9—Bouncing Back.

In *Finding Hot Horses*, I used an example of *England Expects*, a very good two-year-old colt, who went on to beat better. The horse that ran second to *England Expects* was *Living Vicariously*, who went on to win his next start.

START · 6 FURLONGS · BELMONT PARK · FINISH

6 FURLONGS. (1.074) MAIDEN SPECIAL WEIGHT. Purse $23,500. 3-year-olds and upward. Weight, 3-year-olds, 114 lbs. Older, 122 lbs.

Man's Hero

B. c. 3(Feb), by Hero's Honor—Blushing Madame, by Blushing Groom-Fr

VELAZQUEZ J R (130 16 13 10 .12)
Own.—Dileo Philip
Br.—Dileo Philip (Va)
Tr.—Hertler John O (40 7 3 6 .18)

	Lifetime	1992	1	M	1	0	$5,280
114	1 0 1 0						
	$5,280						

17Sep92- 5Bel fst 6f :223 :461 1:11 Md Sp Wt 80 5 1 1½ 1½ 11½ 2¾ Velazquez J R 118 5.40 84-18 LivingVicriously118¾Mn'sHro118noDiggingIn118 Gamely 14
LATEST WORKOUTS Jun 18 Bel 4f fst :473 H

Pro Prospect Dk. b. or br. c. 3(Mar), by Forty Niner—Steel Maiden, by Damascus
BAILEY J D (129 23 27 18 .18) Br.—Stuart S. Janney, III & Ogden Phipp (Ky)
Own.—Janney Stuart S III Tr.—McGaughey Claude III (38 9 9 6 .24) **114**
Lifetime 1 0 1 0 $5,170 | 1993 1 M 1 0 $5,170 | 1992 0 M 0 0
30May93- 5Bel fst 6f :231 :46 1:094 Md Sp Wt 78 5 2 31½ 31 23 27½ Krone J A 122 2.10 83-13 SenorRex1227½ProProspct1222½PlcPipr122 Second best 6
LATEST WORKOUTS Jun 11 Bel 4f fst :48 H May 29 Bel 3f fst :343 H May 24 Bel 4f fst :482 Bg May 19 Bel 5f fst 1:021 B

Afleetwinner Ch. g. 3(May), by Afleet—Baldwinner, by Baldski
DAVIS R G (204 28 32 20 .14) Br.—Thompson Roland E (Ky)
Own.—Meriweither John W Tr.—Freeman Willard C (17 2 4 2 .12) **114**
Lifetime 6 0 2 0 $13,650 | 1993 5 M 1 0 $8,370 | 1992 1 M 1 0 $5,280
30May93- 5Bel fst 6f :231 :46 1:094 Md Sp Wt 71 1 6 54 43½ 47 410¼ Davis R G b 122 3.30 81-13 SenorRx1227½ProProspct1222½PlcPipr122 Broke slowly 6
15May93- 1Bel fst 7f :23 :461 1:24 3↑Md Sp Wt 77 1 2 2hd 2½ 2½ 23 Davis R G b 122 2.40 80-17 Moyer1223Afltwinnr1221¾IrishDoctor-GB122 Held place 6
6Mar93- 2GP fst 6f :22 :452 1:112 Md Sp Wt 56 1 7 67¼ 69½ 55 47 Perret C b 120 *1.30 77-09 InsdConncton1201½MghtyAvnt1202¾EvlBr120 Late rally 10
15Feb93- 3GP fst 7f :222 :452 1:243 Md Sp Wt 70 5 4 2½ 2hd 2hd 41¾ Perret C b 120 6.00 78-13 Recorder120hdSnappyFeli120nkPlntgenet120 Weakened 12
28Jan93- 5GP fst 6f :224 :463 1:122 Md Sp Wt 54 6 2 53¼ 64½ 77 54½ Bailey J D 120 *1.30 74-19 StoneyWolf120½DixielandChief1203Mgico120 Weakened 10
30Jly92- 5Sar fst 5f :22 :453 :58 Md Sp Wt 62 5 4 55½ 56½ 44 25 Davis R G 118 7.50 89-06 InsurdWnnr1185Afltwnnr1182GrmlnGry118 Up for place 6
LATEST WORKOUTS Jun 18 Bel 5f fst 1:013 H Jun 11 Bel 5f fst 1:021 B May 26 Bel 4f fst :483 B May 7 Bel 4f fst :47 H

Western Forte Dk. b. or br. g. 3(Apr), by Gone West—Lido Isle, by Far North
SMITH M E (209 50 28 28 .24) Br.—Foxfield (Ky)
Own.—Kimmel Caesar P Tr.—Kimmel John C (12 2 4 0 .17) **114**
Lifetime 7 0 2 2 $15,980 | 1993 5 M 2 2 $15,980 | 1992 2 M 0 0 | Turf 1 0 0 0
10Jun93- 1Bel gd 7f :231 :462 1:232 Md Sp Wt 76 7 1 31½ 2hd 21 25 Smith M E 122 *1.40 81-17 Pescgni1225WstrnFort1221¾InSplitScond122 Held place 7
21May93- 5Bel fst 7f :223 :46 1:24 3↑Md Sp Wt 84 4 1 1½ 1½ 2hd 21¼ Velasquez J 122 2.10 82-20 Crsey'sPl1221¼WesternForte1224½PrivtePln122 Gamely 7
9May93- 5Bel fm 1 1/16 Ⓣ:462 1:103 1:404 3↑Md Sp Wt 59 1 2 21 32½ 613 720 Velasquez J 115 4.80 72-14 CozzMk1155¾NbzLkShwbz1151¾T.V.Gld115 Forced pace 11
28Apr93- 3Aqu fst 7f :224 :453 1:232 Md Sp Wt 88 5 2 1½ 2hd 1½ 33 Velazquez J R 122 8.70 84-19 PlnPlsr122½MnD'Or1222½WstrnFrt122 Dueled weakened 7
7Apr93- 5Aqu fst 7f :232 :47 1:23 3↑Md Sp Wt 89 5 1 12 11½ 3nk 31¾ Velazquez J R 115 5.60 87-16 All Gone115¾ MineD'Or1101WesternForte115 Weakened 10
29Aug92- 4Sar fst 6f :214 :444 1:104 Md Sp Wt 49 1 3 31½ 43½ 64¾ 710½ McCauley W H 118 34.50 79-07 DancingHunter1185¼Glenbarra1181¼NorwyGry118 Tired 9
12Aug92- 4Sar fst 5f :214 :452 :583 Md Sp Wt 42 5 6 86½ 67½ 78 79 Antley C W 116 6.30 82-07 Birdie'sFly118nkDevilishlyYours118nkBatct118 Checked 9
LATEST WORKOUTS Jun 4 Bel 4f fst :481 B

Wills Ch. c. 4, by His Majesty—Catcha Shiningstar, by Accipiter
PERRET C (60 12 8 13 .20) Br.—Fiumefreddo Anthony (Fla)
Own.—Aldila Farm Tr.—Combs Don (7 3 2 0 .43) **122**
Lifetime 0 0 0 0 | 1991 0 M 0 0 | 1990 0 M 0 0
LATEST WORKOUTS Jun 19 Bel 5f fst 1:021 B Jun 12 Bel 5f fst 1:003 H Jun 7 Bel 5f fst 1:04 Bg Jun 2 Bel 5f fst 1:002 H

In a Split Second Ch. c. 3(Apr), by Time for a Change—Thoroughly Wet, by Great Above
SANTOS J A (121 17 17 14 .14) Br.—Steven Dietz (Ky)
Own.—Dietz Steven Tr.—Schulhofer Flint S (51 12 9 4 .24) **114**
Lifetime 2 0 0 1 $2,990 | 1993 2 M 0 1 $2,990 | 1992 0 M 0 0
10Jun93- 1Bel gd 7f :231 :462 1:232 Md Sp Wt 72 5 2 1½ 1hd 32½ 36¾ Santos J A 122 1.40e 79-17 Pscgn1225WstrnFrt1221¾InSpltScnd122 Duel,weakened 7
2Feb93- 5GP fst 7f :224 :462 1:25 Md Sp Wt 53 5 8 76¾ 74¼ 75¾ 69¾ Santos J A 120 3.90 68-22 MgrtngMoon1201½CrdnlPk120½SyChsGrg120 No threat 11
LATEST WORKOUTS Jun 18 Bel 4f fst :484 H Jun 6 Bel 4f fst :471 H May 31 Bel 4f fst :48 H May 26 Bel 5f fst 1:01 H

Man's Hero made his debut on September 17, 1992. This three-year-old colt obviously was injured after that race and ended his two-year-old career. *Man's Hero* lost by 3/4 of a length to *Living Vicariously* in his first start. On this day, he led every step of the way and failed in the last few strides. The fractions were 22.3, 46.1, and 111/5. This horse showed he was meant to be good before he was injured, as indicated by his breeding. John Velasquez is coming back for the mount after drilling a quick half-mile in 47 3/5 handily with a beneficial five days in between.

Pro Prospect picked up logical jockey Jerry Bailey, who replaced Julie Krone. Looking back to *Pro Prospect's* last race, there were a few tipoffs that should have chased bettors away from this 2-1 choice on May 30, 1993. Julie Krone was riding for Claude McGaughrey. He almost never uses her, and the horse had a 34 3/5 blowout the day before making his first start.

The public was asking too much of this horse. The workout did take too much out of him as he chased Senor Rex and tired down the stretch.

If *Man's Hero* wasn't in the race, I felt that *Pro Prospect* would be a winner, but this three-year-old colt is not going to get the lead, and will be chasing again, as in the race with *Senor Rex*.

Afleet Winner is risky. It really depends how many chances you want to give this colt, who likes to be bet down and run close.

Western Forte is the same as *Afleet Winner*: a shorter distance should help.

Wills doesn't fit here. If speed in the race is dying, this one might pick up the pieces, but it's too tough of a spot for his debut. He would be much better off with a race with much less speed. The trainer has been doing well, but works are too slow to compete with these, also giving eight pounds to everyone.

In A Split Second lost to *Western Forte* and is another who should benefit from less distance, but this one should be watching a couple in front of him.

Man's Hero had the most speed and wired the field in 110³/₅. *England Expects* went on to win over $100,000, which led us to *Living Vicariously*, who went on to win over $75,000. *Living Vicariously* led us to *Man's Hero*. *Man's Hero* returned the best of all three, a payout of $6.80. Any impressive winner who goes on to win against better leads us to another winner next time out. Watch out! Horses that get beaten badly by 10-12 lengths will not come back. I am talking about a horse that runs a very good race, but is just not good enough to win to beat the winner. A fine betting range is 1–4 lengths. This concept applies to maiden special weights and goes on to allowance and stakes horses.

FIRST RACE

Belmont
JUNE 23, 1993

6 FURLONGS. (1.07⁴) MAIDEN SPECIAL WEIGHT. Purse $23,500. 3–year–olds and upward. Weight, 3–year–olds, 114 lbs. Older, 122 lbs. (43RD DAY. WEATHER CLEAR. TEMPERATURE 78 DEGREES).

Value of race $23,500; value to winner $14,100; second $5,170; third $2,820; fourth $1,410. Mutuel pool $128,180. Exacta Pool $250,766

Last Raced	Horse	M/Eqt.A.Wt	PP St	¼	½	Str	Fin	Jockey	Odds $1
17Sep92 5Bel²	Man's Hero	3 114	1 1	1¹	1¹	1²	1ⁿᵏ	Velazquez J R	2.40
10Jun93 1Bel²	Western Forte	3 114	4 2	3²½	3³	3²½	2²	Smith M E	3.50
30May93 5Bel²	Pro Prospect	3 114	2 3	2½	2ʰᵈ	2ʰᵈ	3⁴½	Bailey J D	1.50
	Wills	4 122	5 6	6	4ʰᵈ	4ʰᵈ	4¹½	Perret C	7.20
30May93 5Bel⁴	Afleetwinner	b 3 114	3 4	5³	5ʰᵈ	5¹	5²	Davis R G	12.60
10Jun93 1Bel³	In a Split Second	3 115	6 5	4¹	6	6	6	Santos J A	7.70

OFF AT 1:00 Start good, Won driving. Time, :22², :45², :57³, 1:10³ Track fast.

Official Program Numbers

$2 Mutuel Prices:				
	1-(A)-MAN'S HERO	6.80	3.80	2.20
	4-(D)-WESTERN FORTE		3.80	2.20
	2-(B)-PRO PROSPECT			2.10
	$2 EXACTA 1-4 PAID $29.40			

B. c, (Feb), by Hero's Honor—Blushing Madame, by Blushing Groom–Fr. Trainer Hertler John O. Bred by Dileo Philip (Va).

MAN'S HERO sprinted clear in the early stages, widened his margin in midstretch then was all out to hold off WESTERN FORTE in the closing strides. WESTERN FORTE stalked the pace while three wide into the stretch then closed steadily but could not get up. PRO PROSPECT prompted the pace between horses into upper stretch then lacked a strong closing bid. WILLS was never a serious threat. AFLEETWINNER saved ground to no avail. IN A SPLIT SECOND never reached contention.

Owners— 1, Dileo Philip; 2, Kimmel Caesar P; 3, Janney Stuart S III; 4, Aldila Farm; 5, Meriweither John W; 6, Dietz Steven.

Trainers— 1, Hertler John O; 2, Kimmel John C; 3, McGaughey Claude III; 4, Combs Don; 5, Freeman Willard C; 6, Schulhofer Flint S.

Overweight: In a Split Second 1 pound.

5

6 FURLONGS. **(1.07⁴) MAIDEN CLAIMING. Purse $10,000. Fillies and Mares. 3-year-olds and up. Weights: 3-year-olds, 115 lbs.; older, 122 lbs. Claiming Price $30,000; for each $2,500 to $25,000, 2 lbs.**

Coupled—Forever Crafty and Arc Melody; Yuseppa and Well Of Gold.
LASIX—Mundo Latino, Nat's My Gal, Peb.

Friends R Us — B. f. 3(Apr), by Advocator—Hallomar, by Maribeau
$25,000 Br.—Muriel Harpenau (Ky)
Own.—D M S Farm — Tr.—Spina Chuck (2 0 0 0 .00) — 115
Lifetime 0 0 0 0 — 1992 0 M 0 0
LATEST WORKOUTS May 28 Mth 5f fst 1:02³ Bg — May 22 Mth 5f fst 1:02 B — May 15 Mth 5f fst 1:05 B — Apr 8 Pha 4f fst :54 B

Forever Crafty — Ch. f. 3(May), by Crafty Prospector—Lets Talk Irish, by Irish River
$30,000 Br.—Woods R Todd (Fla)
Own.—Grainger Farms — Tr.—Manning Dennis J (8 0 0 0 .00) — 110⁵
Lifetime 0 0 0 0 — 1992 0 M 0 0
LATEST WORKOUTS ●May 26 Mth 6f fst 1:15¹ Hg — May 19 GS 5f my 1:02⁴ Bg — May 14 GS 4f fst :49 B — May 8 GS 4f fst :48 B

Afternoon Star — Ch. f. 3(Feb), by Circle of Steel—Twice Restored, by Twice Worthy
$25,000 Br.—Vickie Smith & J C III (Fla)
Own.—Aldright Charlie — Tr.—Rispoli Joseph N (—) — 106⁵
Lifetime 2 0 2 0 $1,292 — 1993 2 M 2 0 $1,292 — 1992 0 M 0 0
4Apr93- 1Tam fst 7f :23² :47¹ 1:26³ ⒻMd Sp Wt 45 4 4 43¾ 21½ 23 22 Gomez E R 118 1.70 85-12 Don'tCryforM118²AftrnnStr118⁴MyDrChryl118 2nd best 8
20Mar93- 3Tam fst 7f :24 :48² 1:28 ⒻMd 12500 42 3 5 51¾ 53¼ 4nk 2hd Gomez E R 118 20.40 80-08 BndboutHolm118hdAftrnoonStr118¹½JstJoy116 Led late 8
LATEST WORKOUTS May 29 Mth 3f fst :36 Bg — May 22 Mth 4f fst :49¹ Bg — May 15 GS 4f fst :51 B

Mundo Latino — Ch. f. 3(Feb), by Skip Trial—Big Goldie, by Big Spruce
$30,000 Br.—Cresci Dorothy E (Fla)
Own.—Levine Robert L — Tr.—Levine Robert L (—) — 115
Lifetime 1 0 0 0 $240 — 1993 1 M 0 0 $240 — 1992 0 M 0 0
27Mar93- 3GP fst 6f :22² :46¹ 1:12 ⒻMd Sp Wt 14 9 8 77¼ 89 1023 1026½ Castillo H Jr Lb 120 32.20 54-19 RglSolution120²LTurk120²TwntySecondAv120 Gave way 11
LATEST WORKOUTS Jun 2 Mth 3f fst :36⁴ Bg — May 26 Mth 5f fst 1:01¹ Hg — May 13 Mth 4f fst :49¹ B

Nat's My Gal — B. f. 3(Apr), by Gold Crest—Hello Nat, by Valid Appeal
$25,000 Br.—King Frank L Jr & Young Damon (Ky)
Own.—Tucker Paula J — Tr.—Jennings Lawrence Jr (4 2 0 0 .50) — 111
Lifetime 6 0 1 2 $2,595 — 1993 2 M 1 0 $1,165 — 1992 4 M 0 2 $1,430 — Wet 1 0 0 0
2May93- 3Hia fst 7f :23² :47¹ 1:28 ⒻMd 28000 42 3 3 1hd 1½ 21 53¼ Castillo H Jr b 117 7.90 66-20 RunningReview117hdHstyAppel121½LovlyCrol117 Faded 9
20Apr93-10Hia fst 7f :23² :47¹ 1:27² ⒻMd 16000 48 9 2 3nk 1½ 12½ 22 Castillo H Jr b 121 11.80 70-21 LitigatingLady121²Nt'sMyGl121¹SunnyWish121 Gamely 10
20Aug92-10LaD fst 5½f :22² :46⁴ 1:06⁴ ⒻMd 20000 4 5 3 43 67 916 916¾ Howard D L b 119 7.40 67-12 Holme's Dove115¹½ Surprise K115⁵ ReadyNow113 Tired 12
5Aug92- 4LaD fst 5½f :23 :47⁴ 1:07⁴ ⒻMd 20000 31 6 3 2hd 1hd 1hd 34 Howard D L b 119 2.40 75-15 ExplosivePldg116¹SurprisK116³Nt'sMyGl119 Weakened 12
22Jly92- 6LaD fst 5½f :22¹ :46⁴ 1:07¹ ⒻMd 20000 34 10 1 11 12 12 32 Howard D L b 115 27.00 80-13 JodyJosih115²AssmblyTim115noNt'sMyGl115 Weakened 11
26Jun92- 3LaD my 5f :23¹ :48¹ 1:01⁴ ⒻMd 30000 13 2 2 22 44 68¼ 712¾ Han R W5 111 6.70 74-21 Jiffener116⁴VeiledBride116¹Ctchmeforthekey111 Tired 12
LATEST WORKOUTS May 21 Mth 5f my 1:03⁴ B — ●May 10 Hia 4f fst :49² B — Apr 28 Hia 4f fst :49 B — Apr 16 Hia 4f sly :49 B

Dancing for Gold — Dk. b. or br. f. 3(Apr), by Vaal Reef—Phantom Dancer, by Restless Native
$25,000 Br.—Knight Larry E (Md)
Own.—Farro Michael — Tr.—Farro Michael (1 0 0 0 .00) — 111
Lifetime 1 0 0 0 $110 — 1993 1 M 0 0 $110 — 1992 0 M 0 0
12May93- 7GS gd 6f :22¹ :45² 1:11¹ ⒻMd Sp Wt 3 4 8 88½ 713 816 726¼ Olea R E L 121 21.20 60-18 FightAin'tOver121nkGlcon121⁹CheckrideJuli116 Outrun 9
LATEST WORKOUTS Jun 2 Mth 3f fst :37 B — May 26 Mth 5f fst 1:04 B — May 8 GS 5f fst 1:03 Bg — May 1 GS 5f fst 1:02² B

Mon Montreaux — B. f. 3(Apr), by Tasso—Toque Rouge Ir, by Tarboosh
Lifetime 0 0 0 0 — 1993 0 M 0 0 — 1992 0 M 0 0

$30,000 Br.—Robins Gerald (Ky)
Own.—Martucci William C   Tr.—Crupi James J (12 0 1 2 .00)   115
LATEST WORKOUTS May 29 Mth 6f fst 1:16 B   May 22 Mth 6f fst 1:18 B   May 14 Mth 6f fst 1:161 B

Kaaren's Smile   Dk. b. or br. f. 3(Apr), by Smile—Best Punt, by Best Western   Lifetime 2 0 0 0 $915   1993 2 M 0 0 $915   1992 0 M 0 0
$25,000 Br.—Biggs M Hays (Ky)
Own.—Biggs Hays & Kaaren   Tr.—Wren Steve (1 0 0 0 .00)   111   Wet 1 0 0 0 $510
23May93- 6Pha fst 6f :221 :461 1:131 ⒻMd Sp Wt 32 1 2 1hd 1hd 43½ 57½ Marquez C H Jr 122 5.60 67-24 PublicDefendant122hdMoKitty122nkWjwonder122 Tired 9
10Feb93- 5OP sly 6f :22 :463 1:121 ⒻMd 25000 47 10 10 52¼ 2½ 33½ 49½ Borel C H 116 6.70 68-19 VlncBy1201½SlsBttflsch1202DmmrPn120 Four wide 3/8 12
LATEST WORKOUTS May 14 Mth 5f fst 1:02 Bg

Lost Another   B. f. 3(Apr), by Lost Code—Another Karla, by Fappiano   Lifetime 1 0 0 0 $130   1992 1 M 0 0 $130
$30,000 Br.—Sessa Judy (Fla)
Own.—Sessa John C   Tr.—Croll Warren A Jr (4 1 0 0 .25)   115
13Dec92- 3Crc fst 6f :22 :461 1:124 ⒻMd Sp Wt 30 2 11 129¾111410171016½ Castillo H Jr 120 29.90 70-12 Gipsy Countess1201 CodeBlum1205StarJolie120 Outrun 12
LATEST WORKOUTS Jun 1 Mth 4f sly :51 B   May 27 Mth 6f fst 1:152 B   ●May 21 Mth 5f my 1:011 Bg   May 17 Mth 5f fst 1:022 B

Yuseppa   B. f. 3(May), by Garthorn—Nishe, by Cornish Prince   Lifetime 2 0 0 0   1993 1 M 0 0   1992 1 M 0 0
$27,500 Br.—Bold Arrow Partnership (Fla)
Own.—Winbound Farms   Tr.—Contessa Gary C (2 0 0 0 .00)   1135
26May93- 3Bel fst 7f :231 :471 1:26 3↑Md 32500 48 5 9 911 88 75¼ 78½ Sweeney K H 108 43.60 64-22 Retirement Account1153 Pick'nRoll115½VeryTricky115 9
26May93-Broke slow, clipped heels, stumbled
29Nov92- 4Aqu fst 6f :222 :461 1:112 ⒻMd 35000 33 9 8 62¾ 64 712 710¾ Bravo J 117 5.20 73-11 TanksforLunch1131½EsternTune1171¾Oglgyn113 Outrun 11
LATEST WORKOUTS May 19 Bel 3f fst :374 Bg   May 15 Bel 6f fst 1:144 H   May 9 Bel tr.t 3f fst :35 H   May 4 Bel 6f fst 1:161 B

Peb   Ch. f. 3(Jun), by Exuberant—Mrs Bridges, by Bold Effort   Lifetime 4 0 0 2 $2,640   1993 4 M 0 2 $2,640   1992 0 M 0 0
$25,000 Br.—Bantivoglio Robert (Fla)
Own.—Bantivoglio Robert T   Tr.—Tammaro John J III (6 1 2 1 .17)   111   Wet 1 0 0 0 $110
16Apr93- 7GS sly 6f :22 :454 1:114 ⒻMd Sp Wt 36 3 5 31½ 34½ 57 714 King E L Jr b 121 7.90 69-20 Studntofthwk1215¼CmpbllSlwp1162¼Rminscnc121 Tired 9
9Apr93- 5GS fst 5f :222 :47 1:002 3↑ⒻMd Sp Wt 34 1 2 31 44 33½ 33¾ King E L Jr b 112 *2.20 82-19 Harlem's Starburst1123 Double Irish112¾Peb112 Evenly 9
26Mar93- 2GS fst 6f :223 :463 1:123 ⒻMd Sp Wt 40 5 3 11½ 1hd 21 36 King E L Jr b 122 13.10 73-15 SunshineKim122nkCmpbellSlewp1175¾Pb122 Weakened 7
2Mar93- 6Pha fst 6f :223 :464 1:134 ⒻMd Sp Wt 8 2 5 53¼ 48 612 814¼ King E L Jr b 122 3.70 58-26 NavyManner122½ThrutheNight1221½PublicDefendnt122 9
2Mar93-Drifted in start, tired
LATEST WORKOUTS May 22 Mth 5f fst 1:014 H   May 13 Mth 4f fst :482 B   Apr 5 GS 5f fst 1:062 B

Well Of Gold   B. f. 3(Mar), by Well Decorated—Inward Joy, by Raise a Native   Lifetime 1 0 0 0   1993 1 M 0 0   1992 0 M 0 0
$30,000 Br.—Evans T Willian (Ohio)
Own.—Green Leonard C   Tr.—Contessa Gary C (2 0 0 0 .00)   115
28May93- 3Bel fst 6f :223 :462 1:114 3↑ⒻMd 35000 35 3 5 41¾ 62¼ 66½ 912 Rodriguez R R5 110 14.40 69-14 K'SGoodGrl1132¼RostMAmr1152¼Undvddttntn112 Tired 12
LATEST WORKOUTS May 22 Bel 7f fst 1:35 B   May 14 Bel 3f fst :353 H   May 8 Bel 6f fst 1:17 Bg   May 4 Bel 6f fst 1:16 B

Also Eligible (Not in Post Position Order):

Arc Melody   Ro. f. 3(Mar), by Vigors—Free Weekend, by Honest Pleasure   Lifetime 2 0 0 0 $510   1993 2 M 0 0 $510   1992 0 M 0 0
$25,000 Br.—Tom Grusenmeyer & Alex Brancato (Ky)
Own.—Grainger Farms   Tr.—Manning Dennis J (8 0 0 0 .00)   11[illegible]   Wet 1 0 0 0 $400
26Mar93- 2GS fst 6f :223 :463 1:123 ⒻMd Sp Wt 21 6 2 55½ 69 612 613¾ Olea R E L 122 6.80 65-15 Sunshine Kim122nk CampbellSlewp1175¾Peb122 Outrun 7
13Feb93- 6GS sly 6f :223 :474 1:161 ⒻMd Sp Wt 31 2 6 39 36 45½ 41½ Olea R E L 119 9.20 59-33 MgntMrk114nkAnthrStt1191½CmpbllSiwp114 Some gain 7
LATEST WORKOUTS May 27 Mth 5f fst 1:03 B   May 19 GS 5f my 1:024 Bg   May 14 GS 4f fst :49 B   May 8 GS 4f fst :48 B

Warren Croll Jr. is one of the best trainers of two-year-olds in the country. The fifth race at Monmouth on June 4 featured a Jimmy Croll three-year-old filly by the name of *Lost Another*. *Lost Another* was dropping into maiden claimers off a dismal performance in a maiden special weight contest at Calder. *Lost Another* was apparently injured in the race and was put on the shelf until April or May, when Croll started to train this filly back to the track. *Lost Another* has been working very nicely back, and also worked six furlongs on May 27. Working longer and in some cases the same distance means condition should be a problem. The only reason I say some cases is because, if it is a breezy work, then condition is not a problem, but, if handily, the horse could have been all-out in the workout. Thus going in he might not have the needed endurance. By way of computer and the jockey club information system, I recalled *Lost Another*'s only race when I was handicapping this event.

CALDER RACE COURSE December 13, 1992

race #	dist fur.	trk con	race type	value of race	wnrs time	runners
3	6.00	FST	FO2M	$14,400	1:12.04	12

horse name	fp	lngths	wt	pp	earned	odds	claim	most recent trk/race #
Gipsy Countess	1	1	120	9	$9,200	15.20		061993CRC09

Unite —— Gipsy Princess (CLO) by The Prince's Pants
                Owner   : LA ISLA STABLE
                Trainer: MILLS RANDY
                Jockey : HERNANDEZ R

Code Blum	2	1	120	8	$2,340	16.50		060593MTH08

                Owner   : H & D STABLE
                Trainer: DONOVAN L WILLIAM
                Jockey : THIBEAU R J JR

Star Jolie	3	6	120	10	$1,300	11.80		063093BEL06

                Owner   : FIVE STAR STABLE INC
                Trainer: MCKENZIE RONALD H
                Jockey : VASQUEZ J

Pattijump	4	6 1/2	115	5	$520	23.10		062593CRC08

                Owner   : CIRCLE DISC FARM INC
                Trainer: HERRERA HUMBERTO JR
                Jockey : PORTILLO D A

Muffer's Pet	5	9 1/2	115	4	$130	18.60		062593CRC08

                Owner   : LEWIS JAMES JR
                Trainer: TORTORA EMANUEL
                Jockey : DIAZ M R

Filimint	6	11 1/2	120	6	$130	1.80		121392CRC03

                Owner   : HINE CAROLYN & SEAMAN BERNICE
                Trainer: HINE HUBERT
                Jockey : SANTOS J A

Misty Kris	7	12	120	12	$130	22.90		052793CRC07

                Owner   : TARTAN STABLE
                Trainer: BRACKEN JAMES E
                Jockey : LEE M A

Mystical Flyer	8	12	120	1	$130	19.10		052893CRC06

                Owner   : ROBINSON J MACK
                Trainer: GOMEZ FRANK
                Jockey : MADRID S O

Cabrilla	9	16 1/2	120	11	$130	9.80		061893CRC08

                Owner   : FORD ALICE
                Trainer: TUCKER MARK S
                Jockey : HUNTER M T

```
Lost Another           10 16 1/2 120   2      $130   29.90           060493MTH05
          Owner   : SESSA JUDY
          Trainer: ROOT RICHARD R
          Jockey : CASTILLO H JR
Future Guest           11 19     120   7      $130    1.60           062693HOL06
          Owner   : HOOPER FRED W
          Trainer: PICOU JAMES E
          Jockey : GONZALEZ M A
Cope's Light           12 23 1/2 120   3      $130    1.60           012293GP 03
          Owner   : HOOPER FRED W
          Trainer: PICOU JAMES E
```

Over the next couple of pages, one will see the lifetime races for all of the horses that beat *Lost Another* that day. Many have gone on to stakes company.

```
Gipsy Countess 1990 CH filly, by Unite 82 — Gipsy Princess (CLO) 84
                                       by  The Prince's Pants 73

Breeder:  William J. Veale


(SPR=93)

1993 in USA and Canada:
```

date	trk race#	dist furl	trk con	race type	value of race	wt	pp	fp	lngths	earned	wnrs time	claim price	# rn
0619	CRC 09	7.00	FST	FO3STK	100,000	113	01	10	27 1/2	0	1:23.2		10

```
      AZALEA H.-L (100,000A)
      1st  Kimscountrydiamond           2nd  Nijivision
      3rd  Hollywood Wildcat
      Owner:   The Prince's Pants
      Trainer: Mills Randy
      Jockey:  Hernandez R
```

| 0530 | CRC 10 | 6.00 | SY | FO3H | 22,000 | 114 | 04 | 03 | 7 1/2 | 2,600 | 1:11.3 | | 07 |

```
      1st  Kimscountrydiamond           2nd  Insight to Cope
      3rd  Gipsy Countess
```

| 0502 | HIA 10 | 7.00 | FST | FO3STK | 50,000 | 112 | 03 | 02 | NK | 10,000 | 1:25.1 | | 07 |

```
      POINSETTIA S.-L (50,000A)
      1st  Debbie's Bliss               2nd  Gipsy Countess
      3rd  Kanned Gold
```

| 0411 | HIA 11 | 6.00 | FST | FO3STK | 40,000 | 116 | 01 | 06 | 15 | 0 | 1:10.3 | | 07 |

```
      JASMINE S.-O (40,000A)
      1st  Best in Sale                 2nd  Gater Co Ed
```

```
      3rd   Hidden Fire
0313 GP 08  6.00   FST FO3AL     27,800 113 03 01  1         18,600 1:11.1        09
      1st  Gipsy Countess                        2nd  Crafty Annie
      3rd  Sakura Fubuki
0220 GP 01  6.00   FST FO3AL     21,000 115 01 03     NK    2,520 1:11.3         08
      1st  Jacody                               2nd  Classy Mirage
      3rd  Gipsy Countess
0130 GP 07  6.00   FST FO3AL     20,000 115 03 07 11          200 1:11.2         11
      1st  Circle Command                       2nd  Jacody
      3rd  Evie M.
0101 CRC08  6.00   GD  FO3AL     17,500 117 02 04  2          700 1:13.1         09
      1st  Best in Sale                         2nd  Nikki B. Mine
      3rd  Courtly Attire
```

1992 in USA and Canada:

date	trk race#	dist furl	trk con	race type	value of race	wt	pp	fp	lngths	earned	wnrs time	claim price	# rn
1213	CRC03	6.00	FST	FO2M	14,400	120	09	01	1	9,200	1:12.4		12

```
      1st  Gipsy Countess                       2nd  Code Blum
      3rd  Star Jolie
```

Gipsy Countess has gone on to win $43,190 in her short campaign, only losing by a neck to *Jacody* and *Classy Mirage*.

Code Blum 1990 CH filly, by Lost Code 84 -- Marshesseaux 83, by Dr. Blum 77

Breeder: Fawn Leap Farm

(SPR=96)

1993 in USA and Canada:

date	trk race#	dist furl	trk con	race type	value of race	wt	pp	fp	lngths	earned	wnrs time	claim price	# rn
0605	MTH08	6.00	FST	FO3STK	79,800	115	07	01	1 3/4	47,880	1:11.0		07

```
         MISS WOODFORD BREEDERS' CUP H.-L (50,000A)
      1st  Code Blum                            2nd  Fighting Jet
      3rd  Touch of Love
      Owner:   H & D Stable
      Trainer: Donovan L William
      Jockey:  Turner T G
0509 PIM09  6.00   FST FO3STK     53,625 121 01 03      3/4    5,899 1:11.1       05
         MISS PREAKNESS S.-L (50,000A)
```

```
     1st   My Rosa                       2nd   Fighting Jet
     3rd   Code Blum
0420 PIM08  6.00   FST F03AL       17,640 114 03 01  4 1/4  10,260 1:11.0             05
     1st   Code Blum                     2nd   My Rosa
     3rd   Bocamis
0203 GP 09  7.00   FST F03STK      74,850 113 04 04  6 1/2   4,527 1:23.3             09
          FORWARD GAL BREEDERS' CUP S.-G2 (50,000A)
     1st   Sum Runner                    2nd   Boots 'n Jackie
     3rd   Lunar Spook
0114 GP 08  6.00   FST F03AL       18,000 113 04 01  2 1/2  10,800 1:10.4             08
     1st   Code Blum                     2nd   Circle Command
     3rd   Miss Pride
```

1992 in USA and Canada:

date	trk race#	dist furl	trk con	race type	value of race	wt	pp	fp	lngths	earned	wnrs time	claim price	# rn
1227	CRC03	6.00	FST	F02M	13,000	120	12	01	3		7,800	1:11.4		12

```
     1st   Code Blum                     2nd   Les Etoiles (IRE)
     3rd   High Decision
```

| 1213 | CRC03 | 6.00 | FST | F02M | 14,400 | 120 | 08 | 02 | 1 | | 2,340 | 1:12.4 | | 12 |

```
     1st   Gipsy Countess                2nd   Code Blum
     3rd   Star Jolie
```

| 0919 | PIM02 | 6.00 | FST | F02M | 16,700 | 119 | 08 | 05 | 10 1/2 | | 465 | 1:12.3 | | 10 |

```
     1st   Cormorant's Flight            2nd   Buck Roll
     3rd   Tis a Hooch
```

> *Code Blum* is a winner of $89,971 and captured the Miss Woodford
> Breeders Cup at Monmouth Park.

Star Jolie 1990 DK B/ filly, by John Alden 74 -- La Jolie 78, by Sir Wiggle 67

Breeder: Farnsworth Farms

(SPR=96)

1993 in USA and Canada:

date	trk race#	dist furl	trk con	race type	value of race	wt	pp	fp	lngths	earned	wnrs time	claim price	# rn
0630	BEL06	8.50T	FRM	F3UAL	30,500	110	03	02	2		6,710	1:42.2		09

```
     1st   Winnetka                      2nd   Star Jolie
     3rd   Statuette
     Owner:   Perlow Jeffrey M
     Trainer: Terrill William V
```

```
        Jockey:  Carr D
0605 BELO2  8.50T FRM FO3STK    53.950 116 04 04  4 1/2   3,237 1:40.3         09
        TANYA S.-L (50,000A)
        1st  Russian Bride                2nd  Bright Penny
        3rd  Magic Street (GB)
0522 BELO3  9.00  FST FO3AL     30,500 116 02 04  5 1/4   1,830 1:50.0         08
        1st  Testy Trestle                2nd  Standard Equipment
        3rd  Defense Spending
0508 BELO8  8.00  FST FO3STK   150,000 121 03 05 15 1/4       0 1:35.2         06
        ACORN S.-G1 (150,000A)
        1st  Sky Beauty                   2nd  Educated Risk
        3rd  In Her Glory
0410 HIA11  9.00  FST  O3STK   200,000 117 07 05  5 1/4   6,000 1:51.1         09
        FLAMINGO S.-L (200,000A)
        1st  Forever Whirl                2nd  Bull Inthe Heather
        3rd  Pride Prevails
0320 TAM10  8.50  FST FO3STK   100,000 111 09 01  2      60,000 1:45.3         11
        FLORIDA OAKS-L (100,000A)
        1st  Star Jolie                   2nd  Hollywood Wildcat
        3rd  Jacody
0226 GP 06  8.50  FST FO3AL     23,000 112 01 02  2 1/2   4,370 1:44.3         08
        1st  Sheila's Revenge             2nd  Star Jolie
        3rd  Star Guest
0124 GP 05  8.50  FST FO3AL     19,000 114 04 03  4 1/4   2,280 1:46.2         08
        1st  Dream Mary                   2nd  T. V. Maud
        3rd  Star Jolie
0102 CRC05  7.00  GD  FO3M      16,400 120 03 01  NK     11,200 1:26.1         09
        1st  Star Jolie                   2nd  Muffer's Pet
        3rd  Gana

1992 in USA and Canada:

     trk     dist  trk   race   value of                      wnrs   claim  #
date race#   furl  con   type    race    wt  pp fp lngths earned  time   price  rn
---- -----   ----  ---   ----   -------  --  -- -- ------ ------  ----   -----  --
1213 CRC03  6.00  FST FO2M      14,400 120 10 03  6       1,300 1:12.4         12
        1st  Gipsy Countess               2nd  Code Blum
        3rd  Star Jolie
```

Star Jolie captured the $100,000 Florida Oaks at Tampa Bay Downs and finished fifth beaten by 5¾ lengths to *Forever Whirl* and *Bull in the Heather*.

Pattijump 1990 B filly, by Bailjumper 74 — Hot 83, by Youth 73

Breeder: Arthur I. Appleton

(SPR=78)

1993 in USA and Canada:

date	trk race#	dist furl	trk con	race type	value of race	wt	pp	fp	lngths	earned	wnrs time	claim price	# rn
0625	CRC08	6.00	SY	F03CL	14,400	113	06	03	6	1,690	1:11.1	40,000	07

1st Merry Maudie 2nd Bachata Rosa
3rd Pattijump
Owner: Circle Disc Farm Inc
Trainer: Delgado Oscar
Jockey: Coa E M

0610	CRC07	6.00	FST	F03CL	13,300	113	04	02	5	2,280	1:10.2	32,000	08

1st Merry Maudie 2nd Pattijump
3rd Di's Known Fact

0530	CRC10	6.00	SY	F03H	22,000	111	07	07	18 1/4	200	1:11.3		07

1st Kimscountrydiamond 2nd Insight to Cope
3rd Gipsy Countess

0514	HIA08	7.00	FST	F03CL	14,400	111	04	05	11 1/4	120	1:25.0	50,000	07

1st Mary Morning 2nd So Say all of Us
3rd Future of Gold

0502	HIA10	7.00	FST	F03STK	50,000	111	06	07	18 1/2	0	1:25.1		07

POINSETTIA S.-L (50,000A)
1st Debbie's Bliss 2nd Gipsy Countess
3rd Kanned Gold

0423	HIA09	6.00	FST	F03AL	18,000	108	03	01	5	12,000	1:12.0		10

1st Pattijump 2nd Courtly Attire
3rd Naked Glory

0408	HIA01	6.00	FST	F03MCL	6,500	117	11	01	2 1/2	3,900	1:12.2	16,000	11

1st Pattijump 2nd Sue Sez
3rd Shawnee Sunset

0117	GP 03	7.00	FST	F03M	16,000	115	01	07	9 1/4	160	1:25.3		08

1st Bally Five 2nd Bujama
3rd Magical Queen (IRE)

0107	CRC05	8.50	FST	F03M	14,000	120	01	06	25 3/4	140	1:49.3		06

1st C. U. Later Sal 2nd Trufulla Rose
3rd Beereadyforme

1992 in USA and Canada:

date	trk race#	dist furl	trk con	race type	value of race	wt	pp	fp	lngths	earned	wnrs time	claim price	# rn
1227	CRC03	6.00	FST	F02M	13,000	120	02	04	10	520	1:11.4		12

1st Code Blum 2nd Les Etoiles (IRE)
3rd High Decision

Pattijump made her second career start and finished 10 lengths behind *Code Blum* and broke her maiden three starts later on April 4. On April 23, she came back to win an allowance $18,000 event.

Muffer's Pet 1990 CH filly, by On to Glory 71 —— Mitchel's Pet 73
by Insubordination 67

Breeder: Brad Gay & Shirley Gay

(SPR=87)

1993 in USA and Canada:

date	trk race#	dist furl	trk con	race type	value of race	wt	pp	fp	lngths	earned	wnrs time	claim price	# rn
0625	CRC08	6.00	SY	FO3CL	14,400	118	01	04	9 1/2	650	1:11.1	40,000	07

1st Merry Maudie   2nd Bachata Rosa
3rd Pattijump
Owner: Lewis James Jr
Trainer: Tortora Emanuel
Jockey: Russ M L

0609	CRC09	8.50	FST	FO3STK	20,450	112	05	06	8 1/2	0	1:46.1		07

SILVERED SILK H.-N (20,000A)
1st A Demon a Day   2nd Liberada
3rd Urus

0530	CRC10	6.00	SY	FO3H	22,000	112	02	05	8 3/4	200	1:11.3		07

1st Kimscountrydiamond   2nd Insight to Cope
3rd Gipsy Countess

0516	HIA10	8.50T	FRM	FO3STK	35,000	111	08	09	16 3/4	0	1:42.2		10

PATRICIA S.-O (35,000A)
1st Liberada   2nd Nicely Wild
3rd Debbie's Bliss

0411	HIA10	7.00	FST	FO3AL	18,000	115	12	01	3/4	12,000	1:25.0		12

1st Muffer's Pet   2nd Caanon's Destiny
3rd Nicely Wild

0308	OTC03	8.50	FST	FO3STK	150,000	122	04	05	17	4,500	1:47.4		11

OCALA BREEDERS' SALES CHAMPIONSHIP S.-LR (150,000A)
1st Sum Runner   2nd Dasharoo
3rd Unlaced

0225	GP 04	6.00	FST	FO3MCL	20,300	116	10	01	8 1/2	13,700	1:12.3	70,000	11

1st Muffer's Pet   2nd Anniversary Bliss
3rd Toujours Jolie

0212	GP 04	7.00	FST	FO3M	17,000	120	03	03	5	1,870	1:24.4		10

1st Testy Trestle   2nd Miss Obsession
3rd Muffer's Pet

0121	GP 06	8.50	FST	FO3M	17,000	115	07	04	5 3/4	850	1:46.0		11

```
1st   Gana                            2nd   Harlan Honey
3rd   Vouch
0110 CRC06  6.00  GD  F03M      13,000 120 06 02  4        2,340 1:12.2          11
1st   Jacody                          2nd   Muffer's Pet
3rd   Naked Glory
```

Muffer's Pet broke her maiden in a maiden claiming $70,000 event and has compiled $40,610 in career earnings.

Misty Kris 1990 DK B/ filly, by Kris S. 77 — In all Truth 82, by In Reality 64

Breeder: Sally Andersen

(SPR=37)

1993 in USA and Canada:

date	trk race#	dist furl	trk con	race type	value of race	wt	pp	fp	lngths	earned	wnrs time	claim price	# rn
0527	CRC07	8.50T	FRM	F34M	15,500	114	03	08	26 1/2	140	1:45.0		08

```
1st   Koollanna                       2nd   Al's Memory
3rd   Slew O Tunes
Owner:    Tartan Stable
Trainer: Bracken James E
Jockey:  Nunez E O
```

date	trk race#	dist furl	trk con	race type	value of race	wt	pp	fp	lngths	earned	wnrs time	claim price	# rn
0214	GP 03	6.00	FST	F03M	17,000	120	05	10	25 1/4	170	1:11.1		11

```
1st   Crafty Annie                    2nd   So True
3rd   Clare's Opinion
```

1992 in USA and Canada:

date	trk race#	dist furl	trk con	race type	value of race	wt	pp	fp	lngths	earned	wnrs time	claim price	# rn
1227	CRC03	6.00	FST	F02M	13,000	120	01	10	28	130	1:11.4		12

```
1st   Code Blum                       2nd   Les Etoiles (IRE)
3rd   High Decision
```

date	trk race#	dist furl	trk con	race type	value of race	wt	pp	fp	lngths	earned	wnrs time	claim price	# rn
1213	CRC03	6.00	FST	F02M	14,400	120	12	07	12	130	1:12.4		12

```
1st   Gipsy Countess                  2nd   Code Blum
3rd   Star Jolie
```

Misty Kris is the only horse to beat *Lost Another* that has not broken her maiden, but her light race schedule is probably due to injury.

Mystical Flyer 1990 CH filly, by Jeblar 82 -- Misty Current 81

                                              by Little Current 71

Breeder: Farnsworth Farm

(SPR=75)

1993 in USA and Canada:

date	trk race#	dist furl	trk con	race type	value of race	wt	pp	fp	lngths	earned	wnrs time	claim price	# rn
0528	CRC06	7.00	FST	FO3CL	12,000	116	01	07	18 1/2	120	1:24.4	30,000	07
	1st Caanon's Destiny								2nd Othila				
	3rd Eskimo Slush												
	Owner: Robinson J Mack												
	Trainer: Gomez Frank												
	Jockey: Velez J a Jr												
0502	HIA06	7.00	FST	FO3CL	13,200	118	05	05	20 1/2	110	1:24.4	40,000	06
	1st Future of Gold								2nd Eskimo Slush				
	3rd Slew Knew												
0410	HIA06	6.00	FST	FO3CL	11,500	116	04	01	1 1/4	7,700	1:12.3	32,000	07
	1st Mystical Flyer								2nd Quaker Bonnet				
	3rd Nezzie Baby												
0312	GP 07	8.32	FST	FO3CL	20,000	114	03	08	12 1/4	200	1:43.2	45,000	08
	1st Royal Explosive								2nd Common Scheme				
	3rd Mystic Tower												
0204	GP 01	7.00	FST	FO3MCL	15,500	120	10	01	NO	10,500	1:27.1	50,000	12
	1st Mystical Flyer								2nd Gin Joint				
	3rd Alluring Secretary												
0118	GP 02	6.00	FST	FO3MCL	12,000	120	04	04	2 1/4	480	1:12.3	50,000	12
	1st Native Niki								2nd Toujours Jolie				
	3rd Southern Nature												

1992 in USA and Canada:

date	trk race#	dist furl	trk con	race type	value of race	wt	pp	fp	lngths	earned	wnrs time	claim price	# rn
1213	CRC03	6.00	FST	FO2M	14,400	120	01	08	12	130	1:12.4		12
	1st Gipsy Countess								2nd Code Blum				
	3rd Star Jolie												
1115	CRC03	6.00	FST	FO2M	14,400	119	04	05	13 1/2	130	1:12.1		08
	1st Best in Sale								2nd Liliha				
	3rd Muffer's Pet												
0905	CRC03	6.00	FST	FO2M	14,400	117	08	05	5 1/4	130	1:13.1		09
	1st Princess Mypromise								2nd Mystic Tower				
	3rd Sophisticatedblend												
0816	CRC03	7.00	FST	FO2M	14,400	116	02	05	7 1/2	130	1:26.4		07
	1st Mary Morning								2nd More Freedom				
	3rd You Spoiled Brat												

Mystical Flyer broke her maiden in the claiming $50,000 ranks in her second start after racing against *Lost Another*. *Mystical Flyer* has also come back to win again.

Cabrilla 1990 CH filly, by Cabrini Green 75 -- Scream 79, by Nostrum 71

Breeder: Oscar Penn

(SPR=79)

1993 in USA and Canada:

date	trk race#	dist furl	trk con	race type	value of race	wt	pp	fp	lngths	earned	wnrs time	claim price	# rn
0618	CRC08	6.00	FST	F3UAL	15,500	113	07	10	14	140	1:10.3		11
	1st Twenty Second Ave									2nd Lucky Ho			
	3rd Bridle Show												
	Owner: Ford Alice												
	Trainer: Tucker Mark S												
	Jockey: Henry W T												
0526	CRC09	6.00	FST	FO3AL	15,500	111	01	02	3 3/4	2,660	1:12.3		07
	1st Real Bucks									2nd Cabrilla			
	3rd Nezzie Baby												
0205	GP 05	8.50	SY	FO3AL	21,000	115	05	04	2	1,050	1:49.1		07
	1st Gana									2nd Explicit Export			
	3rd Luro's Law												
0109	CRC08	9.00	SY	FO3AL	15,000	115	03	08	29 1/4	150	1:56.3		08
	1st A Demon a Day									2nd Congo Queen			
	3rd Crying Eyes												

1992 in USA and Canada:

date	trk race#	dist furl	trk con	race type	value of race	wt	pp	fp	lngths	earned	wnrs time	claim price	# rn
1229	CRC06	9.00	FST	FO2M	14,000	114	06	01	4 1/2	8,400	1:59.3		08
	1st Cabrilla									2nd Sharp Tracy			
	3rd Trufulla Rose												
1213	CRC03	6.00	FST	FO2M	14,400	120	11	09	16 1/2	130	1:12.4		12
	1st Gipsy Countess									2nd Code Blum			
	3rd Star Jolie												
1129	CRC04	6.00	FST	FO2M	13,000	119	03	02	1	2,470	1:13.1		07
	1st Lee's Lost									2nd Cabrilla			
	3rd Peaceful Pam												
1115	CRC03	6.00	FST	FO2M	14,400	119	03	06	20	130	1:12.1		08
	1st Best in Sale									2nd Liliha			
	3rd Muffer's Pet												

After finishing just a nose in front of *Lost Another*, *Cabrilla* went on to win by 4½ lengths in a maiden special weight contest in her next start.

What does all this tell us? It tells us that the competition that *Lost Another* faced was tough, and all except one were able to go on and break their maiden. Two questions had to be answered before *Lost Another* was playable.

1) Was *Lost Another* in a winnable position?

2) Was *Lost Another* in top condition?

The class level was fine, as we saw horses win in claiming $70,000. By working 6 furlongs in good time, plus her other workout of 101⅕ breezing from the gate and 02 breezing, she became an excellent play.

The rest of the June 4 field at Monmouth didn't stack up to be too much. *Afternoon Star*, *Kaaren's Smile*, and *Peb* were unplayable because of the two to three start theory.

Friends R Us workouts were too slow and she probably would be happier on the claiming $10,000 level.

Nundo Catino didn't show a thing in her debut at Gulfstream. She has lasix and blinkers, and those are bad signs for her debut. Lasix and blinkers are supposed to correct a problem. It seems when trainers install one or both of these tactics for an initial start, they are already guessing and trying to make improvements before the horse runs.

Dancing for Gold is another one who did not show much in her debut at a less competitive track, Garden State. Check *Ride Julie*, who was 17 lengths ahead of this one, running in maiden, claiming $10,000.

Mon Montreaux not been working fast, but has been working at this distance, and that is a plus.

Well of Gold showed good early speed in her debut at Belmont. Blinkers will help, but she will have to hustle from this post and that is something she doesn't need. A definite winner going long, with the conditioning not being a problem.

Lost Another was just better than this field. She stalked the pace and drew away to a 1½ length victory. *Lost Another* paid $10.40 and keyed a 196.60 exacta with *Mon Montreaux*, a first time starter who worked the same distance.

FIFTH RACE

Monmouth

JUNE 4, 1993

6 FURLONGS. (1.07⁴) MAIDEN CLAIMING. Purse $10,000. Fillies and Mares. 3-year-olds
and up. Weights: 3-year-olds, 115 lbs.; older, 122 lbs. Claiming Price $30,000; for each $2,500
to $25,000, 2 lbs.

Value of race $10,000; value to winner $6,000; second $1,900; third $1,100; fourth $500; balance of starters $100 each. Mutuel
pool $59,055. Exacta Pool $55,340 Trifecta Pool $57,452

Last Raced	Horse	M/Eqt.A.Wt	PP	St	¼	½	Str	Fin	Jockey	Cl'g Pr	Odds $1
13Dec92 3Crc¹⁰	Lost Another	3 115	7	1	4½	3½	11½	11½	Santagata N	30000	4.20
	Mon Montreaux	b 3 115	5	6	7³	5²	2hd	21¾	Squartino RA	30000	15.20
	Friends R Us	3 111	1	8	61½	6³	4³	35¼	Bravo J	25000	7.20
4Apr93 1Tam²	Afternoon Star	b 3 106	2	5	3hd	4hd	5³	4²	HomstrRBJr⁵	25000	2.20
16Apr93 7GS⁷	Peb	Lb 3 112	8	2	22½	11½	31½	5⁷	Nied D	25000	5.50
23May93 6Pha⁵	Kaaren's Smile	3 112	6	4	1½	21½	62½	62¼	MrquezCHJr	25000	3.20
28May93 3Bel⁹	Well Of Gold	b 3 115	9	3	5½	7⁸	7¹⁴	7¹⁸	Torres C A	30000	19.70
12May93 7GS⁷	Dancing for Gold	L 3 112	4	7	9	8	8	8	Olea R E	25000	69.30
27Mar93 3GP¹⁰	Mundo Latino	L 3 115	3	9	3⁴	—	—	—	Rivera L Jr	30000	12.90

Mundo Latino, Pulled up.

OFF AT 3:01 Start good Won driving Time, :22 , :46¹, :59⁴, 1:13² Track fast.

$2 Mutuel Prices:

10-LOST ANOTHER	10.40	6.40	5.20
8-MON MONTREAUX		16.40	10.00
2-FRIENDS R US			4.80

$2 EXACTA 10-8 PAID $196.60 $2 TRIFECTA 10-8-2 PAID $1,257.20

B. f, (Apr), by Lost Code—Another Karla, by Fappiano. Trainer Croll Warren A Jr. Bred by Sessa Judy (Fla).

LOST ANOTHER moved to the front approaching the furlong marker then held MON MONTREAUX safe. The
latter advanced outside turning for home and finished well. FRIENDS R US, five wide into the lane advanced into
midstretch then lacked the needed late response. AFTERNOON STAR was steadied some along the rail nearing the
stretch, eased out and tired. PEB drew clear on the turn and gave way in the drive. KAAREN'S SMILE showed the
early way, saved ground and was steadied slightly when appearing to shy some nearing the quarter pole then gave
way. WELL OF GOLD was through turning for home. MUNDO LATINO was pulled up nearing the turn and fell after
hemorrhaging. DANCING FOR GOLD wore mud caulks.

Owners— 1, Sessa John C; 2, Martucci William C; 3, D M S Farm; 4, Aldright Charlie; 5, Bantivoglio Robert
T; 6, Biggs Hays & Kaaren; 7, Green Leonard C; 8, Farro Michael; 9, Levine Robert L.

Trainers— 1, Croll Warren A Jr; 2, Crupi James J; 3, Spina Chuck; 4, Rispoli Joseph N; 5, Tammaro John J
III; 6, Wren Steve; 7, Contessa Gary C; 8, Farro Michael; 9, Levine Robert L.

Corrected weight: Friends R Us 111 pounds. Overweight: Peb 1 pound; Kaaren's Smile 1; Dancing for Gold 1. .
Scratched—Forever Crafty; Nat's My Gal (2May93 3Hia⁵); Yuseppa (26May93 3Bel⁷); Arc Melody (26Mar93 2GS⁶).

On June 25 in the fifth race, eight two-year-olds were headed
postward to this Maiden Special Weight contest. This race is another
prime example of "Stupidity." The morning line favorite was *Wildest
Dreams*, a failure as the 3-2 favorite twice. In *Wildest Dreams's* first start
she beat *Lori's Passion* by a head. *Lori's Passion* also came to Monmouth
Park and failed miserably against *Pagofire*, losing by 21¾ lengths. *Wildest
Dreams's* incentive is running against New Jersey bred horses for the enhancement in purse, and maybe to catch a easy field. As I looked down
the entries, there was nothing that was working consistently, except
My Protege, who was working up a storm and received a comment for her
47 drill from the gate.

5

5 FURLONGS. (.561) MAIDEN SPECIAL WEIGHT. Purse $21,200 (purse reflects $4,200 NJ–bred enhancement). Fillies. 2–year–olds. Registered New Jersey–breds. Weight: 117 lbs.

Coupled—Jersey Gold and My Protege.

Holyterial
B. f. 2(May), by Magesterial—Holy Water, by Divine Royalty
Br.—Edwards Robert L (NJ)
Tr.—McKee John D (1 0 0 0 .00)

117

Own.—Edwards Robert L

Lifetime 1993 1 M 0 0
1 0 0 0

18Jun93- 4Pha fst 5f :222 :46 :594 ⒻMd Sp Wt 20 9 10 109 99¾ 811 68½ Dupuis T J 118 14.50 76-18 Amvldhop118½NormndyBll118²¼MdclRcrd113 No factor 10

LATEST WORKOUTS ●Jun 12 CT 4f fst :483 Hg   May 29 CT 4f fst :502 Hg   May 21 CT 4f fst :493 H   May 14 CT 3f fst :372 H

Paula's Day
Ch. f. 2(Apr), by Henbane—Dancing Karla, by Green Dancer
Br.—Judy Sessa (NJ)
Tr.—Scanlon Robert N (2 1 0 0 .50)

117

Own.—Sessa John C

Lifetime 1993 0 M 0 0
0 0 0 0

LATEST WORKOUTS Jun 19 Mth 4f fst :483 Hg   Jun 12 Mth 4f fst :482 Hg   Jun 5 Mth 3f fst :363 Bg

Aspiring Proof
Ch. f. 2(Apr), by Proof—Aspire, by Baldski
Br.—Daniel Ljoka (NJ)
Tr.—Pregman John S Jr (5 1 0 1 .20)

117

Own.—Ljoka Daniel

Lifetime 1993 0 M 0 0
0 0 0 0

LATEST WORKOUTS Jun 19 Mth 4f fst :482 Hg   Jun 13 Mth 4f fst :494 Bg   Jun 8 Mth 3f fst :381 B   Jun 2 Mth 5f fst 1:043 B

One Free Spirit
Ch. f. 2(Apr), by Free Reality—One Trick Pony, by Johnny Appleseed
Br.—Corsiglia Beatrice (NJ)
Tr.—Medio Walter L (—)

117

Own.—Scott Kenneth

Lifetime 1993 2 M 0 0 $560
2 0 0 0
$560

Entered 23Jun93- 1 ATL

5Jun93- 1Atl fst 4½f :23 :471 :534 ⒻMd Sp Wt 26 4 5 53½ 45 43 Olea R E 117 8.40 89-11 Allen'sCheer117½AlaCasey117½EmerldFever117 No bid 6
29Apr93- 3GS fst 4½f :23 :471 :534 ⒻMd Sp Wt 2 5 3 56½ 513 510½ Olea R E 117 6.20 86-16 Sixmore117¾ House Divided117³ Aye Blue117 Outrun 7

LATEST WORKOUTS May 29 Atl 3f fst :363 B   May 22 Atl 3f gd :37 B

Tj's Tuff as Nails
Gr. f. 2(Mar), by Bates Motel—Wears Like Iron, by Iron Ruler
Br.—Lindsay Simon & Carol Ahearn (N.J.)
Tr.—Demasi Kathleen A (1 0 0 0 .00)

117

Own.—Pewter Stable

Lifetime 1993 0 M 0 0
0 0 0 0

LATEST WORKOUTS ●May 29 GS 3f fst :364 B

Melanie Mark
B. f. 2(Feb), by Elocutionist—First Heaven, by Cyane
Br.—Bronwyn Pait (NJ)
Tr.—Bonaventura Paul (10 1 2 2 .10)

112⁵

Own.—Bonaventura Paul

Lifetime 1993 0 M 0 0
0 0 0 0

LATEST WORKOUTS Jun 23 Mth 3f fst :363 Bg   Jun 11 Mth 5f fst 1:034 B   Jun 4 Mth 5f fst 1:032 B   May 13 Hia 4f fst :484 Hg

Wildest Dreams
Dk. b. or br. f. 2(May), by Talc—Valentine Kiss, by Reflected Glory
Br.—Dianne Boyken (NJ)
Tr.—Nu Equestar Stable

117

Own.—Nu Equestar Stable

Lifetime 1993 2 M 2 0 $10,340
2 0 2 0
$10,340

2Jun93- 3Bel fst 5½f :223 :464 1:053 ⒻMd Sp Wt 41 3 1 2½ 2¹ 2³ 2¹¹ Davis R G 117 *1.50 76-12 RedSoul117¹¹WildestDrems117³JenGin117 Second best 7
24May93- 3Bel fst 5f :222 :464 1:00 ⒻMd Sp Wt 62 5 3 2ʰᵈ 1½ 2¹½ 2¾ Davis R G 117 1.50e 80-22 Warta117²WildestDreams117ʰᵈLori'sPassion117 Gamely 6

LATEST WORKOUTS Jun 16 Bel 5f fst 1:013 H   May 8 Bel 4f fst :484 Hg   Apr 30 Bel tr.t 4f fst :483 H

Judicial Power
Dk. b. or br. f. 2(Jan), by Horatius—Nottaten, by Smarten
Br.—Marjorie R. Francis (NJ)
Tr.—Manning Dennis J (29 3 6 1 .10)

117

Own.—Southview Farm

Lifetime 1993 0 M 0 0
0 0 0 0

LATEST WORKOUTS Jun 19 Mth 4f fst :484 Bg   Jun 13 Mth 4f fst :503 Bg   Jun 7 Mth 4f fst :52 B   May 31 Mth 3f fst :372 B

Ala Casey
Dk. b. or br. f. 2(Mar), by Two Davids—Sizzling Skirt, by Tentam
Br.—Hallmark Farm (NJ)
Tr.—Biamonte Sharon (—)

117

Own.—Hallmark Farm

Lifetime 1993 1 M 1 0 $1,500
1 0 1 0
$1,500

5Jun93- 1Atl fst 4½f :23 :471 :534 ⒻMd Sp Wt 32 3 3 1ʰᵈ 2¹ 2¹½ Chavis S T b 117 2.20 91-11 Allen'sCheer117½AlaCsey117½EmerldFever117 2nd best 6

LATEST WORKOUTS Jun 15 Atl 5f fst 1:02 B   May 28 Atl 4f fst :492 Bg   May 24 Atl 4f fst :492 Bg   May 22 Atl 3f gd :371 B

Jersey Gold
B. f. 2(Apr), by Great Prospector—Retton's Gold, by Miteas Well Laff
Br.—Stanley Panco (NJ)
Tr.—Deville Carl (3 0 0 0 .00)

117

Own.—Panco Stanley M

Lifetime 1993 0 M 0 0
0 0 0 0

LATEST WORKOUTS Jun 11 Mth 4f fst :48 H   May 29 Mth 4f fst :49 B   May 22 Mth 3f fst :36 Bg

My Protege
Ch. f. 2(Apr), by Apalachee—Maitz's Lady, by Slady Castle
Br.—Corsiglia Beatrice & Panco Stanley (NJ)
Tr.—Deville Carl (3 0 0 0 .00)

117

Own.—Tracy Celest & Panco Stanley I

Lifetime 1993 0 M 0 0
0 0 0 0

LATEST WORKOUTS ●Jun 21 Mth 3f fst :35 H   Jun 11 Mth 4f fst :471 H   ●May 29 Mth 4f fst :47 Hg   May 22 Mth 4f fst :493 Bg

FIFTH RACE

Monmouth

5 FURLONGS. (.561) MAIDEN SPECIAL WEIGHT. Purse $21,200 (purse reflects $4,200 NJ–bred enhancement). Fillies. 2–year–olds. Registered New Jersey–breds. Weight: 117 lbs.

JUNE 25, 1993

Value of race $21,200; value to winner $12,720; second $4,240; third $2,332; fourth $1,060; balance of starters $212 each.
Mutuel pool $62,947. Exacta Pool $69,568 Trifecta Pool $62,069

Last Raced	Horse	M/Eqt.A.Wt	PP	St	⅛	⅜	Str	Fin	Jockey	Odds $1
	My Protege	2 117	8	1	1 1½	1 2	1 4½	1 3½	Wilson R	1.20
	Melanie Mark	2 112	5	3	6½	5½	4½	2 4½	Homeister R BJr5	18.30
	Aspiring Proof	2 117	3	8	7 6	4 3	3 hd	3 1½	Lopez C C	20.20
	Tj's Tuff as Nails	2 117	4	4	2 1½	2½	2 2	4 3¾	Ferrer J C	23.60
2Jun93 3Bel2	Wildest Dreams	2 117	6	5	3 3	3 2	5 6	5 hd	Bravo J	1.50
18Jun93 4Pha6	Holyterial	2 117	1	7	8	8	7 2	6 2	Lopez C	37.00
5Jun93 1Atl2	Ala Casey	b 2 117	7	2	5 hd	6 hd	6 hd	7 9	Chavis S T	19.20
	Paula's Day	b 2 117	2	6	4 1½	7 3	8	8	Santagata N	5.00

OFF AT 2:56 Start good Won ridden out Time, :22 , :461, :594 Track fast.

$2 Mutuel Prices:	1-MY PROTEGE	4.40	3.40	3.20
	6-MELANIE MARK		9.60	6.20
	4-ASPIRING PROOF			6.20

$2 EXACTA 1–6 PAID $61.80 $2 TRIFECTA 1–6–4 PAID $471.00

Ch. f, (Apr), by Apalachee—Maltz's Lady, by Slady Castle. Trainer Deville Carl. Bred by Corsiglia Beatrice & Panco Stanley (NJ).

MY PROTEGE, a bit slow to load, broke to command and held a clear advantage to the lane, widened into midstretch then was ridden out. MELANIE MARK, in tight quarters briefly soon after entering the turn, moved to the rail and finished well. ASPIRING PROOF, jostled between foes at the start, advanced outside on the turn and raced five wide into the lane then weakened late. TJ'S TUFF AS NAILS broke inward, advanced inside to the turn, eased out on the bend and weakened in the drive. WILDEST DREAMS loomed a threat from the outside to the drive and gave way. HOLYTERIAL broke outward and was outrun. ALA CASEY gave way on the turn. PAULA'S DAY, in tight at the start, gave way on the turn.

Owners— 1, Tracy Celest & Panco Stanley I; 2, Bonaventura Paul; 3, Ljoka Daniel; 4, Pewter Stable; 5, Equestar Racing Stable; 6, Edwards Robert L; 7, Hallmark Farm; 8, Sessa John C.

Trainers— 1, Deville Carl; 2, Bonaventura Paul; 3, Pregman John S Jr; 4, Demasi Kathleen A; 5, Rice Linda; 6, McKee John D; 7, Biamonte Sharon; 8, Scanlon Robert N.

Scratched—One Free Spirit (23Jun93 1Atl4), Judicial Power; Jersey Gold.

As I expressed throughout this book, maidens who ship to a better track usually fail, but do get bet down, especially the ones from New York. For all the readers out there that think Monmouth is not more competitive than Belmont, they are definitely wrong. Belmont tends to be top heavy, where all the good animals win their stakes and the rest are below average. If you claim a horse for $15,000 that is consistently running well at Belmont and bring him to Monmouth, he or she would not even finish in the money, while being at the same claiming $15,000 level. You will consistently see this, now that you are aware. Bet on it.

Even though *Wildest Dreams* was a New Jersey bred and that was the reason for coming to Monmouth Park, I have to believe that Linda

Rice thought she could have won there, and if Monmouth Park's competition is tougher, how is she going to win here? If we as handicappers think about the horses we are wagering upon and do our homework, we will increase profits.

Even as a maiden expert, I have to admit I do like to shy away from bad maiden claimers, but two-year-olds can still be very profitable. The reason I say this is that in two-year-old maiden claiming races, one horse usually sticks out above the rest. The exactas and trifectas might be close to impossible, but usually, we can be guaranteed a stick out.

3

5 ½ FURLONGS. (1.03) MAIDEN CLAIMING. Purse $11,500. Fillies, 2–year–olds. Weight, 117 lbs. Claiming Price $35,000, for each $2,500 to $30,000 2 lbs.

Euphoric Interlude
Dk. b. or br. f. 2(May), by Ziggy's Boy—Discreet Matinee, by Our Native
KRONE J A (203 37 25 32 .18) $35,000 Br.—Kimran Stables (Ky)
Own.—Nicholson Ronald Tr.—Toner James J (10 0 0 0 .00) **117**
Lifetime 0 0 0 0 1993 0 M 0 0
LATEST WORKOUTS Jun 17 Bel 4f fst :491 B Jun 2 Bel tr.t 5f fst 1:03 B May 26 Bel 4f fst :493 Hg May 20 Bel 5f gd 1:03 B

K Bomb
Dk. b. or br. f. 2(Mar), by Explosive Bid—Kristin S, by Kris S
MAPLE E (96 15 18 12 .16) $35,000 Br.—Chevalier Stable (NY)
Own.—Chevalier Stable Tr.—Shapoff Stanley R (46 8 5 5 .17) **117**
Lifetime 0 0 0 0 1993 0 M 0 0
LATEST WORKOUTS Jun 21 Bel tr.t 4f sly :491 B Jun 17 Bel tr.t 3f fst :361 H Jun 12 Bel tr.t 3f fst :37 B

Safe At Home
Dk. b. or br. f. 2(May), by Homebuilder—Dazzled, by Majestic Light
SMITH M E (212 50 29 29 .24) $35,000 Br.—Stilz Brothers & Pin Oak Stable Inc (Ky)
Own.—Minassian Harry Tr.—Barbara Robert (40 8 5 3 .20) **117**
Lifetime 0 0 0 0 1993 0 M 0 0
LATEST WORKOUTS Jun 12 Bel 5f fst 1:021 Hg Jun 4 Bel 4f fst :483 H May 29 Bel tr.t 3f fst :371 B

Susans Melody
B. f. 2(Mar), by Compliance—Viking Melody, by Viking
CHAVEZ J F (174 31 23 15 .18) $35,000 Br.—Newe John F (NY)
Own.—Newe John F Tr.—O'Brien Colum (13 1 0 0 .08) **117**
Lifetime 0 0 0 0 1993 0 M 0 0
LATEST WORKOUTS Jun 17 Bel 4f fst :512 B Jun 11 Bel 5f fst 1:05 B Jun 4 Bel 5f fst 1:06 B May 17 Bel 3f fst :371 Hg

Majestic Goose
B. f. 2(Feb), by Simply Majestic—Gander Crude, by Quack
SANTOS J A (126 19 17 15 .15) $35,000 Br.—Curtis C. Green (Ky)
Own.—Blue Goose Stable Tr.—Kelly Thomas J (4 2 0 0 .50) **117**
Lifetime 2 0 0 0 1993 2 M 0 0

5May93- 4Bel fst 5f :221 :452 :574 ⓕMd Sp Wt 29 5 3 41½ 63½ 66 612¾ Santos J A 117 8.00 79-08 Cmcordr117⁶Lori'sPssion117¹½Amvlidhop117 No factor 7
20Apr93- 5Kee fst 4½f :224 :462 :524 ⓕMd Sp Wt 29 3 8 87½ 78½ 69 Santos J A L 117 2.90 86-12 QnAthn1175SrFrn117½WrldPrdcts117 Went to knees st 8
LATEST WORKOUTS Jun 18 Bel 4f fst :494 B Jun 12 Bel tr.t 3f fst :371 B Jun 7 Bel tr.t 5f fst 1:06 B ●May 29 Bel tr.t 3f fst :361 H

Cannon Road
Ch. f. 2(May), by Loose Cannon—Dorset Road, by Riva Ridge
LEON F (79 2 6 9 .03) $30,000 Br.—Raymond Roncari (Md)
Own.—Script R Farm Tr.—Miceli Michael (5 0 1 0 .00) **106⁷**
Lifetime 0 0 0 0 1993 0 M 0 0
LATEST WORKOUTS Jun 7 Bel tr.t 5f fst 1:044 B May 29 Bel 5f fst 1:031 B May 23 Bel 5f fst 1:034 Bg May 15 Bel 4f fst :514 B

Goldlee
Ch. f. 2(Jan), by Gold Alert—Jessie Lee, by Kaskaskia
CRUGUET J (57 6 5 7 .11) $30,000 Br.—Mr. & Mrs. Robert F. Bussman (Fla)
Own.—Lowe Ernest A Tr.—Lowe Ernest A Jr (—) **113**
Lifetime 0 0 0 0 1993 0 M 0 0
LATEST WORKOUTS May 28 Suf 3f fst :373 Hg May 22 Suf 4f fst :501 Hg May 17 Suf 3f fst :384 Hg

Native Warning
B. f. 2(Mar), by Caveat—Frozen Native, by Exclusive Native
MCCAULEY W H (57 4 11 6 .07) $35,000 Br.—Ryehill Farm (Md)
Own.—Ryehill Farm Tr.—Boniface J William (9 1 2 1 .11) **117**
Lifetime 1 0 0 0 1993 1 M 0 0 $200 $200
3Jun93- 3Pim fst 4½f :231 :471 :532 ⓕMd 25000 —0 6 9 914 817 919½ Sheridan E M 119 8.20 — — MrineCourt119¹SpunkyProspct114⁶½SwtFrn114 Outrun 9
LATEST WORKOUTS ●May 12 Del 3f fst :373 Hg

Stardust Girl
Gr. f. 2(Apr), by Kona Tenor—Stardust Jane, by Distinctive
DAVIS R G (209 29 32 22 .14) $35,000 Br.—Louie B. Rogers (Fla)
Own.—Matses Charles T Tr.—Trimmer Richard K (2 1 1 0 .50) **117**
Lifetime 0 0 0 0 1993 0 M 0 0
LATEST WORKOUTS Jun 17 Rkm 5f fst 1:042 B Jun 12 Rkm 5f fst 1:033 Hg Jun 7 Rkm 4f my :494 B Jun 2 Rkm 4f my :503 B

Placido Princess
TOSCANO P R (52 2 3 2 .M)
Own.—Larson Stables
LATEST WORKOUTS   Jun 21 Aqu 3f my :38 Bg

B. f. 2(Apr), by Chief Steward—Leelark, by Giboulee
$35,000 Br.—Berens F & Garazi S (Fla)
Tr.—Parisella John (6 2 0 1 .33)

Lifetime   1993 0 M 0 0
0 0 0 0

117

K Bomb was that stick out for the simple reason of consistent works and a comment. *K Bomb* worked 37 breezing on June 12, 1993. For this workout, *K Bomb* received a comment of "*K Bomb* bested *La Torque Blanc* in company". When I handicapped the rest of the competition, this gave me the go-ahead on *K Bomb*. Good workouts, trainer, jockey and comment all lead to a winning combination.

BELMONT PARK – (Training) Track Fast

Three Furlongs				Five Furlongs	
Addy Nashua	:36¹ H	Onestepstheline :37⁴ B	Gini McCown :52¹ B		
Big Weekend	:37² B	Rosalind :37³ B	Imah :49¹ B	Cannon Opera	1:01⁴ H
Brittney Erin	:40 B	Royce Joseph :37 B	**Jaded Image** :48³ B	Flags R Up	1:04 B
Francella	:35³ H	SpechlssColony :38 B	Kim's Image :48⁴ H	Hickory Lake	1:05 B
K. Bomb	:37 B	Thor Thors :35⁴ B	Lauren Melissa :49 B	Proud of All	1:02¹ B
Latorque Blanc	:37³ B	**Four Furlongs**	MstrBoomBoom :50⁴ B	Tomahawk Man	1:01¹ H
Litigation Rex	:37 B	Asaracket :49¹ B	Mr. Vesuvio :51¹ B		
M. D. Katie	:36 H	Big Kudu :51³ B	**Ocean Course** :48³ B	**Six Furlongs**	
Majestic Goose	:37¹ B	Bill of Rights :49⁴ B	Shades of Pink :52⁴ B		
Nelson's Navy	:34³ H	Eggless :49² B	Skip the Rest :49 B	A. J. Warbucks	1:17 B
		Electret :49 B	Take A Powder :52⁴ B	Very Fast	1:18 B

K. BOMB (3f) bested LATORQUE BLANC (3f) in company. NELSON'S NAVY galloped out 1/2 in :47 3/5.

Now if *K Bomb* worked that 37 on June 12 and received a comment, then went on to run poor or inconsistent works, we might get suspicious because of the claiming tag. She worked back well and Stanley Shapoff is just putting her where she could win.

```
BELMONT PARK June 24, 1993

          dist  trk   race         value of  wnrs
race #    fur.  con   type             race   time    runners
-----     ----  ----  -----        --------  -----    --------
  3       5.50  FST   F02MCL       $11,500   1:06.04    10

                                                            most recent
horse name                  fp lngths wt  pp      earned   odds   claim      trk/race #
-----------                 -- ------ --  --      ------   ----   -----      ---------
```

Horse								
K Bomb	1	1/2 117	2	$6,900	6.80	$35,000	062493BEL03
Explosive Bid — Kristin S. by Kris S.							
Owner : CHEVALIER STABLE							
Trainer: SHAPOFF STANLEY R							
Jockey : MAPLE E							
Safe At Home	2	1/2 117	3	$2,530	4.30	$35,000	062493BEL03
Owner : MINASSIAN HARRY							
Trainer: BARBARA ROBERT							
Jockey : SMITH M E							
Euphoric Interlude	3	5 1/2 117	1	$1,380	7.60	$35,000	062493BEL03
Owner : NICHOLSON RONALD							
Trainer: TONER JAMES J							
Jockey : KRONE J A							
Stardust Girl	4	9 1/2 117	9	$690	4.60	$35,000	062493BEL03
Owner : MATSES CHARLES T							
Trainer: TRIMMER RICHARD K							
Jockey : DAVIS R G							
Placido Princess	5	10 3/4 117	10	$0	3.90	$35,000	062493BEL03
Owner : LARSON STABLES							
Trainer: PARISELLA JOHN							
Jockey : TOSCANO P R							
Susans Melody	6	17 3/4 117	4	$0	21.60	$35,000	062493BEL03
Owner : NEWE JOHN F							
Trainer: O'BRIEN COLUM							
Jockey : CHAVEZ J F							
Native Warning	7	18 117	8	$0	25.90	$35,000	062493BEL03
Owner : RYEHILL FARM							
Trainer: BONIFACE J WILLIAM							
Jockey : MCCAULEY W H							
Cannon Road	8	18 1/4 106	6	$0	29.70	$30,000	062493BEL03
Owner : SCRIPT R FARM							
Trainer: MICELI MICHAEL							
Jockey : LEON F							
Goldlee	9	19 1/4 113	7	$0	12.60	$30,000	062493BEL03
Owner : LOWE ERNEST A							
Trainer: LOWE ERNEST A JR							
Jockey : CRUGUET J							
Majestic Goose	10	20 117	5	$0	3.70	$35,000	062493BEL03
Owner : BLUE GOOSE STABLE							
Trainer: KELLY THOMAS J							

K Bomb took the lead from the outset and never looked back, winning by a half of a length and paying $15.60. *Safe at Home*, who finished second, was the only one to have halfway decent works, but *K Bomb* was much the best and the best value playing her across the board. In this maiden claimer, the public did not know what to bet, as they bet two shippers, one from Suffolk and the other from Rockingham, sending one off at $12.60-1 and the other at $4.60-1. *Majestic Goose* had an excuse in her first start, as she went off at $2.90-1 and then was abandoned when she showed speed at $8.00-1 in her second start, then was bet down to

$3.70-1 today. If blinkers were added, we may consider her for second, but I did not like the time off, even though she was working out.

The comment is so important, as I have stressed throughout this book. If a horse received a comment and was placed in a race like this one with hardly any competition, if she looked impressive that day, she would not need to much to win against these. Comments equal Profits. Pay attention to this.

If you are learning from this book, you should be able to spot what angle is coming up.

---

5 START **6 FURLONGS** BELMONT PARK FINISH

6 FURLONGS. **(1.07^{4}) MAIDEN SPECIAL WEIGHT. Purse $23,500. 3-year-olds and upward. Weights, 3-year-olds, 114 lbs.; older, 122 lbs.**

Here's Noah — Dk. b. or br. c. 3(Apr), by Demons Begone—Famous Gail, by Cut Throat
SANTOS J A (71 9 11 5 .13) — Br.—Cohen B I (Ky) — Lifetime 0 0 0 0 — 1993 0 M 0 0 — 1992 0 M 0 0
Own.—Cohen Bertram I — Tr.—O'Connell Richard (7 0 1 2 .00) — **114**
LATEST WORKOUTS May 30 Bel 4f fst :47^{2} H — May 24 Bel 5f fst 1:01^{2} Hg — ●May 19 Bel 5f fst 1:00^{4} H — May 14 Bel 4f fst :47^{4} H

Gulable — B. c. 3(Apr), by Gulch—Able Maid, by Good Behaving
BAILEY J D (58 13 12 8 .22) — Br.—Donnelly Faith & Walter (Cal) — Lifetime 3 0 0 2 $8,400 — 1992 3 M 0 2 $8,400
Own.—McDonald James C — Tr.—Lukas D Wayne (7 2 2 2 .29) — **114**
15Jly92- 4Hol fst 6f :22^{1} :45^{2} 1:10^{1} Md Sp Wt 63 2 2 33½ 4^{3} 33½ 36¼ Nakatani C S Bb 117 6.80 83-12 Gilded Time117^{4} Chayim1172¼ Gulable117 No mishap 8
21Jun92- 4Hol fst 5f :21^{4} :45^{1} :56^{4} Md Sp Wt 64 8 5 43½ 44½ 3^{5} 3^{9} Nakatani C S Bb 117 11.60 89-08 Altazarr117^{8}FleetWizrd117^{1}Gulble117 Wide backstretch 8
31May92- 6Hol fst 4½f :21^{4} :45^{2} :52 Md Sp Wt 43 8 8 6^{9} 97¾ 97¼ Stevens G L B 117 29.50 91-06 Ecologist117^{hd} I'm An Issue1141¼ Kalembo117 No rally 10
LATEST WORKOUTS May 30 Bel 4f fst :49^{3} Bg — May 21 Bel 5f fst 1:01^{1} H — May 15 Bel 5f fst 1:01 H — May 1 Bel 5f fst 1:02^{4} H

Swindle — Dk. b. or br. c. 4, by Private Account—Number, by Nijinsky II
SWEENEY K H (7 0 0 1 .00) — Br.—Claiborne Farm & The Gamely Corp. (Ky) — Lifetime 0 0 0 0 — 1991 0 M 0 0 — 1990 0 M 0 0
Own.—Hobeau Farm — Tr.—Jerkens H Allen (19 6 2 4 .32) — **122**
LATEST WORKOUTS May 31 Bel 4f fst :49^{3} B — ●May 27 Bel 6f fst 1:12^{2} H — May 22 Bel 5f fst 1:01 B — May 16 Bel 3f fst :35^{3} Hg

Splendid Buck — B. c. 4, by Spend a Buck—Jolly Mariner, by Fifth Marine
SMITH M E (103 26 14 17 .25) — Br.—Sabarese Theodore M (Fla) — Lifetime 5 0 1 1 $8,610 — 1993 1 M 0 0 $1,530 — 1991 4 M 1 1 $7,080 — Turf 1 0 0 0 $1,530
Own.—Khaled Saud B — Tr.—Clement Christopher (11 3 1 1 .27) — **122**
17May93- 5Bel fm 1$\frac{1}{16}$ Ⓣ:46^{1} 1:11 1:42^{1} 3↑Md Sp Wt 72 10 2 2^{1} 2½ 3½ 4^{5} Smith M E 124 16.10 80-17 JhnnysGlry1151½MystcGr115^{3}HlfACrn115 Bid weakened 10
8Sep91- 5Bel fst 6f :22^{3} :46 1:10^{2} Md Sp Wt 48 4 2 74¼ 72¼ 86½ 814¼ Santos J A 118 5.60 74-11 Freight Bill1183½ Chapito1182½ Dignitas118 Outrun 8
26Aug91- 4Sar fst 6f :22^{2} :45^{2} 1:10^{3} Md Sp Wt 76 2 5 2^{hd} 41½ 3^{2} 33¼ Krone J A 118 8.60 88-10 TritoWatch1181¼SeBb118^{2}SplendidBuck118 Bumped st 6
21Jly91- 9EIP fst 6f :22^{4} :46^{1} 1:11^{3} S Kenton 64 6 9 97¾ 9^{10} 69¼ 5^{6} D'Amico A J B 110 25.80 82-17 PlaceDancer113^{1}NeverWavering121^{2}Thntopsis111 Tired 10
23Jun91- 6CD fst 5½f :23 :47^{3} 1:06^{2} Md Sp Wt 59 9 9 55½ 4^{4} 4^{2} 2^{2} Woods C R Jr B 120 5.00 88-14 PrizFight120^{2}SplndidBuck1203½AsburyPrk120 2nd best 11
LATEST WORKOUTS May 13 Bel 4f fst :48^{3} H — ●Apr 23 Pay tr.t 3f fst :37^{4} B — Apr 19 Pay tr.t 3f fst :38 B — ●Apr 11 Pay tr.t 5f fst 1:05^{4} B

Jason Dean — B. g. 3(Mar), by Timeless Native—Kaikilani, by Wavering Monarch
MIGLIORE R (86 14 12 11 .16) — Br.—Glencrest Farm (Ky) — Lifetime 2 0 0 1 $4,230 — 1993 2 M 0 1 $4,230 — 1992 0 M 0 0
Own.—Three Kit Stable — Tr.—Klesaris Robert P (16 3 2 2 .19) — **114**
9May93- 3Bel fst 6f :22^{1} :45^{2} 1:10^{2} Md Sp Wt 84 11 7 3^{2} 3^{2} 2^{2} 32½ Migliore R b 122 3.00 85-13 RedRiverGorge122^{2}Crsey'sPl122½JsonDen122 Bid, wknd 11
28Apr93- 3Aqu fst 7f :22^{4} :45^{3} 1:23^{2} Md Sp Wt 82 2 5 31½ 3^{2} 4^{1} 45½ Bravo J 122 11.50 81-19 PlnoPlsur122½MinD'Or1222½WstrnFort122 Lacked rally 7
LATEST WORKOUTS May 30 Bel tr.t 4f fst :51 B — May 21 Bel tr.t 4f fst :49^{4} B — May 7 Bel tr.t 4f fst :50^{2} B — Apr 21 Bel tr.t 5f fst 1:01^{2} B

Pat's Pickle — B. c. 4, by Cocalus—Pat's Peak, by Patrician
ALVARADO F T (19 2 2 6 .11) — Br.—Daniel Cummings (N.Y.) — Lifetime 0 0 0 0 — 1991 0 M 0 0 — 1990 0 M 0 0
Own.—Cummings Daniel — Tr.—Cummings Daniel (—) — **122**
LATEST WORKOUTS May 27 Sar tr.t 3f fst :41 Bg — May 19 Sar Ⓣ 4f fm :52^{3} B — May 12 Sar Ⓣ 4f fm :53^{3} B

Majesty's Man — B. c. 3(Feb), by His Majesty—Little Luiana, by Mill Reef
VELAZQUEZ J R (67 9 8 4 .13) — Br.—Galbreath Daniel M (Ky) — Lifetime 1 0 0 0 — 1992 1 M 0 0
Own.—Dileo Philip — Tr.—Hertler John O (20 5 2 2 .25) — **114**
13Jly92- 5Bel fst 5½f :22^{1} :45^{2} 1:03 Md Sp Wt 38 9 7 78¼ 78¼ 7^{11} 719¾ Santos J A 118 59.60 80-10 StrollngAlng1182½DvlshlyYrs1188½Dr.Alfs118 No factor 10
LATEST WORKOUTS May 27 Bel 5f fst 1:01 H — May 22 Bel 5f fst 1:00^{3} H — May 16 Bel 4f fst :49^{4} B

If you said it had something to do with *Swindle*, you are correct! If you thought it was looking up his workout, you are wrong! Actually, that workout on May 27 is great, and he did receive a comment for the work. His workouts are also consistent, and he has one of the best trainers in the business. So why would we throw this horse out? One simple reason: if this horse was that good, why would Allen Jerkins, who could have any jockey in the country, be using Kathy Sweeney on a horse that just worked tremendously for a maiden race. Why Kathy Sweeney?

As a handicapper, one has to use his head. I am going to give another example in the same race. *Gulable*, who was the morning line favorite, failed three times against maidens at Hollywood Park. After these three starts, he was obviously injured and turned out for the year. Even if this horse came back from his injury to his full potential, he still would not be able to win at Hollywood. His workouts here do not raise my eyebrows, and if he cannot win at Hollywood Park, he is not going to win here. Also, for all handicappers that noticed that he finished 6¼ lengths behind *Gilded Time* (1992 Breeder's Cup Juvenile winner) this means nothing, and here's why. In the example of *England Expects*, *Living Vicariously* and *Man's Hero*, they were all first-time starters, who won their next start. *Gulable* had his opportunities in his first two starts, and could not get the job done. Also, *Gulable* finished ninth by 7¼ and third by nine lengths, at odds of $29.50-1 and $11.60-1. Now in his third start against a monster like *Gilded Time*. *Gulable* was sent off at $6.80-1, showing that besides *Gilded Time*, who probably went off at even money, that there was no other competition. One must use his head when handicapping. If *Gulable* was any good, he still would be at Hollywood Park. If *Swindle* was anything, Jerkins would not have Kathy Sweeney aboard, who has ridden only seven times at the meet with one third place finish to her credit. Throwing out a 3-2 shot and a 7-2 shot will increase profitability tremendously.

BELMONT PARK June 02, 1993

race #	dist fur.	trk con	race type	value of race	wnrs time	runners
5	6.00	FST	3UM	$23,500	1:10.03	6

horse name	fp	lngths	wt	pp	earned	odds	claim	most recent trk/race #
Jason Dean	1	1/2	114	4	$14,100	1.70		062393BEL07
Timeless Native — Kaikilani by Wavering Monarch								
Owner : THREE KIT STABLE								
Trainer: KLESARIS ROBERT P								
Jockey : MIGLIORE R								
Splendid Buck	2	1/2	122	3	$5,170	4.80		062793BEL06
Owner : KHALED SAUD BIN								
Trainer: CLEMENT CHRISTOPHER								
Jockey : SMITH M E								
Swindle	3	6 1/2	122	2	$2,820	1.70		060293BEL05
Owner : HOBEAU FARM								
Trainer: JERKENS H ALLEN								
Jockey : SWEENEY K H								
Gulable	4	8 1/2	114	1	$1,410	3.60		062593BEL09
Owner : MCDONALD JAMES C								
Trainer: LUKAS D WAYNE								
Jockey : BAILEY J D								
Majesty's Man	5	23 1/2	114	6	$0	22.10		062093BEL05
Owner : DILEO PHILIP								
Trainer: HERTLER JOHN O								
Jockey : VELAZQUEZ J R								
Pat's Pickle	6	45 1/2	122	5	$0	24.80		062593FL 05
Owner : CUMMINGS DANIEL								
Trainer: CUMMINGS DANIEL								
Jockey : ALVARADO F T								

Searchs Shuffle is the perfect blinkers horse. She had early speed
against Maiden Special Weights and was shorting up on distance. Even
though she went slowly, those fractions would get the job done here.

5 ½ FURLONGS. (1.041) MAIDEN CLAIMING. Purse $10,500. Fillies and mares. 3–year–olds and upward. Weight, 3–year–olds, 112 lbs., older, 122 lbs. Claiming Price $18,500; for each $1,000 to $16,500, 1 lb.

LASIX—Searchs Shuffle, Jessica Jean, Spring Alone, North Charm, Tu Marphe.

Passive Star — Ch. f. 3(Mar), by Pas Seul—Number One Star, by Diamond Prospect — Lifetime 1992 0 M 0 0 — 0 0 0 0
$18,500 Br.—Jenkins Enis R (Va) — **112**
Own.—White Rose Stable — Tr.—Campitelli Francis P (65 9 13 7 .14)
LATEST WORKOUTS — May 22 Pim 4f fst :49¹ Bg — May 18 Pim 3f fst :37¹ B — May 14 Pim 4f fst :49¹ Bg — May 8 Pim 6f fst 1:14⁴ H

Searchs Shuffle — Ch. f. 3(May), by Dancing Again—Island Search, by Search for Gold — Lifetime 1993 1 M 0 0 $310 — 1 0 0 0 1992 0 M 0 0
$18,500 Br.—Heil John C (Md) — $310 — **112**
Own.—Stonechurch Farm — Tr.—DiNatale John F (13 2 1 2 .15)
23May93- 7Pim fst 6f :23³ :48 1:13³ 3 ↑ ⓜMd Sp Wt 39 8 5 1½ 1hd 2nd 67 Saumell L — L 114 7.10 70-16 LttlFlght113⁵ⓓRb'sPlsr112²⅓BckysBrd113 Bore in start 12
LATEST WORKOUTS ● May 4 Pim 5f fst 1:00 Hg

Nacumi — Ch. f. 3(Jun), by Naevus—Curly Mint, by Key to the Mint — Lifetime 1992 0 M 0 0 — 0 0 0 0
$18,500 Br.—Judy Klosterman (Ohio) — **112**
Own.—Pearce Suzanne — Tr.—Fisher Janon III (—)

Woody's Date | Dk. b. or br. f. 3(Apr), by Medieval Man—Paula Paula, by Mr Paul

$18,500   Br.—Cutrona Jerry M (Fla)

Own.—Southern Oaks Inc   Tr.—Mount Jack L (3 0 1 0 .00)   **112**

Lifetime   1992   0 M 0 0
0 0 0 0

Jessica Jean | Ro. f. 3(Jun), by Aichise—Beachhead, by Bellypha

$18,500   Br.—Bebe Dalton (Fla)

Own.—Burns Wendye   Tr.—Frock Charles L (2 0 0 0 .00)   **107⁵**

Lifetime   1993   2 M 0 1 $632
2 0 0 1   1992   0 M 0 0 $632

11May93- 1Pim fst 5½f :22³ :46⁴ 1:07 3+ⒻMd 18500 —0 1 5 32½ 34 6¹¹ 819¾ Saumell L   b 112   4.30   70-12 StrikingBrod112¾PrssthBt114½OurCndySu108   Fell back 8
18Apr93- 4Tam fst 7f :23² :47³ 1:26³ ⒻMd Sp Wt 35 5 5 66 67½ 56 38 Burns C W   118   *1.90   79-10 DixieShine118³GrpeDncer118⁵JessicJen118   Steadied st 9

LATEST WORKOUTS   ●Apr 7 Tam 5f fst 1:01² Hg   ●Apr 1 Tam 5f gd 1:01⁴ Hg

---

Spring Alone | Dk. b. or br. f. 3(Apr), by Pas Seul—Spring Rite, by Cyane

$18,500   Br.—Blackhurst Phyllis P-Smiley Harold (Pa)

Own.—Sterling Michael P   Tr.—Sterling Michael E (1 1 0 0 1.00)   **107⁵**

Lifetime   1992   0 M 0 0
0 0 0 0

LATEST WORKOUTS   May 27 Bow 4f fst :50 Bg   May 22 Bow 3f fst :38¹ Bg   May 15 Bow 4f fst :49 B   May 8 Bow 4f fst :49 Hg

---

Mickies Best | Dk. b. or br. f. 3(Apr), by Nale the Crow—Raise Em Up, by Upper Nile

$18,500   Br.—Ragan Billy H (Tex)

Own.—Ragan Billy H   Tr.—Ragan Billy H (5 0 0 0 .00)   **107⁵**

Lifetime   1992   0 M 0 0
0 0 0 0

North Charm | Ch. f. 3(May), by North Tower—Silver Charmer, by Hoist the Silver

$18,500   Br.—Ayres Fountain Spring Farm (Md)

Own.—Ayres Fountain Spring Farm   Tr.—Ayres Joseph W Jr (20 3 3 4 .15)   **112**

Lifetime   1993   1 M 0 1 $990
1 0 0 1   1992   0 M 0 0
$990

16May93- 1Pim fst 5½f :23 :48 1:08 3+ⒻMd 14500 30 1 6 67½ 66 43½ 35 Saumell L   114   6.10   80-16 Equal Donna112¾ JeanFolly114²¾NorthCharm114   Wide 6
LATEST WORKOUTS   May 13 Pim 3f fst :37 Bg   Apr 29 Pim 5f fst 1:03² Bg   Apr 18 Pim 5f fst 1:02³ B   Apr 14 Pim 5f fst 1:04³ B

Tu Marphe | Gr. f. 3(Apr), by Waquoit—Tulindas, by Shelter Half

$18,500   Br.—Dr. & Mrs. William Devoe (Md)

Own.—Devoe William   Tr.—Witte Lisa (2 0 0 0 .00)   **112**

Lifetime   1993   2 M 0 0 $600
2 0 0 0   1992   0 M 0 0
$600

14May93- 7Pim fst 6f :23³ :47² 1:13⁴ 3+ⒻMd Sp Wt 4 8 3 44 58 712 821 Guerra W A   Lb 112   20.50   55-18 CozyScene107ⁿᵒSrtogMgic114²¾Cvt'sLssi112   Gave way 8
1May93- 5Pim fst 6f :23¹ :46² 1:12² 3+ⒻMd Sp Wt 27 4 8 8¹³ 9¹⁹ 920 817¼ Johnston M T   L 114   25.70   66-14 MmsWndChrm112ⁿᵏSltthplrl112⁴¼CldsAmbr113   Outrun 9
LATEST WORKOUTS   ●May 11 Pim 3f fst :35³ Hg   Apr 26 Pim 5f fst 1:02⁴ B   Apr 21 Pim 5f fst 1:05² B   Apr 15 Pim 4f fst :50 Bg

---

When I turned to the front of the entries, I noticed that there was not an addition of blinkers. For all of those who do not know, blinkers extend speed and it seems that they make the horse go longer. Since there were no blinkers, this turned *Searchs Shuffle* from a valuable play to a sucker's bet. She was most likely going to do the same thing she did in her last start, lead and fail.

Since we had to look elsewhere, *Passive Star*, who caught my attention, was getting a lot of attention at the betting windows. With the longer workout, she seemed the logical play. The rest of the field was nothing special. Actually, it was just nothing. *Nacumi* and *Woody's Date's* workouts were announced as 51²/₅ breezing and 51 breezing, and, as expected, they ran out.

ELEVENTH RACE   5½ FURLONGS. (1.04¹) MAIDEN CLAIMING. Purse $10,500. Fillies and Mares. 3–year–olds

Pimlico   and upward. Weights, 3–year–olds, 112 lbs. Older, 122 lbs. Claiming Price $18,500; for each $1,000 to $16,500, 1 lb.

MAY 31, 1993

Value of race $11,100; value to winner $5,985; second $2,205; third $1,155; fourth $630; fifth $315; sixth $210; balance of starters $200 each. Mutuel pool $21,810. Exacta Pool $31,844 Triple Pool $33,741

Last Raced	Horse	M/Eqt.A.Wt	PP St	¼	⅜	Str	Fin	Jockey	Cl'g Pr	Odds $1
	Passive Star	3 114	1 5	3¹	2ʰᵈ	1ʰᵈ	1ʰᵈ	Rocco J	18500	2.20

16May93	1Pim3	North Charm	L	3 112	8	1	2hd	34	2hd	23½	Guerra W A	18500	4.00
23May93	7Pim6	Searchs Shuffle	L	3 114	2	3	12½	11½	35	31½	Samuel L	18500	2.10
		Spring Alone	Lb	3 108	6	4	51½	53	4½	46¼	Salazar A C5	18500	8.70
		Nacumi		3 112	3	7	73	61½	63½	5no	Luzzi M J	18500	13.80
11May93	1Pim8	Jessica Jean	Lb	3 107	5	2	43	42	54	67½	Cullum W5	18500	8.20
14May93	7Pim8	Tu Marphe	b	3 112	9	6	61½	7½	83	7nk	Johnston MT	18500	21.40
		Mickies Best		3 117	7	9	9	84	7hd	8½	Korte K†	18500	33.30
		Woody's Date		3 112	4	8	8hd	9	9	9	Hamilton S D	18500	29.80

OFF AT 6:01 Start good. Won driving. Time, :22⁴, :47², 1:00³, 1:07² Track fast.

$2 Mutuel Prices:

1—PASSIVE STAR	....	6.40	5.00	2.80
8—NORTH CHARM			4.60	3.20
2—SEARCHS SHUFFLE	....			2.60

$2 EXACTA 1–8 PAID $37.60 $2 TRIPLE 1–8–2 PAID $66.40

Ch. f, (Mar), by Pas Seul—Number One Star, by Diamond Prospect. Trainer Campitelli Francis P. Bred by Jenkins Enis R (Va).

PASSIVE STAR disputed the pace between horses and gamely prevailed under brisk urging. NORTH CHARM, three wide, prompted the pace in a sharp effort. SEARCHS SHUFFLE had speed along the rail and weakened. SPRING ALONE passed tired ones. NACUMI was no factor. JESSICA JEAN weakened.

Owners— 1, White Rose Stable; 2, Ayres Fountain Spring Farm; 3, Stonechurch Farm; 4, Sterling Michael P; 5, Pearce Suzanne; 6, Burns Wendye; 7, Devoe William; 8, Ragan Billy H; 9, Southern Oaks Inc.

Trainers— 1, Campitelli Francis P; 2, Ayres Joseph W Jr; 3, DiNatale John F; 4, Sterling Michael E; 5, Fisher Janon III; 6, Frock Charles L; 7, Witte Lisa; 8, Ragan Billy H; 9, Mount Jack L.

† **Apprentice allowance waived:** Mickies Best 5 pounds. **Corrected weight:** Mickies Best 112 pounds. **Overweight:** Passive Star 2 pounds; Searchs Shuffle 2; Spring Alone 1.

This field was terrible, and that is why even *Passive Star's* six furlong workout was not great, but it was good enough in here. Also, the backing at the windows supported her other workouts. That six- furlong workout gave her the conditioning and stamina to win in 107 flat for the five and one-half furlongs. *Passive Star* returned $6.40 and proved again that working farther than running often means profits.

If I said that the following horse was entered in a Maiden Claiming event at Monmouth Park would anyone bet him?

5 FURLONGS. (.56¹) MAIDEN CLAIMING. Purse $10,000. 2-year-olds. Weight, 118 lbs. Claiming Price $32,000; for each $1,000 to $28,000, 1 lb.

Coupled—Gifted Son and Paper Weight; Distinct Effort and Defense of Liberty.

River Clare		Ch. c. 2(May), by Irish River—Lady of Arathorn, by Stage Door Johnny	Lifetime	1993	2 M 0 1	$1,340
	$28,000	Br.—Nursery Place & Rayberg M (Ky)	2 0 0 1			
Own.—Krakower L J		Tr.—Taylor Ronald J (12 1 2 1 .08)	114	$1,340		
16Jun93- 1Mth fst 5f	:23¹ :47³ 1:00¹	Md 30000	32 1 2 11½ 1hd 21½ 39½ Lopez C	114	*1.60	70-22 DuellingKnight1185CrryRose118¾4½RiverClr114 Gave way 7
29Apr93- 3Hia fst 3f	:21² :32²	Md Sp Wt	— 7 4 52¾ 65¾ Ferrer J C	118	*1.60	— — Bye Guys118no Frank Knew118¾4 El Chiquito118 9
29Apr93–Brushed start, failed to menace						
LATEST WORKOUTS	Jun 4 Mth 4f fst :50² B		May 15 Mth 4f fst :49² B			

Sonny's Bruno		B. c. 2(Apr), by Queen City Lad—Settlers Cabin, by Cabin	Lifetime	1993	0 M 0 0	-
	$32,000	Br.—Hancock Arthur (Ky)	0 0 0 0			
Own.—Garafolo Bruce		Tr.—Crupi James J (64 10 13 11 .16)	118			
LATEST WORKOUTS	Jun 26 Mth 4f fst :49³ Bg					

Easy Buck B. c. 2(Feb), by Silver Buck—Creta-Br, by Millenium Lifetime 1993 0 M 0 0
$32,000 Br.—Haras Santa Maria De Araras (Fla) 0 0 0 0
Own.—Romero Jorge E Tr.—Romero Jorge E (10 2 1 2 .20) **118**
LATEST WORKOUTS Jun 22 Mth 5f my 1:07 B Jun 15 Mth 3f fst :36 B Jun 12 Mth 3f fst :38 B Jun 1 Mth 3f sly :37^2 B

Wiloso Dk. b. or br. c. 2(Apr), by Jeloso—Wildren, by Rash Prince Lifetime 1993 3 M 1 1 $3,730
$28,000 Br.—Dalton Bebe (Fla) 3 0 1 1 $3,730
Own.—Dalton Bebe R Tr.—Smith A Archie Jr (1 0 0 0 .00) **109^5**
20Jun93- 1Pha fst 5f :23 :46^2 :59 Md Sp Wt 20 3 1 2^1 4^5 5^8 5$^{15\frac{3}{4}}$ Black A S 118 8.60 72-18 Sprtn'sHro118$^{3\frac{1}{2}}$LightningShow118$^{1\frac{3}{4}}$BritishRj118 Tired 8
11Jun93- 5Pha fst 4½f :23^4 :47^4 :54 Md Sp Wt 32 4 2 3$^{1\frac{1}{2}}$ 3$^{2\frac{1}{2}}$ 3$^{5\frac{1}{4}}$ Black A S 118 3.30 86-22 Three Timer118½ Burn TheToast118$^{4\frac{3}{4}}$Wiloso118 Evenly 7
25May93- 5Pha fst 4½f :23^3 :48^2 :55 Md 20000 17 5 4 2^1 2^2 2$^{2\frac{1}{2}}$ Ryan K 116 *1.60 83-19 GlidingLady116$^{2\frac{1}{2}}$Wiloso116^{4}DestinyAppeal116 2nd best 5
LATEST WORKOUTS Jun 4 Pha 3f fst :36^2 B May 20 Pha 5f sly 1:02^2 Bg May 15 Pha 4f fst :48^4 Bg May 11 Pha 3f fst :38^3 B

Just Chester Ch. g. 2(Jan), by Who's Fleet—Very Impresive, by No Sale George Lifetime 1993 0 M 0 0
$28,000 Br.—Great Luck Farm (Fla) 0 0 0 0
Own.—Kielty Donald E Tr.—Kielty Donald E (—) **114**
LATEST WORKOUTS Jun 23 Rkm 5f fst 1:02 Hg Jun 10 Rkm 4f fst :49 Hg Jun 5 Rkm 4f fst :49^2 Hg

Gifted Son B. g. 2(Mar), by Rexson's Hope—Hot Times Ahead, by Cutlass Lifetime 1993 0 M 0 0
$32,000 Br.—Yeoman Jean & John (Fla) 0 0 0 0
Own.—Minassian Harry Tr.—Serpe Philip M (18 4 2 2 .22) **118**
LATEST WORKOUTS Jun 20 Mth 4f fst :49^3 Bg Jun 14 Mth 4f fst :50 Bg Jun 8 Mth 4f fst :50^2 B May 26 Mth 3f fst :39 B

Private Enough Ch. c. 2(Mar), by Enough Reality—Private Secretary, by Secretary of War Lifetime 1993 0 M 0 0
$32,000 Br.—Sessa John (Fla) 0 0 0 0
Own.—Sessa John C Tr.—Scanlon Robert N (3 1 0 0 .33) **118**
LATEST WORKOUTS Jun 19 Mth 4f fst :48^3 Hg Jun 11 Mth 4f fst :48^3 Hg May 29 Mth 3f fst :38^1 B

Late Night Dk. b. or br. c. 2(Feb), by Bet Big—Elmer's Affair, by Clandestine Lifetime 1993 0 M 0 0
$32,000 Br.—Croll W A (Fla) 0 0 0 0
Own.—Croll Warren A Jr Tr.—Croll Warren A Jr (23 4 2 5 .17) **118**
LATEST WORKOUTS Jun 25 Mth 5f fst 1:01^2 Bg Jun 15 Mth 5f fst 1:03^4 B Jun 9 Mth 5f my 1:04 Bg Jun 4 Mth 4f fst :49^4 Bg

Mickeray B. c. 2(Feb), by Blood Royal—Logical Confusion, by Hagley Lifetime 1993 1 M 0 0 $100
$32,000 Br.—Argiannis Elizabeth P (Fla) 1 0 0 0 $100
Own.—Mamone Raymond Tr.—Vincitore Michael J (12 0 0 1 .00) **113^5**
16Jun93- 1Mth fst 5f :23^1 :47^3 1:00^1 Md 35000 2 4 3 5^6 6^{10} 6^{14} 6$^{19\frac{1}{2}}$ Lopez C C 118 32.40 60-22 DuellingKnight118^{5}CrryRose118$^{4\frac{1}{2}}$RivrClr114 Thru early 7
LATEST WORKOUTS Jun 24 Mth 4f fst :48^2 H Jun 9 Mth 5f my 1:04^2 B Jun 3 Mth 5f fst 1:07 B May 27 Mth 4f fst :52 Bg

Paper Weight Gr. c. 2(Apr), by Cutlass—Wicked Good, by Distinctive Pro Lifetime 1993 0 M 0 0
$32,000 Br.—Minassian Harry (NJ) 0 0 0 0
Own.—Minassian Harry Tr.—Serpe Philip M (18 4 2 2 .22) **118**
LATEST WORKOUTS Jun 22 Mth 4f my :48^4 Bg Jun 17 Mth 3f fst :37 B Jun 11 Mth 3f fst :37^2 B

Distinct Effort B. c. 2(May), by Distinctive Pro—Angel Dance, by Classical Ballet Lifetime 1993 1 M 0 0 $170
$32,000 Br.—Century Thoroughbreds (Fla) 1 0 0 0 $170
Own.—Snowden Guy B Tr.—Salzman John E (6 2 1 0 .33) **118**
4Jun93- 6Mth fst 5f :22^3 :46^3 :59^1 Md Sp Wt 26 5 6 3$^{3\frac{1}{2}}$ 4$^{4\frac{1}{2}}$ 5^9 5$^{15\frac{3}{4}}$ HomistrRBJr^5 b 113 2.70e 69-23 ScrdHonour118^{11}BritishRj118$^{1\frac{3}{4}}$PrllFll118 Saved ground 9
LATEST WORKOUTS Jun 23 Mth 4f fst :49 B Jun 15 Mth 5f fst 1:05 B May 25 Mth 4f fst :49^2 B May 11 Lrl Ⓣ 4f fm :49^3 Bg

Amarillo Slim B. g. 2(Apr), by Bet Big—Mins, by Rajab Lifetime 1993 0 M 0 0
$32,000 Br.—Friedman Gladys (Fla) 0 0 0 0
Own.—Campbell Gilbert G Tr.—Allard Edward T (11 0 2 1 .00) **118**
LATEST WORKOUTS Jun 18 Mth 5f fst 1:06 •Bg Jun 13 Mth 4f fst :54 B Jun 8 Mth 3f fst :38^1 Bg Jun 2 Mth 3f fst :37^4 Bg

Also Eligible (Not in Post Position Order):

Defense of Liberty B. c. 2(Mar), by Eskimo—Dana Calqui-Ar, by Dan Kano Lifetime 1993 0 M 0 0
$32,000 Br.—Four Horsemen Inc (Fla) 0 0 0 0
Own.—Four Horsemen's Ranch Tr.—Salzman John E (6 2 1 0 .33) **113**
LATEST WORKOUTS Jun 23 Mth 5f fst 1:03^2 B Jun 15 Mth 4f fst :50 B Jun 8 Mth 5f fst 1:03^1 B Jun 1 Mth 4f sly :49^1 B

If anyone said yes, he would have been part of the suckers at Monmouth Park. They bet him down to 1.90-1 and he returned with a fifth place finish beaten by 7½ lengths. Unlike *Swindle* in an example previously discussed in this chapter, *Just Chester* had his jockey, but there is a different tipoff to this horse. This horse shipped all the way down from Rockingham, which is approximately 800 miles from Monmouth Park, and his connections are going to enter him in a claiming race. If the owners were looking for a higher purse, they would have entered him in a maiden special weight contest at Monmouth or Rockingham. If he was not good enough to race in a maiden special weight conditions at Monmouth where the purse is $21,000, then it would be reasonable to stay on his home track, where the purse for a maiden special weight contest is $14,000 at Rockingham. The maiden claiming event at Monmouth Park is tougher than the maiden special weight contest at Rockingham. The purse for the maiden claiming race is $10,000, compared to $14,000 at Rockingham. One must remember to use his head when handicapping and eliminating these nags at $1.90-1. That leads the way to a great day at the races.

race #	dist fur.	trk con	race type	value of race	wnrs time	runners
5	5.00	FST	02MCL	$10,000	1:00.00	9

horse name	fp	lngths	wt	pp	earned	odds	claim	most recent trk/race #
Private Enough	1	2 3/4	118	7	$6,000	10.10	$32,000	062993MTH05

Enough Reality — Private Secretary by Secretary of War
        Owner : SESSA JOHN C
        Trainer: SCANLON ROBERT N
        Jockey : KING E L JR

Gifted Son	2	2 3/4	118	6	$1,900	6.40	$32,000	062993MTH05

        Owner : MINASSIAN HARRY
        Trainer: SERPE PHILIP M
        Jockey : BRAVO J

Sonny's Bruno	3	3	118	2	$1,100	8.40	$32,000	062993MTH05

        Owner : GARAFOLO BRUCE
        Trainer: CRUPI JAMES J
        Jockey : SQUARTINO R A

River Clare	4	5 1/4	114	1	$500	4.00	$28,000	062993MTH05

        Owner : KRAKOWER LAWRENCE J
        Trainer: TAYLOR RONALD J
        Jockey : LOPEZ C

Just Chester	5	7 1/2	114	5	$100	1.90	$28,000	062993MTH05

        Owner : KIELTY DONALD E
        Trainer: KIELTY DONALD E
        Jockey : VEGA H

Wiloso	6	10 1/2	109	4	$100	10.40	$28,000	062993MTH05

        Owner : DALTON BEBE R
        Trainer: SMITH A ARCHIE JR
        Jockey : UMANA J L

Mickeray	7	10 3/4	113	8	$100	67.20	$32,000	062993MTH05

        Owner : MAMONE RAYMOND
        Trainer: VINCITORE MICHAEL J

```
                 Jockey : RUSSELL W B
Distinct Effort          8 12 3/4 118  9        $100    4.00      $32,000    062993MTH05
                 Owner  : SNOWDEN GUY B
                 Trainer: SALZMAN JOHN E
                 Jockey : WILSON R
Easy Buck                ff          118  3      $100   21.40      $32,000    062993MTH05
                 Owner  : ROMERO JORGE E
                 Trainer: ROMERO JORGE E
                 Jockey : MARQUEZ C H JR
```

Trainers

15

Most trainers do their best training in claiming or allowance company. In the examples below, I will show you some of the trainers to keep an eye out for when you are handicapping. In those examples, I have selected a group of trainers from all over the country depicting who's, good with first time starters, wins with the biggest payout, consistently strong with all types of maidens, and who's unbeatable after their horses make their first start.

We start the examples with one of the best teams training today, Ben Perkins Jr. and Ben Perkins Sr.

This team has always had success with maidens and the 1993 meet at Monmouth Park was no different.

ERKINS BENJAMIN W — TRAINER SUMMARY FOR SPECIFIC YEAR FOR MONMOUTH PARK

N NORTH AMERICA FOR ALL TRACKS:

               1976 – 1993   05/30 – 06/28

    STARTERS   56   11

```
WINNERS      34( 61%)        7( 64%)
PLACERS      39( 70%)        5(  0%)
STARTS       291            15
   WINS      52( 18%)        9( 60%)
 PLACES      98( 34%)        5( 33%)
```

1993 FOR MONMOUTH PARK

	STARTS	1ST (%)	2ND (%)	3RD (%)	UNPL%	EARNINGS	ROWB
TOTALS	12	6 (50)	4 (33)	1 (8)	(9)	$77,890	+$4
AVERAGE FOR ALL TRAINERS		(11)	(12)		(13)	(64)	-$3
COLTS	5	3 (60)	1 (20)	0 (0)	(20)	$34,355	+$5
FILLIES	7	3 (43)	3 (43)	1 (14)	(0)	$43,535	-$1
GRADED							
BLACKTYPE	0	0 (0)	0 (0)	0 (0)	(0)	$0	+$0
ALL BLACKTYPE	0	0 (0)	0 (0)	0 (0)	(0)	$0	+$0
ALLOWANCE	3	1 (33)	1 (33)	0 (0)	(34)	$16,710	-$2
CLAIMING	4	2 (50)	1 (25)	1 (25)	(0)	$23,110	+$0
MAIDEN	5	3 (60)	2 (40)	0 (0)	(0)	$38,070	+$6
DIRT	12	6 (50)	4 (33)	1 (8)	(9)	$77,890	+$4
FAST TRACK	12	6 (50)	4 (33)	1 (8)	(9)	$77,890	+$4
OFF TRACK	0	0 (0)	0 (0)	0 (0)	(0)	$0	+$0
TURF	0	0 (0)	0 (0)	0 (0)	(0)	$0	+$0
FIRM TURF	0	0 (0)	0 (0)	0 (0)	(0)	$0	+$0
OFF TURF	0	0 (0)	0 (0)	0 (0)	(0)	$0	+$0
MILE OR MORE	5	2 (40)	2 (40)	0 (0)	(20)	$31,655	-$3
< 1 MILE	7	4 (57)	2 (29)	1 (14)	(0)	$46,235	+$7
FAVORITES	8	5 (63)	2 (25)	0 (0)	(12)	$56,485	+$4
ODDS < 5 TO 1	3	1 (33)	2 (67)	0 (0)	(0)	$20,140	+$2
ODDS 5 TO 1– 10 TO 1	1	0 (0)	0 (0)	1(100)	(0)	$1,265	-$2
ODDS > 10 TO 1	0	0 (0)	0 (0)	0 (0)	(0)	$0	+$0
FIRST TIME STARTERS	5	3 (60)	2 (40)	0 (0)	(0)	$38,070	+$6
RACES WITH APPRENTICES	0	0 (0)	0 (0)	0 (0)	(0)	$0	+$0

Ben Perkins Sr. started the meet winning six of his first twelve, and eleven of those twelve starters finished in the money. All of the horses were maidens. With first time starters he has a 60 percent winning percentage and is five for five with horses finishing on the board. One of the reasons for the success of Team Perkins is the fact that they do not embarrass themselves by only bringing in quality horses that can win at Monmouth Park.

PERKINS BEN W JR — TRAINER SUMMARY FOR SPECIFIC YEAR FOR ALL TRACKS IN
NORTH AMERICA

IN NORTH AMERICA FOR ALL TRACKS:

	1982 – 1993	05/30 – 06/28
STARTERS	262	24
WINNERS	172(66%)	9(38%)
PLACERS	189(72%)	9(0%)
STARTS	1,854	31
WINS	418(23%)	9(29%)
PLACES	547(30%)	11(35%)

1992 IN NORTH AMERICA

	STARTS	1ST (%)	2ND (%)	3RD (%)	UNPL%	EARNINGS	ROWB
TOTALS	416	105 (25)	73 (18)	52 (13)	(44)	$1,888,227	–$66
AVERAGE FOR ALL TRAINERS		(9)	(9)	(9)	(73)		–$19
COLTS	210	57 (27)	36 (17)	21 (10)	(46)	$1,093,576	–$34
FILLIES	206	48 (23)	37 (18)	31 (15)	(44)	$794,651	–$33
GRADED BLACKTYPE	14	0 (0)	3 (21)	1 (7)	(72)	$128,075	–$28
ALL BLACKTYPE	56	10 (18)	9 (16)	6 (11)	(55)	$648,503	–$36
ALLOWANCE	150	40 (27)	29 (19)	21 (14)	(40)	$688,465	–$1
CLAIMING	71	16 (23)	15 (21)	8 (11)	(45)	$166,288	–$18
MAIDEN	139	39 (28)	20 (14)	17 (12)	(46)	$384,971	–$12
DIRT	382	98 (26)	70 (18)	51 (13)	(43)	$1,786,965	–$52
FAST TRACK	307	80 (26)	60 (20)	38 (12)	(42)	$1,436,418	+$0
OFF TRACK	75	18 (24)	10 (13)	13 (17)	(46)	$350,547	$52
TURF	34	7 (21)	3 (9)	1 (3)	(67)	$101,262	–$14
FIRM TURF	32	7 (22)	3 (9)	1 (3)	(66)	$101,107	–$10
OFF TURF	2	0 (0)	0 (0)	0 (0)	(100)	$155	–$4
MILE OR MORE	125	28 (22)	21 (17)	10 (8)	(53)	$627,781	–$32
< 1 MILE	291	77 (26)	52 (18)	42 (14)	(42)	$1,260,446	–$36
FAVORITES	146	63 (43)	31 (21)	22 (15)	(21)	$935,818	+$5
ODDS < 5 TO 1	147	28 (19)	30 (20)	18 (12)	(49)	$593,957	–$58
ODDS 5 TO 1– 10 TO 1	74	12 (16)	10 (14)	7 (9)	(61)	$254,574	+$40
ODDS > 10 TO 1	49	2 (4)	2 (4)	5 (10)	(82)	$103,878	–$52
FIRST TIME STARTERS	47	12 (26)	10 (21)	2 (4)	(49)	$145,485	–$15
RACES WITH APPRENTICES	14	2 (14)	2 (14)	0 (0)	(72)	$23,691	–$12

LACKTYPE WINS

DATE	STAKES NAME	VALUE	HORSE NAME
921205	MARYLAND JUVENILE CHAMPIONSHIP S. --LR (LRL)	125,000	Woods of Windsor
920215	WHIRLAWAY BREEDERS' CUP S. --L (AQU)	116,350	Dr. Unright
920628	JERSEY SHORE BUDWEISER BREEDERS' CUP H. --L (ATL)	107,050	Surely Six
920719	DAVONA DALE H. --L (LRL)	54,550	Crowned
920725	VERY SUBTLE BREEDERS' CUP H. --O (LRL)	52,750	Dhaka
920315	MISTER DIZ S. --LR (LRL)	50,000	North Carroll
920726	TYRO S. --L (MTH)	50,000	Wild Zone
920104	MARSHUA S. --O (LRL)	43,500	Luramore
920703	PRIMER BREEDERS' CUP S. --O (LRL)	42,925	Wild Zone
920703	REGRET S. --O (MTH)	40,000	Dhaka

Ben Perkins Jr., gained national fame in 1993 with his Kentucky Derby hopeful, *Storm Tower*. *Storm Tower* failed in the derby but Perkins did not let that stop him.

In 1992, Ben Perkins Jr. finished the year with a healthy 25 percent winning percentage and 56 percent finished in the money. His 1.8 million in earning for 1992, was grinded out all year as he did not have one stand out. With maidens that have started more than once, Perkins has his highest winning percentage, 39 for 139 or 28 percent. *Storm Tower* led the charge in 1992 with the first time starters that connected for Perkins. He won 12 of 47 and finished 24 of 47 in the money. Though not in the maiden category, Ben Perkins Jr.'s most impressive stats come with the favorites, winning an incredible 43 percent of the time. An even better 79 percent were in the money.

Team Perkins usually does most of their training and racing on the east coast but with simulcasting the team is a force all over the country. They are most effective with maidens, as seen with the stats in the above examples.

Daniel Vella is a good example of a trainer that has obviously changed his tactics with his training maidens. From 1985 - 1992, Vella has struggled with maidens and has not posted impressive statistics.

VELLA DANIEL J - TRAINER SUMMARY FOR SPECIFIC YEAR FOR ALL TRACKS IN NORTH
                 AMERICA

IN NORTH AMERICA FOR ALL TRACKS:

	1985 - 1993	06/03 - 07/02
STARTERS	122	20
WINNERS	65(53%)	4(20%)
PLACERS	76(62%)	10(0%)
STARTS	751	29
WINS	117(16%)	4(14%)
PLACES	197(26%)	12(41%)

1992 IN NORTH AMERICA

	STARTS	1ST (%)	2ND (%)	3RD (%)	UNPL%	EARNINGS	ROWB
TOTALS	321	51 (16)	51 (16)	34 (11)	(57)	$1,720,991	-$181
AVERAGE FOR ALL TRAINERS		(9)	(9)	(9)	(73)		-$19
COLTS	147	25 (17)	30 (20)	13 (9)	(54)	$1,102,259	-$113
FILLIES	174	26 (15)	21 (12)	21 (12)	(61)	$618,732	-$67
GRADED							
BLACKTYPE	15	0 (0)	3 (20)	2 (13)	(67)	$133,996	-$30
ALL BLACKTYPE	64	5 (8)	7 (11)	7 (11)	(70)	$789,113	-$87
ALLOWANCE	101	18 (18)	23 (23)	11 (11)	(48)	$476,945	-$15
CLAIMING	74	13 (18)	6 (8)	9 (12)	(62)	$193,384	-$17
MAIDEN	82	15 (18)	15 (18)	7 (9)	(55)	$261,549	-$63
DIRT	221	33 (15)	33 (15)	20 (9)	(61)	$786,377	$174
FAST TRACK	155	19 (12)	18 (12)	16 (10)	(66)	$495,323	-$166
OFF TRACK	66	14 (21)	15 (23)	4 (6)	(50)	$291,054	-$8
TURF	100	18 (18)	18 (18)	14 (14)	(50)	$934,614	-$5
FIRM TURF	60	12 (20)	11 (18)	9 (15)	(47)	$399,487	+$14
OFF TURF	40	6 (15)	7 (18)	5 (13)	(54)	$535,127	$19
MILE OR MORE	185	31 (17)	29 (16)	18 (10)	(57)	$1,195,814	$90
< 1 MILE	136	20 (15)	22 (16)	16 (12)	(57)	$525,177	-$91
FAVORITES	67	25 (37)	19 (28)	5 (7)	(28)	$538,017	$18
ODDS < 5 TO 1	67	16 (24)	12 (18)	6 (9)	(49)	$578,549	+$6
ODDS 5 TO 1 -							
10 TO 1	83	9 (11)	14 (17)	11 (13)	(59)	$399,529	-$16
ODDS > 10 TO 1	104	1 (1)	6 (6)	12 (12)	(81)	$204,896	-$151
FIRST TIME							
STARTERS	18	3 (17)	4 (22)	2 (11)	(50)	$57,385	-$6
RACES WITH							
APPRENTICES	3	0 (0)	0 (0)	0 (0)	(100)	$170	$6

BLACKTYPE WINS

DATE	STAKES NAME		VALUE	HORSE NAME
920816	BREEDERS' S. -LR (WO)		500,000	Blitzer
920927	CUP AND SAUCER S. -LR (WO)		135,800	Explosive Red
920524	HERESY BREEDERS' CUP S. -L (WO)		111,860	Blitzer
920412	ACHIEVEMENT S. -LR (GRD)		108,400	Blitzer
920712	OCEAN HOTEL S. -L (MTH)		35,000	Diamonds Galore

In 1992, Daniel Vella produced winners fifteen times out of the 82 maiden starters or 18 percent. His in-the-money percentage was also low. Only 45 percent finished on the board. With first time starters, Vella's winning percentage dropped slightly to 17 percent.

VELLA DANIEL J - TRAINER SUMMARY FOR SPECIFIC YEAR FOR ALL TRACKS IN NORTH AMERICA

IN NORTH AMERICA FOR ALL TRACKS:

	1985 - 1993	06/03 - 07/02
STARTERS	122	20
WINNERS	65(53%)	4(20%)
PLACERS	76(62%)	10(0%)
STARTS	751	29
WINS	117(16%)	4(14%)
PLACES	197(26%)	12(41%)

1993 IN NORTH AMERICA

	STARTS	1ST (%)	2ND (%)	3RD (%)	UNPL%	EARNINGS	ROWB
TOTALS	86	20 (23)	18 (21)	13 (15)	(41)	$643,740	+$116
AVERAGE FOR ALL TRAINERS		(9)	(9)	(10)	(72)		$11
COLTS	38	9 (24)	8 (21)	7 (18)	(37)	$355,069	+$1
FILLIES	48	11 (23)	10 (21)	6 (13)	(43)	$288,671	+$115
GRADED BLACKTYPE	9	2 (22)	1 (11)	2 (22)	(45)	$181,960	+$0
ALL BLACKTYPE	23	3 (13)	3 (13)	6 (26)	(48)	$308,236	+$67
ALLOWANCE	25	6 (24)	4 (16)	5 (20)	(40)	$137,582	+$26
CLAIMING	22	6 (27)	8 (36)	1 (5)	(32)	$118,404	+$15
MAIDEN	16	5 (31)	3 (19)	1 (6)	(44)	$79,518	+$8

DIRT	53	12 (23)	10 (19)	8 (15)	(43)	$320,114	+$31
FAST TRACK	38	10 (26)	7 (18)	5 (13)	(43)	$260,130	+$4
OFF TRACK	15	2 (13)	3 (20)	3 (20)	(47)	$59,984	+$27
TURF	33	8 (24)	8 (24)	5 (15)	(37)	$323,626	+$84
FIRM TURF	26	6 (23)	8 (31)	4 (15)	(31)	$233,663	+$80
OFF TURF	7	2 (29)	0 (0)	1 (14)	(57)	$89,963	+$4
MILE OR MORE	52	11 (21)	9 (17)	9 (17)	(45)	$465,950	+$77
< 1 MILE	34	9 (26)	9 (26)	4 (12)	(36)	$177,790	+$39
FAVORITES	23	8 (35)	6 (26)	4 (17)	(22)	$196,450	$5
ODDS < 5 TO 1	30	6 (20)	8 (27)	2 (7)	(46)	$225,351	-$17
ODDS 5 TO 1-							
10 TO 1	18	4 (22)	3 (17)	6 (33)	(28)	$137,780	+$33
ODDS > 10 TO 1	15	2 (13)	1 (7)	1 (7)	(73)	$84,159	+$104
FIRST TIME							
STARTERS	10	4 (40)	1 (10)	0 (0)	(50)	$55,398	+$16
RACES WITH							
APPRENTICES	3	1 (33)	1 (33)	0 (0)	(34)	$21,880	+$1
BLACKTYPE WINS							

DATE	STAKES NAME	VALUE	HORSE NAME
930524	ECLIPSE S. --G3 (WO)	107,800	Blitzer
930421	FORERUNNER S. --G3 (KEE)	83,450	Explosive Red
930131	JOE NAMATH H. --L (GP)	50,000	Hero's Love

In 1993, Vella had to change tactics. His maidens responded very well to his new methods. It is very important for the handicapper to realize that a trainer that may have been unsuccessful in the past with maidens may be worth a bet once he has started to prove that he may have changed his ways. Daniel Vella has increased his maiden winning percentage by 13 percent from 18 percent to 31 percent. With first time starters he has an even bigger improvement from 17 percent to 40 percent. From a minus $6 in 1992 this leads to a plus $16 in 1993, based on a two dollar bet.

Daniel Vella has changed tactics for the better. Handicappers must revaluate their position and stay aware of current fluctuations with trainers and their methods. This will increase profits and make one a better handicapper.

Claude McGaughey III is in the upper echelon of trainers and only trains the best. He does not race any of his horses in claiming company and if they cannot make it in allowance company, he will turn them over to someone else. Claude is a handicapper's friend, because he places all of his horses in a position to win. In 1993, with maidens, Claude was not doing his best training winning with maidens, but as I mentioned he does have a very good in-the-money percentage of 65 percent. Once again, this shows that he knows where to place his horses and always puts them in a winning position. A great trainer to use in exactas and trifectas.

MCGAUGHEY CLAUDE III -- TRAINER SUMMARY FOR SPECIFIC YEAR FOR ALL TRACKS IN NORTH AMERICA

IN NORTH AMERICA FOR ALL TRACKS:

	1980 -- 1993	06/03 -- 07/02
STARTERS	412	22
WINNERS	270(66%)	7(32%)
PLACERS	296(72%)	7(0%)
STARTS	2,892	26
WINS	751(26%)	7(27%)
PLACES	949(33%)	8(31%)

1992 IN NORTH AMERICA

	STARTS	1ST (%)	2ND (%)	3RD (%)	UNPL%	EARNINGS	ROWB
TOTALS	236	51 (22)	51 (22)	43 (18)	(38)	$4,115,992	$162
AVERAGE FOR ALL TRAINERS		(9)	(9)	(9)	(73)		-$19
COLTS	108	25 (23)	22 (20)	14 (13)	(44)	$1,977,498	-$28
FILLIES	128	26 (20)	29 (23)	29 (23)	(34)	$2,138,494	-$133
GRADED BLACKTYPE	67	10 (15)	21 (31)	10 (15)	(39)	$3,111,259	-$73
ALL BLACKTYPE	75	12 (16)	23 (31)	12 (16)	(37)	$3,238,159	-$83
ALLOWANCE	87	20 (23)	15 (17)	15 (17)	(43)	$495,200	-$77
CLAIMING	2	0 (0)	0 (0)	1 (50)	(50)	$2,640	-$4
MAIDEN	72	19 (26)	13 (18)	15 (21)	(35)	$379,993	+$0
DIRT	215	47 (22)	49 (23)	39 (18)	(37)	$3,487,672	-$153
FAST TRACK	152	32 (21)	36 (24)	25 (16)	(39)	$2,650,607	-$118
OFF TRACK	63	15 (24)	13 (21)	14 (22)	(33)	$837,065	-$35
TURF	21	4 (19)	2 (10)	4 (19)	(52)	$628,320	-$9
FIRM TURF	14	4 (29)	1 (7)	2 (14)	(50)	$576,400	+$5
OFF TURF	7	0 (0)	1 (14)	2 (29)	(57)	$51,920	-$14

M1LE OR MORE	119	26 (22)	27 (23)	17 (14)	(41)	$3,292,214	-$95
< 1 MILE	117	25 (21)	24 (21)	26 (22)	(36)	$823,778	$67
FAVORITES	80	32 (40)	14 (18)	17 (21)	(21)	$1,490,801	$39
ODDS < 5 TO 1	79	14 (18)	21 (27)	18 (23)	(32)	$1,211,574	$54
ODDS 5 TO 1							
10 TO 1	42	3 (7)	13 (31)	3 (7)	(55)	$1,152,144	$49
FIRST TIME							
STARTERS	25	5 (20)	6 (24)	3 (12)	(44)	$110,180	-$22
RACES WITH							
APPRENTICES	0	0 (0)	0 (0)	0 (0)	(0)	$0	+$0

BLACKTYPE WINS

DATE	STAKES NAME	VALUE	HORSE NAME
921031	BREEDERS' CUP MILE -G1 (GP)	916,000	Lure
920404	GOTHAM S. -G2 (AQU)	250,000	Lure
921010	FRIZETTE S. -G1 (BEL)	250,000	Educated Risk
920223	RAMPART H. -G2 (GP)	200,000	Fit for a Queen
920907	JEROME H. -G1 (BEL)	200,000	Furiously
920906	GO FOR WAND S. -G1 (BEL)	200,000	Easy Now
920920	RUFFIAN H. -G1 (BEL)	200,000	Versailles Treaty
920704	MOLLY PITCHER H. -G2 (MTH)	150,000	Versailles Treaty
920919	FUTURITY S. -G1 (BEL)	120,200	Strolling Along
920926	MARYLAND MILLION OAKS -LR (PIM)	95,000	Deputation
920111	AFFECTIONATELY H. -G3 (AQU)	87,750	Get Lucky
920328	BOURBONETTE S. -L (TP)	60,000	Preach

Certain trainers have tip-offs as to when they have a horse that will win. Stanley Hough is an example. With first time starters, Stanley Hough did not send out many two-year-olds, but when he did, he had eight starters with three wins and six of eight in the money. The more astonishing fact is when Jerry Bailey was on these first time starters he was three for three. If you are at a track where Bailey is on a Hough-trained maiden, guess what you should do.

HOUGH STANLEY M — TRAINER SUMMARY FOR SPECIFIC YEAR FOR ALL TRACKS IN NORTH
        AMERICA

IN NORTH AMERICA FOR ALL TRACKS:

        1976 - 1993   06/03 - 07/02

```
STARTERS      895                17
 WINNERS      495( 55%)           2( 12%)
 PLACERS      628( 70%)           7(  0%)
  STARTS    6,083                22
    WINS    1,088( 18%)           2(  9%)
  PLACES    1,756( 29%)           8( 36%)
```

1992 IN NORTH AMERICA

	STARTS	1ST (%)	2ND (%)	3RD (%)	UNPL%	EARNINGS	ROWB
TOTALS	136	21 (15)	20 (15)	23 (17)	(53)	$688,402	-$60
AVERAGE FOR ALL TRAINERS		(9)	(9)	(9)	(73)		-$19
COLTS	87	13 (15)	14 (16)	13 (15)	(54)	$413,230	-$69
FILLIES	49	8 (16)	6 (12)	10 (20)	(52)	$275,172	+$8
GRADED BLACKTYPE	10	3 (30)	1 (10)	2 (20)	(40)	$279,390	+$4
ALL BLACKTYPE	18	3 (17)	2 (11)	4 (22)	(50)	$307,082	-$12
ALLOWANCE	36	4 (11)	6 (17)	7 (19)	(53)	$119,740	-$43
CLAIMING	50	6 (12)	9 (18)	7 (14)	(56)	$119,260	-$2
MAIDEN	32	8 (25)	3 (9)	5 (16)	(50)	$142,320	-$4
DIRT	96	16 (17)	14 (15)	19 (20)	(48)	$489,392	-$56
FAST TRACK	73	11 (15)	12 (16)	14 (19)	(50)	$406,302	$45
OFF TRACK	23	5 (22)	2 (9)	5 (22)	(47)	$83,090	-$11
TURF	40	5 (13)	6 (15)	4 (10)	(62)	$199,010	-$5
FIRM TURF	27	3 (11)	4 (15)	4 (15)	(59)	$99,650	-$27
OFF TURF	13	2 (15)	2 (15)	0 (0)	(70)	$99,360	+$22
MILE OR MORE	54	6 (11)	7 (13)	8 (15)	(61)	$225,790	-$4
< 1 MILE	82	15 (18)	13 (16)	15 (18)	(48)	$462,612	-$56
FAVORITES	25	9 (36)	3 (12)	4 (16)	(36)	$217,240	-$8
ODDS < 5 TO 1	50	8 (16)	11 (22)	9 (18)	(44)	$315,309	-$30
ODDS 5 TO 1 - 10 TO 1	31	2 (6)	4 (13)	7 (23)	(58)	$92,620	-$29
ODDS > 10 TO 1	30	2 (7)	2 (7)	3 (10)	(76)	$63,233	+$7
FIRST TIME STARTERS	8	3 (38)	1 (13)	2 (25)	(24)	$48,240	-$3
RACES WITH APPRENTICES	4	0 (0)	0 (0)	2 (50)	(50)	$3,780	-$8

Mark Reid is the type of trainer that does exceptionally well once his maidens have made their first starts. He obviously makes changes and adjustments. Also, he may be placing first time starters too high and then dropping them where they can win. The winning percentages are almost the same but the dollar figure is a minus $1 with first time starters and a plus $32 with maidens that have already started.

REID MARK J — TRAINER SUMMARY FOR SPECIFIC YEAR FOR ALL TRACKS IN NORTH
AMERICA

IN NORTH AMERICA FOR ALL TRACKS:

	1977 - 1993	05/30 - 06/28
STARTERS	1,018	43
WINNERS	621(61%)	11(26%)
PLACERS	755(74%)	13(0%)
STARTS	9,792	73
WINS	1,589(16%)	13(18%)
PLACES	2,705(28%)	17(23%)

1992 IN NORTH AMERICA

	STARTS	1ST (%)	2ND (%)	3RD (%)	UNPL%	EARNINGS	ROWB
TOTALS	1,180	221 (19)	179 (15)	188 (16)	(50)	$2,628,917	−$339
AVERAGE FOR ALL TRAINERS		(9)	(9)	(9)	(73)		-$19
COLTS	628	115 (18)	97 (15)	99 (16)	(51)	$1,279,658	−$177
FILLIES	552	106 (19)	82 (15)	89 (16)	(50)	$1,349,259	-$165
GRADED BLACKTYPE	14	1 (7)	2 (14)	0 (0)	(79)	$69,032	-$25
ALL BLACKTYPE	60	9 (15)	6 (10)	8 (13)	(62)	$428,883	−$67
ALLOWANCE	299	42 (14)	58 (19)	43 (14)	(53)	$805,869	−$161
CLAIMING	681	137 (20)	100 (15)	115 (17)	(48)	$1,092,045	−$144
MAIDEN	140	33 (24)	15 (11)	22 (16)	(49)	$302,120	+$32
DIRT	1094	210 (19)	170 (16)	178 (16)	(49)	$2,389,535	−$242
FAST TRACK	773	162 (21)	119 (15)	120 (16)	(48)	$1,762,777	−$19
OFF TRACK	321	48 (15)	51 (16)	58 (18)	(51)	$626,758	−$223
TURF	86	11 (13)	9 (10)	10 (12)	(65)	$239,382	−$97
FIRM TURF	70	9 (13)	8 (11)	9 (13)	(63)	$168,690	-$73
OFF TURF	16	2 (13)	1 (6)	1 (6)	(75)	$70,692	−$24
MILE OR MORE	423	74 (17)	68 (16)	70 (17)	(50)	$1,114,150	−$114
< 1 MILE	757	147 (19)	111 (15)	118 (16)	(50)	$1,514,767	−$227
FAVORITES	306	107 (35)	59 (19)	44 (14)	(32)	$1,049,948	−$93
ODDS < 5 TO 1	400	75 (19)	69 (17)	75 (19)	(45)	$943,753	−$161
ODDS 5 TO 1−							

10 TO 1	269	28 (10)	36 (13)	49 (18)	(59)	$404,015	−$99
ODDS ⟩ 10 TO 1	205	11 (5)	15 (7)	20 (10)	(78)	$231,201	+$12
FIRST TIME STARTERS	36	8 (22)	2 (6)	5 (14)	(58)	$78,251	−$1
RACES WITH APPRENTICES	115	15 (13)	19 (17)	18 (16)	(54)	$114,764	−$97

BLACKTYPE WINS

DATE	STAKES NAME	VALUE	HORSE NAME
921108	EAST VIEW S. --LR (AQU)	88,950	Our Shopping Spree
920827	MOHAWK S. --LR (SAR)	84,600	Our Shopping Spree
921128	NEW YORK STALLION S. --LR (AQU)	80,000	Our Shopping Spree
920912	LADY FINGER S. --OR (FL)	66,013	Our Shopping Spree
920530	VINELAND H. --G3 (GS)	50,000	Le Famo
920503	MISS PREAKNESS S. --O (PIM)	44,175	Toots La Mae
920217	CARRY BACK H. --O (GS)	32,790	Doctor Fish
920927	ALYSHEBA S. --O (MTH)	31,850	Doctor Fish
920315	JUNIPER S. --OR (PHA)	27,200	Major Danger
920118	CINDERELLA S. --NR (GS)	21,800	All the Vees

Warren "Jimmy" Croll Jr. has been a force on the East Coast with two-year-old first-time starters since 1976. Jimmy is the type of trainer who wins at first asking and if he doesn't, do not bet the horse again. With first time starters, Jimmy is winning 35 percent of the time and only 17 percent with horses that have started more than once. Also, like Team Perkins, Jimmy is excellent with favorites, winning 37 percent of the time.

CROLL WARREN A JR — TRAINER SUMMARY FOR SPECIFIC YEAR FOR ALL TRACKS IN NORTH AMERICA

IN NORTH AMERICA FOR ALL TRACKS:

	1976 − 1993	05/30 − 06/28
STARTERS	434	20
WINNERS	289(67%)	4(20%)
PLACERS	318(73%)	9(0%)
STARTS	3,889	29
WINS	796(20%)	5(17%)
PLACES	1,139(29%)	9(31%)

1992 IN NORTH AMERICA

	STARTS	1ST (%)	2ND (%)	3RD (%)	UNPL%	EARNINGS	ROWB
TOTALS	198	35 (18)	39 (20)	31 (16)	(46)	$799,715	−$131
AVERAGE FOR ALL TRAINERS		(9)	(9)	(9)	(73)		−$19
COLTS	100	15 (15)	21 (21)	17 (17)	(47)	$376,070	−$79
FILLIES	98	20 (20)	18 (18)	14 (14)	(48)	$423,645	−$52
GRADED BLACKTYPE	9	1 (11)	0 (0)	1 (11)	(78)	$52,500	−$12
ALL BLACKTYPE	25	5 (20)	5 (20)	2 (8)	(52)	$297,188	−$14
ALLOWANCE	81	16 (20)	16 (20)	13 (16)	(44)	$286,935	−$16
CLAIMING	21	2 (10)	7 (33)	3 (14)	(43)	$44,837	−$29
MAIDEN	71	12 (17)	11 (15)	13 (18)	(50)	$170,755	−$70
DIRT	145	26 (18)	27 (19)	25 (17)	(46)	$478,965	−$103
FAST TRACK	112	21 (19)	23 (21)	18 (16)	(44)	$391,645	−$64
OFF TRACK	33	5 (15)	4 (12)	7 (21)	(52)	$87,320	−$39
TURF	53	9 (17)	12 (23)	6 (11)	(49)	$320,750	−$27
FIRM TURF	45	6 (13)	11 (24)	5 (11)	(52)	$245,938	−$36
OFF TURF	8	3 (38)	1 (13)	1 (13)	(36)	$74,812	+$9
MILE OR MORE	109	20 (18)	23 (21)	12 (11)	(50)	$545,605	−$55
< 1 MILE	89	15 (17)	16 (18)	19 (21)	(44)	$254,110	−$76
FAVORITES	51	19 (37)	14 (27)	9 (18)	(18)	$313,435	−$16
ODDS < 5 TO 1	72	12 (17)	16 (22)	15 (21)	(40)	$322,375	−$45
ODDS 5 TO 1− 10 TO 1	33	2 (6)	3 (9)	5 (15)	(70)	$50,380	−$36
ODDS > 10 TO 1	42	2 (5)	6 (14)	2 (5)	(76)	$113,525	−$34
FIRST TIME STARTERS	17	6 (35)	0 (0)	2 (12)	(53)	$55,255	−$4
RACES WITH APPRENTICES	40	8 (20)	7 (18)	8 (20)	(42)	$120,515	−$11

BLACKTYPE WINS

DATE	STAKES NAME	VALUE	HORSE NAME
921003	PALISADES BREEDERS' CUP H. −L (MED)	77,200	Bidding Proud
920328	FAIRWAY FUN S. −L (TP)	62,900	Trumpet's Blare
920403	APPALACHIAN S. −L (KEE)	55,400	White Corners
921225	CHRISTMAS DAY H. −G3 (CRC)	50,000	Bidding Proud
920802	RESTORATION S. −O (MTH)	40,000	Bidding Proud

Sometimes knowing trainers to avoid is as helpful as the other way around. Trainers who are horrible with maidens devour money. Gary Jones, Gary Contessa, Nicholas Zito, and Thomas Bohannan are examples.

Gary Jones finished the 1992 season with 4.7 million dollars in earnings. He had an incredible winning percentage in graded blacktype races, where he won 14 of 42 or 33 percent. Although he has shown greatness throughout his 17 year training career, he has consistently struggled with maidens. In 1992, Jones struggled once again only winning 15 of 97, or 15 percent with maidens that have already started. Compared to his other percentages of Graded Blacktype - 33 percent, All Blacktype - 26 percent, Allowance - 27 percent and Claiming - 19 percent, his maiden stats are much lower than these other conditions.

JONES GARY — TRAINER SUMMARY FOR SPECIFIC YEAR FOR ALL TRACKS IN NORTH AMERICA

IN NORTH AMERICA FOR ALL TRACKS:

	1976 – 1993	05/30 – 06/28
STARTERS	1,075	0
WINNERS	535(50%)	0(0%)
PLACERS	630(59%)	0(0%)
STARTS	6,742	0
WINS	1,224(18%)	0(0%)
PLACES	1,745(26%)	0(0%)

1992 IN NORTH AMERICA

	STARTS	1ST (%)	2ND (%)	3RD (%)	UNPL%	EARNINGS	ROWB
TOTALS	329	71 (22)	50 (15)	45 (14)	(49)	$4,720,519	−$57
AVERAGE FOR ALL TRAINERS		(9)	(9)	(9)	(73)		−$19
COLTS	169	38 (22)	27 (16)	23 (14)	(48)	$3,070,025	−$23
FILLIES	160	33 (21)	23 (14)	22 (14)	(51)	$1,650,494	−$34
GRADED BLACKTYPE	43	14 (33)	5 (12)	4 (9)	(46)	$2,911,950	+$0
ALL BLACKTYPE	70	18 (26)	8 (11)	9 (13)	(50)	$3,268,994	−$17
ALLOWANCE	88	24 (27)	14 (16)	18 (20)	(37)	$782,675	+$35
CLAIMING	74	14 (19)	16 (22)	11 (15)	(44)	$369,775	+$26
MAIDEN	97	15 (15)	12 (12)	7 (7)	(66)	$299,075	−$102
DIRT	209	41 (20)	33 (16)	24 (11)	(53)	$2,749,494	−$87
FAST TRACK	171	37 (22)	28 (16)	15 (9)	(53)	$2,590,844	−$33
OFF TRACK	38	4 (11)	5 (13)	9 (24)	(52)	$158,650	−$54

TURF	120	30 (25)	17 (14)	21 (18)	(43)	$1,971,025	+$30
FIRM TURF	114	29 (25)	16 (14)	21 (18)	(43)	$1,890,350	+$34
OFF TURF	6	1 (17)	1 (17)	0 (0)	(66)	$80,675	−$4
MILE OR MORE	171	37 (22)	28 (16)	28 (16)	(46)	$3,704,375	+$7
⟨ 1 MILE	158	34 (22)	22 (14)	17 (11)	(53)	$1,016,144	−$63
FAVORITES	86	36 (42)	10 (12)	12 (14)	(32)	$2,763,125	−$1
ODDS ⟨ 5 TO 1	105	24 (23)	21 (20)	19 (18)	(39)	$1,343,850	−$6
ODDS 5 TO 1−							
10 TO 1	81	9 (11)	15 (19)	8 (10)	(60)	$413,144	−$12
ODDS ⟩ 10 TO 1	57	2 (4)	4 (7)	6 (11)	(78)	$200,400	−$38
FIRST TIME STARTERS	37	8 (22)	4 (11)	4 (11)	(56)	$177,000	−$12
RACES WITH APPRENTICES	2	0 (0)	1 (50)	0 (0)	(50)	$6,800	−$4

BLACKTYPE WINS

DATE	STAKES NAME	VALUE	HORSE NAME
920120	SAN MARCOS H. −G3 (SA)	158,100	Classic Fame
920115	CALIFORNIA BREEDERS' CHAMPION S. −LR (SA)	135,150	Alpine Queen
920101	SAN GABRIEL H. −G3 (SA)	109,300	Classic Fame

Gary Contessa follows in the pattern of Gary Jones with great winning percentages in graded and all blacktypes races. Gary, though, is only 1 for 13 with first time starters and 11 for 81 with maidens that have already started. Gary does well with favorites and is winning 33 percent of the time but is only 1 for 78 with horses over 10 to 1. As a handicapper, bet Contessa in the blacktype races but that's it.

CONTESSA GARY C — TRAINER SUMMARY FOR SPECIFIC YEAR FOR ALL TRACKS IN NORTH
          AMERICA

IN NORTH AMERICA FOR ALL TRACKS:

	1989 − 1993	05/30 − 06/28
STARTERS	303	22
WINNERS	169(56%)	4(18%)
PLACERS	195(64%)	5(0%)
STARTS	1,933	35
WINS	317(16%)	4(11%)
PLACES	519(27%)	5(14%)

1993 IN NORTH AMERICA

	STARTS	1ST (%)	2ND (%)	3RD (%)	UNPL%	EARNINGS	ROWB
TOTALS	245	30 (12)	32 (13)	31 (13)	(62)	$662,461	-$153
AVERAGE FOR ALL TRAINERS		(9)	(9)	(10)	(72)		-$11
COLTS	137	18 (13)	14 (10)	19 (14)	(63)	$297,210	-$43
FILLIES	108	12 (11)	18 (17)	12 (11)	(61)	$365,251	-$110
GRADED BLACKTYPE	6	2 (33)	0 (0)	2 (33)	(34)	$135,183	+$61
ALL BLACKTYPE	11	4 (36)	1 (9)	2 (18)	(37)	$277,095	+$57
ALLOWANCE	41	2 (5)	7 (17)	4 (10)	(68)	$74,480	-$64
CLAIMING	112	13 (12)	14 (13)	18 (16)	(59)	$189,841	-$88
MAIDEN	81	11 (14)	10 (12)	7 (9)	(65)	$121,045	-$59
DIRT	226	29 (13)	30 (13)	30 (13)	(61)	$637,922	-$129
FAST TRACK	187	18 (10)	26 (14)	23 (12)	(64)	$407,804	-$157
OFF TRACK	39	11 (28)	4 (10)	7 (18)	(44)	$230,118	+$28
TURF	19	1 (5)	2 (11)	1 (5)	(79)	$24,539	-$24
FIRM TURF	17	1 (6)	2 (12)	1 (6)	(76)	$24,539	-$20
OFF TURF	2	0 (0)	0 (0)	0 (0)	(100)	$0	$4
MILE OR MORE	110	14 (13)	13 (12)	21 (19)	(56)	$375,787	-$77
< 1 MILE	135	16 (12)	19 (14)	10 (7)	(67)	$286,674	-$76
FAVORITES	36	12 (33)	5 (14)	8 (22)	(31)	$245,381	-$19
ODDS < 5 TO 1	66	8 (12)	13 (20)	11 (17)	(51)	$172,478	-$75
ODDS 5 TO 1- 10 TO 1	65	9 (14)	7 (11)	6 (9)	(66)	$150,078	+$31
ODDS > 10 TO 1	78	1 (1)	7 (9)	6 (8)	(82)	$94,524	-$90
FIRST TIME STARTERS	13	1 (8)	1 (8)	0 (0)	(84)	$18,300	-$6
RACES WITH APPRENTICES	13	1 (8)	1 (8)	1 (8)	(76)	$9,495	-$18

BLACKTYPE WINS

DATE	STAKES NAME	VALUE	HORSE NAME
930410	NATIONAL JOCKEY CLUB OAKS -L (SPT)	150,000	True Affair
930214	BUSHER BREEDERS' CUP H. -G3 (AQU)	87,750	True Affair
930529	ROSEBEN H. -G3 (BEL)	85,500	Codys Key
930306	SENSATIONAL S. -L (AQU)	52,900	True Affair

Nicholas Zito is awful with maiden and handicappers should stay clear from this trainer in these races. With first time starters, in 1992, Zito was 0-20 and only placed four in the money of those twenty. In 1993, Zito was slightly better. He did win one of nine but still had a miserable winning percentage of 11 percent. Maidens who have already started did make a difference. In 1992, he was 12 of 125 and in 1993, he was 4 of 20.

Thomas Bohannan gained national fame with premier runners such as *Pine Bluff, Praire Bayou,* and *Dalhart.* Bohannan has not showed consistency with first time starters but does improve with horses that have made more than one start. He is only 2 for 28, or 8 percent with first time starters, compared to 18 percent winners with experienced maidens. This shows that Bohannan makes the necessary adjustments, but is not good at preparing horses for their debut or does not care about winning the first time a horse races.